1,001 More Things You Always Wanted to Know About the Bible

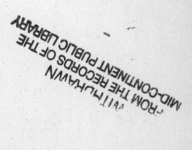

1,001 More Things You Always Wanted to Know About the Bible

J. STEPHEN LANG

OLIVER
NELSON
TM

THOMAS NELSON PUBLISHERS
Nashville

Published in Nashville, Tennessee, by Thomas Nelson, Inc.

Library of Congress Cataloging-in-Publication Data
ISBN 0-7852-6790-5

Printed in the United States of America
1 2 3 4 5 6 7 QWD 06 05 04 03 02 01

Contents

1

So Many Legends

1. colored eggs at Easter

No, the Bible has nothing whatever to say about Easter eggs. But there is an old legend connected with Simon of Cyrene, the man forced by the Romans to carry Jesus' cross to Calvary (Mark 15:21). Legend has it that Simon was an egg merchant, and when he returned from seeing the Crucifixion, he found that all the eggs in his produce basket had miraculously turned a variety of bright colors. In an alternate version of the story, his eggs did not take on their beautiful coloring until the day of Christ's resurrection—Easter, that is.

2. King Arthur and the Last Supper table

There may have been a King Arthur in Britain's distant past, but mostly he was pure legend. Arthur may have started out in the stories as a pagan chieftain, but eventually a lot of biblical imagery came to be associated with him. According to one legend, Arthur's amazing spear (named Ron, believe it or not) was the spear used by the Roman soldier to pierce the side of Jesus on the cross. Another legend: Arthur's sword Excalibur was the sword used to behead John the Baptist. And still another: the famous Round Table used by Arthur and his knights was actually the table used by Jesus and His disciples at the Last Supper.

3. the wandering Jew

One of the more somber legends connected with Christ is the old story that on His way to His crucifixion, He was heckled and slapped by a spiteful old Jew who told him to "move along faster." Christ replied, the story goes, by saying, "I go, but you tarry until I come again." Thus the surly Jew was doomed to walk the earth as a remorseful outcast until the second coming of Christ. In the story, widely spread in the Middle Ages and afterward, he is sometimes called Ahasuerus, sometimes Cartiphilus. In some versions of the story he was a servant of Pilate's. In all versions, his punishment is seen as a symbol of the Jews' rejecting Jesus as their Messiah. "Wandering Jew" is best known to people today as the common name for *Zebrina pendula*, a popular garden vine.

4. the lion's cubs

Many animals, such as cats, are born blind (or, more accurately, with their eyes closed). An old legend has it that lion cubs are actually born dead, but come to life on the third day when the father lion breathes life into them. Tradition makes this a symbol of Christ, who came to life after the third day in the grave.

5. the donkey's cross

The donkey is a much-mentioned Bible creature, notable in the life of Jesus for being the beast that carried Him into Jerusalem. Some people discern a sort of cross-shaped mark on the donkey's shoulders, which is, they say, a symbol of having carried Christ.

6. robin redbreast

People have vivid imaginations. In answer to the question "Why does the robin have a red breast?" folk wisdom came up with this answer: a robin picked a thorn from the crown of thorns on Jesus' head, and a spurt of blood from Jesus dyed the bird's breast red, which has remained so ever since.

7. why the aspen quakes

What wood was Jesus' cross made of? No one knows. The lovely trees of the American West known as "quaking aspens" are said to quake in shame because Jesus' cross was made from aspen wood.

8. Judas and the redbud

According to legend the blossoms of the redbud tree are red (either from shame or from blood) because it is the tree on which Judas Iscariot hanged himself. (For the record, the tree's flowers are really more lavender or pink than red.) The tree is the state tree of Oklahoma, and became so only after state forestry officials convinced ladies' garden clubs that the redbud was *not* the tree Judas hung from (since it grows in America, not Israel).

9. the dogwood legend

People love the white and pink blossoms of the dogwood tree. The trees rarely grow to be more than twenty feet tall, and their branches spread more horizontally than vertically, making them a popular tree for lawns. Legend has it that in the past the dogwood grew as tall as the mighty oak, and its sturdy wood was used for the cross on which Jesus was crucified. After this, the tree (out of shame, some say) never again grew tall and straight but grew low, with narrow, twisting branches that could never be made into the beams of a cross.

10. the man in the moon

For centuries people have thought that the full moon resembles a human face, and many legends have sprung up about who the "man in the moon" is. One legend that circulated widely was that he was the Israelite mentioned in Numbers 15:32–36: because he broke the law of Moses by gathering sticks on the Sabbath, he was stoned to death by the people. His forlorn face became the man in the moon.

11. no "three kings" in the Bible

Nativity scenes usually depict the wise men (or "Magi") of Christmas as three kings, as does the popular song "We Three Kings of Orient Are." But this is legend, not the Bible. The story in Matthew's gospel gives no hint that the wise men were kings, only that they were seeking the newborn "king of the Jews," that is, the baby Jesus. Later legend had it that they were kings themselves, paying their respects to a greater king than they. And, strictly speaking, the wise men don't belong in the Nativity scene at all; they came later than the shepherds, when Joseph, Mary, and the baby were no longer in a stable but in a house (Matt. 2:11).

12. Lazarus's second life

What became of Lazarus after Jesus raised him from the dead (John 11)? The Bible doesn't say, but the people of the island of Cyprus have an idea: Lazarus became an evangelist and later became the island's bishop. He is buried, tradition says, in the white limestone Church of St. Lazarus—his *second* grave. Over his tomb is the inscription "Lazarus, a friend of Christ."

13. the Mar Thoma church

Legend has it that the apostle Thomas took the gospel all the way to India, founding what is called the Mar Thoma ("Lord Thomas") Church. Even if this isn't true (and it probably isn't), it *is* true that a Christian group has existed in India for many centuries. More probable is the tradition that around the year 345 a group of Syrian Christians settled in India, under the leadership of a man called Thomas of Cana.

14. Solomon and the Ethiopians

The Ethiopians have for centuries traced their rulers' ancestry back to King Solomon of Israel. According to their legends, the queen of Sheba paid a visit to Solomon (see 1 Kings 10) and returned to her home country not only impressed with Solomon's wisdom and his building projects (as the Bible says), but pregnant by him. Legend has it that the queen (named Makeda, though her name does not appear in the Bible) bore a son, Menelik, who at age twenty-two journeyed to Jerusalem to learn the Hebrew Scriptures, visit his wise father, and carry the true faith back to his homeland. Down to the twentieth century the Ethiopians insisted that all their rulers were descendants of Solomon and the queen of Sheba.

15. Orpah and Goliath?

In the book of Ruth, Orpah and Ruth are the two daughters-in-law of Naomi, whose husband and sons have died. Naomi told the two to return to their home in Moab, and while Orpah obeyed and parted tearfully, Ruth stayed with Naomi. Ruth, as the book tells us, later bore a child and became the great-grandmother of King David. According to Jewish legend, Orpah also had a famous descendant: Goliath the giant, who was slain by the shepherd boy David. In other words, when David faced Goliath, the two descendants of Ruth and Orpah were standing face-to-face. The legend further states that Orpah, after returning to Moab, became a harlot, thus Goliath and his giant brothers were the sons of prostitution.

16. creating the pig and cat

After spending so long afloat, wasn't Noah's ark a filthy place? The Bible says nothing about it, but logically it would have become pretty rank. According to an old Jewish legend, God created the pig to eat up food refuse. And because rats were becoming a problem (apparently the original two reproduced astoundingly), God created the cat to eliminate the rats.

17. Satan the winemaker

Genesis attributes the first making of wine to the righteous Noah (Gen. 9:20). Because of all the ills that have come from alcohol abuse, some Jews attributed Noah's winemaking to Satan himself. According to the legend, Satan fertilized the grape vines with blood from a lamb, a lion, an ape, and a pig. The meaning of the four beasts' blood: when drinking, a man becomes docile (the lamb), then fierce (the lion), then silly (the ape), and ends up wallowing in the mud (the pig).

18. British Israelites

What became of the "ten lost tribes of Israel," the northern tribes that were conquered by the Assyrians (2 Kings 17)? In the mid-1800s, it became a common (though silly) belief that some descendants of Israel's royal house had settled in the British Isles, with England's royalty being descended from Israel's line. Following this line of thought, many of the Old Testament prophecies to Israel were actually fulfilled in the history of Britain. No scholars have ever taken these beliefs very seriously, and no church or sect has ever been founded based on the beliefs, but they have provided some amusement for more than a few people.

19. Awan

Genesis doesn't tell us where Cain got his wife—which has
led to much speculation, since at the time he took a wife,
the only people on earth were Cain and his parents, Adam
and Eve. The Jewish writing known as the book of Jubilees
supplied an answer: Adam and Eve had a daughter named
Awan, and Cain took her (his own sister) as his wife.

20. the crown of thorns, later

Medieval Christians prized relics connected with Jesus
and the apostles—even though some of the relics were, we
now know, obvious fakes. In 1238, King Louis IX of
France was given what was supposed to be the crown of
thorns placed on Jesus' head. For centuries this supposed
relic was housed in a specially built chapel in Paris, then
later moved to the famous cathedral of Notre Dame there.
An elaborate silver container with jewels housed the
crown of thorns. It is still there, though now consists only
of the plant stems, the thorns themselves being absent.

21. the spear that wounded Christ

John 19:34 reports that one of the Roman soldiers
pierced the side of the crucified Jesus with a spear. Since
it touched Christ, the spear was (in the minds of medieval
Christians) a sacred relic. Supposedly that actual spear

ended up centuries later in the city of Constantinople, and in 1492 the Ottoman ruler of Constantinople sent it to Pope Innocent VIII. The pope placed the spear's shaft in one of the pillars supporting the dome of St. Peter's Basilica in Rome. Was this the actual spear that pierced Jesus' side? Doubtful, but a good story nonetheless.

22. the true cross

An old story—or legend—relates that Helena, mother of the Roman emperor Constantine, traveled to the Holy Land in 326 and there discovered the cross on which Jesus had died. The Catholic Church proceeded to disperse fragments of the "true cross," as it was called, which were worshiped as sacred relics in elaborate containers known as reliquaries. So many of the fragments—often no more than splinters—were around that in the 1500s Protestant leader John Calvin sneered that if all the splinters were put together, there would be enough wood to fill a large ship. Calvin and other Protestant leaders condemned the whole practice of relics, one reason being that so many were obviously fakes. However, many Catholic theologians defended the true cross and claimed that, through a miracle, the cross was able to "multiply" itself far beyond the original wood that it contained.

2

The Bible Versus the Modern World

23. divine creation vs. Darwin

According to intellectuals, the 1925 Scopes trial (also known as the "monkey trial") settled forever the question of whether the Bible was reliable as a science textbook. Technically, teacher John Scopes was found guilty for teaching evolution in his science class, but the worldwide audience that followed the trial felt that Scopes—and Darwin's theory of evolution—won the day. But not so fast: in the 1990s some school boards began to modify their views on the subject. Scientists who take new findings seriously began to question whether Darwin was as wise as they thought. And Christians, not always willing to roll over and play dead when confronted with a secular worldview, had pressed for school systems to at least teach the *possibility* that God created the world (and not necessarily in six twenty-four-hour

11

days, following Genesis 1). The battle is still on, a battle not just between religion and secularism, but between unbelievers and those who think the deep kernel of truth in Genesis 1 (that a personal God created the world with a purpose) is still deserving a hearing in our schools.

24. Butler's *Analogy*

The bishop of Durham in England, Joseph Butler (1692–1752), was one of the best theologians of the 1700s. His most famous work was *The Analogy of Religion, Natural and Revealed.* Butler lived in an age when many people, particularly intellectuals, talked a lot about "nature" and "reason" and were more and more skeptical about the truths of the Bible. In his book Butler claimed that we could learn a lot from both nature and the Bible—and that one without the other was incomplete. Both—together—lead us to full truth, and those who think they can rely on nature and discard the Bible are simply wrong.

25. the comet man

Halley's comet is named for English astronomer Edmund Halley (1656–1742). Like his friend and fellow scientist Isaac Newton, Halley saw no real conflict between science and faith. Halley had an interesting theory: the Great Flood in Genesis 7 was caused by a comet.

26. the rotund Mr. Chesterton

Journalist and author G. K. Chesterton (1874–1936) was a devout Catholic and frequent critic of secular society. Chesterton produced such still-read masterpieces as *The Everlasting Man, Orthodoxy,* and the popular Father Brown detective stories. Regarding the quarrel between religion and science, Chesterton wrote, "Private theories about what the Bible ought to mean, and premature theories about what the world ought to mean, have met in loud and widely advertised controversy, especially in the Victorian time; and this clumsy collision of two very impatient forms of ignorance was known as the quarrel of Science and Religion." Chesterton himself believed in the Bible, but he didn't always believe in the wisdom of some of its defenders.

27. Benjamin Silliman

Here was a noble effort: try to reconcile the Bible with the findings of science. Silliman (1779–1864), a science professor at Yale, was also a devout Christian. He was disturbed that new findings in geology indicated that the earth was much, much older than Christians had ever believed. Silliman was one of the first to suggest that the six "days" of creation in Genesis were not twenty-four-hour days but were actually "ages."

28. Edward Hitchcock

The pupil of geologist Benjamin Silliman (see 27), Hitchcock felt certain that the findings of geology should not disturb Christians. In his book *The Religion of Geology* (1851), Hitchcock insisted that the great age of the earth was merely another illustration of God's constancy and creative power.

29. Louis Agassiz

Not every scientist jumped on the evolution bandwagon after Charles Darwin published his *Origin of Species* in 1859. Darwin sent a copy to the most famous American scientist of the day, Louis Agassiz (1807–1873). He rejected just about everything Darwin said, and insisted that only a special creative act of God could account for the past and present world, including fossils. Agassiz took a curious view of Genesis, though: he said the account was true, but incomplete, for the Bible did not record every act of God's creation, including His creation of other human races. Agassiz was, however, widely praised by many Christians as defender of traditional beliefs against the atheist Darwin.

30. Spencer the skeptic

Almost forgotten today, English philosopher Herbert Spencer (1820–1903) was widely read in his own day.

He helped popularize the evolutionary views of Charles Darwin, and even applied them to human ethics and politics. (By the way, it was Spencer, not Darwin, who coined the phrase "survival of the fittest.") Thinking himself very scientific, Spencer (like many intellectuals then and today) believed that science had somehow "disproved" the Bible and Christianity, and that what we call "God" is really just an impersonal force or energy in the world. Spencer believed strongly in two things that are still typical of secular thinkers: life is perpetual progress, and science is the key instrument of progress. He didn't foresee how science could be abused in places like Nazi Germany and Soviet Russia.

31. *The Genesis of Species*

Charles Darwin's 1859 book *The Origin of Species* set the world on its ear. Christians generally reacted by rejecting it all together or, in some cases, by admitting that evolution might be *somewhat* true, but not totally. In 1871 a Catholic biologist, St. George Mivart, published *The Genesis of Species.* He argued that, scientifically speaking, evolution definitely did occur, but that Darwin's theory of "natural selection" could not account for it all. There had to be (and many Christians agreed with this) an Intelligence, indeed a Person, guiding the whole amazing process, and that Person was, of course, the God of the book of Genesis.

32. Henry Mansel

Can science answer all our questions? Many people asked that question in the 1800s, and still ask it today. One who tried to answer it was Henry Mansel (1820–1871), a Church of England minister and Oxford professor. In *The Limits of Religious Thought*, Mansel hammered home an old (but valid) idea: the human mind has its limits, and it should recognize those limits. If people have an inadequate conception of God, he said, that doesn't mean that belief in God is impossible. We must recognize that there is mystery in God. According to Mansel we must also recognize what the Bible is intended to be: not a manual to answer all of humanity's questions, but a way to regulate man's moral and spiritual life. The Bible's principles "do not serve to satisfy the reason, but to guide the conduct." In other words, the scientists and other skeptics are wrong to expect the Bible to satisfy all man's doubts, for the Bible is intended to tell us how to love God and our neighbor.

33. polygenesis

It means "many origins," and it came into use in the 1800s as some so-called scientists put forward the idea that mankind did not have one ancestor but several. In other words, the old idea that all people descended from

Adam was wrong, for there were several ancestors of humankind. The people who believed in this theory of polygenesis had found a convenient way to account for the differences in the races: obviously (they thought), white Americans and Europeans were descended from a superior ancestor, while Africans and others were descended from inferior stock. In other words, polygenesis was a perfect justification for treating some races worse than others.

Curiously, slaveholders in the South in the 1800s were appalled at this theory. While they tried to justify their holding of slaves (even when they were supposedly Christian), no slaveholder ever contended that blacks and whites had a different ancestor, for they believed all mankind was descended from Adam.

34. Paley's *Evidences*

The 1700s, the Enlightenment era, put many Christians on the defensive as philosophers and scientists became skeptical about the truths of the Bible. One defender of traditional belief was English author William Paley, whose 1794 book *Christian Evidences* tried to show that the Bible was indeed reliable. His 1802 book *Natural Theology* contains his famous watchmaker analogy: if we find a watch, we must assume that some watchmaker designed and made it; thus, looking at the created world, we must assume that some wise Designer made it.

35. "homo-brutalism"

This word was coined by an American Jew, Rabbi Isaac Mayer Wise, to apply to the evolutionary teachings of Charles Darwin. Many Jewish leaders, as many Christian leaders, were extremely disturbed by Darwin's teachings, believing they tore down people's faith in the Bible. More than a few Jewish scholars wrote books attempting to prove that the Bible's story of creation was true. Wise's term "homo-brutalism" refers to Darwin's theory that man (*homo*) descended from animals (that is, the brutes).

THE LIBERAL-CONSERVATIVE BATTLE

36. Clarke's transformation

The experience of William Newton Clarke (1840–1912) is a good illustration of what happened to many Christians in the late 1800s. Clarke, a Baptist pastor's son, grew up trusting and loving the Bible, taking its truths at face value. But in the 1880s Clarke began to read about the biblical criticism coming out of European universities, and he had serious doubts about the truth of the Bible. He left his pastorate, taught at a seminary, and in 1898 published his *Outline of Christian Theology*, probably the first genuinely liberal book of theology in America. Clarke claimed he still believed the Bible was (in some way) inspired, but that it contained numerous errors. Caught up in the intellectual skepticism of his time, Clarke claimed that the average Christian could not interpret the Bible properly (after all, they might take it at face value, as he himself had once done). Thus Christians needed guides—intellectuals, professors, skeptical scholars like himself—to help them read and understand the Bible. He was a typical example of liberal snobbery, an elitist believing that the ignorant Christians in the pews simply could not understand the Bible without the "professionals'" help.

37. Chapter and Verse

Author Mike Bryan, a professed agnostic, did a curious thing: he enrolled in Criswell College, an extremely conservative Southern Baptist college in Dallas, to find out if Bible-believing Christians were as horrible as he thought. To his surprise, he liked them, and they treated him with warmth and kindness. His 1991 book, *Chapter and Verse,* has the subtitle *A Skeptic Revisits Christianity.* After his stay at Criswell, Bryan is still a skeptic, but one with a fresh respect for Christians who take the Bible seriously. The title, of course, comes from conservative Christians' habit of backing up their beliefs with specific quotes from the Bible—"chapter and verse."

38. Fosdick the great liberal

Harry Emerson Fosdick (1878–1969) was one of America's most famous preachers, and also a noted liberal. In 1922 he preached a famous sermon, "Shall the Fundamentalists

Win?" in which he criticized conservative Christians. He took the typical liberal view that fundamentalism was an embarrassment to Christianity, and that intelligent believers could not hold to the traditional view of the Bible. So in 1924 he published *The Modern Use of the Bible*. In that book he insisted that "the heart of the Bible is its reproducible experiences. The spirit and quality of Jesus were meant to be reproduced in its followers. In the New Testament, the Master's life, like music, was meant to be reproduced." Does that sound liberal? Hardly. Fosdick held to a high moral standard, one reason that some people referred to him as an "evangelical liberal."

39. Bishop Robinson, less liberal than before

The "poster child" for liberal Christianity in the 1960s was probably John A. T. Robinson, an English bishop who penned the popular (and very controversial) book *Honest to God*, which made it clear that Robinson was anything but a traditional Christian. In that notorious book and in other writings, the bishop was clearly a skeptic about the Bible, particularly the New Testament, which he believed was written not by people who had known Jesus but by people living more than a century later. But in the 1970s Robinson had a change of heart. Digging into the Bible deeply, Robinson became convinced that all of the New Testament had been written before the year 70—in other words, completed within forty years of Jesus' earthly life. His book *Redating the New Testament* publicized his findings.

40. the Jesus Seminar

Because Christianity is composed of hundreds and even thousands of different denominations and groups, no one, and no "official body," can speak for all Christians. This is certainly true for the infamous Jesus Seminar, a group of notoriously liberal academics who have taken on the task of reading the New Testament and deciding which parts are real and which aren't. Of course, individuals (Thomas Jefferson, for example) have been doing this for centuries—the old process of throwing out the parts of the Bible we happen not to like. But in our media age, the Jesus Seminar has apparently relished playing the role of "Christian skeptics," people claiming to be Christian but extremely doubtful if much of the Bible is really true. Beginning in the 1980s, the participants used colored balls to "vote" on whether a verse from the New Testament is "certainly" authentic, "might be" authentic, or is "definitely not" authentic. The Seminar has, needless to say, found a lot of "definitely nots" in the Gospels. In 1996 the Seminar's so-called scholars claimed that the four Gospels were "notoriously unreliable," and the Seminar threw out the Nativity, the Sermon on the Mount, and the Resurrection. To no one's surprise, the group has decided to publish its own "authentic" version of the Gospels—i.e., the four Gospels using various colors to mark which parts are real (not many) and which aren't (quite a few). The Seminar's findings tell us much more about these scholars than about the truths of the Bible.

41. Henry Van Dyke

In the late 1800s, one of the most-read writers was Henry Van Dyke, an American whose poetry and fiction were phenomenally popular. He is best remembered for his Christmas story, "The Other Wise Man." In fact, Van Dyke was quite liberal in his religion, and he expressed his liberal Christianity in such books as *The Gospel for an Age of Doubt.*

42. Washington Gladden (1836–1918)

Gladden is remembered today mostly as a hymn writer, having written such classics as "O Master, Let Me Walk with Thee." In his own day Gladden was a noted liberal, a key mover in the Social Gospel movement, one who supported labor unions and other liberal causes of the day. Like others in the Social Gospel movement, he wished to apply Christ's teachings (particularly the Sermon on the Mount) to all social problems. He popularized his liberal ideas in such books as *Who Wrote the Bible?*

43. National Association of Evangelicals

For good reasons, many people have long suspected that the National Council of Churches and the World Council of Churches are slightly (or more than slightly) liberal, de-emphasizing the Bible and putting more stress on social action and trendy theologies. Founded in 1942, the National Association of Evangelicals has stuck closely to the Bible and traditional Christian beliefs and morals. Denominations, churches, and individuals may join if they are willing to subscribe to the Association's statement of faith.

44. the RSV fracas

Few Bible versions have been greeted with as much animosity as the Revised Standard Version, published in 1952. A few preachers actually burned the new Bible to show their feeling for it, and there were numerous pamphlets with titles such as *The Bible of Antichrist*, *The New Blasphemous Bible*, *Whose Unclean Fingers Have Been Tampering with God's Holy Bible?*, *The New Bible: Why Christians Should Not Accept It*, and so on. History was repeating itself: most great versions of the past, such as Luther's, Tyndale's, even (centuries ago) the Latin Vulgate, faced opposition for the obvious reason that people are bothered by change. Of course, the fact that the RSV was sponsored by the National Council of Churches (with a well-deserved reputation for being liberal) bothered many conservatives. Another factor to remember: no translation is perfect, and there were some valid criticisms of the RSV, as there will be of any translation. But some criticisms were downright silly—changing "thou" to "you," for example, a change that most people would now approve.

45. the ecumenical movement

There is no shortage of Christian denominations and independent churches. Most Christians accept this situation, but others claim that the many divisions are a scandal. Many Christians have taken seriously Jesus' words to His disciples regarding the "one fold, and one shepherd" (John 10:16 KJV) and His prayer that His followers "all may be one" (John 17:21 KJV). The ecumenical movement is the basic attempt to unite Christians—spiritually, if not organizationally. This has resulted in interdenominational cooperation and, sometimes, the merging of denominations. Regrettably, the attempt to unite has sometimes resulted in some very liberal bureaucracies, notably the National Council of Churches and the World Council of Churches.

LIVING IN A SECULAR WORLD

46. back to Middletown

One of the most famous sociological studies ever done in America was undertaken by Robert and Helen Lynd, who did a close-up study of the city of Muncie, Indiana, and published the famous book *Middletown: A Study in Contemporary American Culture* (1929). The Lynds considered "Middletown" to be a typical American town, and when they studied it in the 1920s, they found that most of its residents believed in the sacredness of the Bible, the reality of heaven and hell, and the divinity of Jesus. But something changed radically in the 1930s, for when the Lynds studied Muncie during that decade, they found that people no longer held to their old beliefs, or at least not with the same certainty. Their 1937 book *Middletown in Transition* showed that science and secularism had taken their toll on Americans' belief systems.

47. 1981, B'nai B'rith

The Anti-Defamation League of B'nai B'rith is noted for fighting anti-Jewish sentiment in America. While its purpose is laudable, the League has often taken positions that seem, well, anti-Christian. One example: in 1981, B'nai B'rith worked to prevent public school boards from allowing the Gideons to distribute copies of the New Testament in schools. Why? Apparently the League sees the Gideons' free Testaments as an attempt to "Christianize" public schools.

48. Feuerbach's Holy Spirit

The German philosopher Ludwig Feuerbach (1804–1872) was an extreme skeptic, and his many books led readers away from Christianity and toward Feuerbach's vague "religion of humanity." Feuerbach would use biblical expressions like "Holy Spirit," but impose an entirely new meaning on them. (For him, Holy Spirit was really the spirit of human love.) Doubting the Bible and all Christian beliefs, Feuerbach claimed that what we have always called "God" is really humanity itself. Feuerbach was a powerful influence on an even more influential thinker, Karl Marx.

49. Franz Overbeck

Sometimes professors of religion are the most vicious enemies of Christianity. Overbeck (1837–1905) taught Christian history and New Testament at a Swiss university, but from 1870 he was an open atheist who never ceased to criticize the Bible and Christianity. He wrote a large—and extremely skeptical—commentary on Acts. He was a friend of the noted anti-Christian philosopher Friedrich Nietzsche.

50. ACLU vs. Ten Commandments

In May 2000, the American Civil Liberties Union found another reason to complain (and sue): it seems the county seal of Richmond County, Georgia, contains an image of two stone tablets with Roman numerals I through X. Obviously the stone tablets represent the Ten Commandments. The ACLU, no friend of the Bible, cited the usual argument about "separation of church and state," and thus the county seal could not have an image from the Bible, and so on and so forth.

51. Horace Mann (1796–1859)

American public schools moved, in a relatively short time, from mandatory prayer and Bible reading to prohibiting or even penalizing such activities. One prime shaper of America's public schools probably would have approved. Horace Mann was the great educational crusader of the 1800s, a man who had been brought up in a devout Christian home and who abandoned the faith of his parents. Mann believed that a vital public school system would make the nation great, and the less religion in them, the better. Having been brought up Christian, however, Mann let words and phrases from the Bible sneak into his writings. One example: "If we can but turn the wonderful energy of this people into right channels, what a new heaven and earth might be realized among us!" Mann took the "new heaven and earth" from Revelation 21:1.

52. Ohio, the Bible, and the modern world

The state motto of Ohio is a quote from the Bible: "With God all things are possible" (Matt. 19:26). Inevitably the forces of secularism had to protest this, citing the usual issue of "separation of church and state." In May 2000 a federal appeals court ruled that the motto was indeed unconstitutional.

POLITICAL CORRECTNESS

53. the NCC lectionary

The issue of "sexist language" has had a serious effect on recent Bible translations. Most new versions of the Bible are content to change traditional words like *men* and *mankind* to *humankind,* while not daring to change the male images applied to God and Jesus. But in 1983 the National Council of Churches (not exactly noted for being conservative) sponsored a new "inclusive" lectionary. (A defining note: many churches use a lectionary, a preset series of readings for the various Sundays of each year, usually an Old Testament passage, Gospel passage, Epistle passage, and psalm for each Sunday and holy day.) The "inclusive" lectionary raised a few eyebrows not just by changing "sons of God" to "children of God" (which most people find acceptable) but also by referring to God as both Mother and Father of humankind. This raises the obvious question: Are people really capable of thinking of God as a two-sexed (or sexless) being? Critics said it not only altered the words and meanings of the Bible, but also made for very clumsy use of the English language.

54. *Is the Bible Sexist?*

Hard-core feminists usually answer "Yes!" to this question. Theologian Donald G. Bloesch used it as the title of his 1982 book, which is an interesting study of this ticklish subject. He points out that so-called "inclusive" language does not necessarily overcome "sexism." He also points out that much of radical feminism is a revolt against all authority, not just male authority, and no Christian can have a part in an antiauthority movement, since all of us are under God's authority.

3

Moving Images:
Films and Video

55. *The Prince of Egypt*

Dreamworks, Hollywood's inventive (and moneymaking) production company that includes movie mogul Steven Spielberg, took a real chance with this animated version of the story of Moses and the exodus from Egypt. Let's admit it: Cecil B. DeMille's classic movie *The Ten Commandments*, starring Charlton Heston as Moses, was a tough act to follow. But the animation in this new film was superb, and somehow it managed to be both entertaining and reverent, with no serious departures from the story in the Bible. As a safeguard against offending anyone, the movie involved more than five hundred religious consultants, both Christians and Jews. One result: goofy comic relief such as a wisecracking camel was dropped from the movie. The movie was a commercial success and continues to do well on video.

56. *Jesus*

Can you picture Jesus dancing at a wedding, laughing often, being the object of a girl's crush? Such was the Jesus played by Jeremy Sisto in this four-hour TV movie, first broadcast in May 2000. All in all, the movie followed the Bible closely, but it showed an extremely *human* Jesus, which bothered some viewers more accustomed to the "reverent" portrayals in movies of the past. Perhaps as a bow to contemporary expectations, the movie even featured some special visual effects—notably in a very dramatic temptation scene (with Satan in a contemporary black suit and hip hairdo). Worth noting: the movie drew enough viewers to beat out the phenomenally popular quiz show *Who Wants to Be a Millionaire?*

57. *End of Days*

In 1999, this was the surefire formula for a hit: combine Y2K paranoia, Arnold Schwarzenegger, the book of Revelation, gore, and jaw-dropping special effects. This heart-stopping action/horror film covered some of the same ground as *The Omen* series, with a Satan-Antichrist wreaking havoc. The suave Satan (played by Gabriel Byrne) engages in a sort of "temptation scene" with Arnold (who has the biblical name Jericho), telling him that the Bible is "an overblown press kit." Interestingly, the movie opens with text from Revelation, both in English and Greek. Like many such movies from

Hollywood, this one manages to be both anti-Satan *and* anti-church. With serious profanity and some sexual scenes, the movie deserved its R rating.

58. *The Miracle Maker*

Here was a pleasant TV surprise, aired on Easter 2000: a clay animation retelling of the life of Jesus, done as a collaboration between British and Russian producers. The animation was excellent, and the production featured the voices of such respected actors as Ralph Fiennes and Julie Christie. As with the popular movie *The Prince of Egypt* several months earlier, this one enlisted a large number of clergymen to serve as consultants (and to ensure that nothing irreverent would enter into the film). One curiosity: the character Mary Magdalene was not depicted as a prostitute (a tradition, though not found in the Bible), but as a demon-possessed woman healed by Jesus (definitely found in the Bible—see Luke 8:2).

59. *The Search for Jesus*

In 2000, ABC aired this two-hour special hosted by Peter Jennings. While the program conveyed some useful information about Jesus' life, the "experts" interviewed for the show were (with one exception) extremely skeptical about the truth of the stories told in the Gospels. The show might have been called "Deconstructing Jesus."

60. *Sodom and Gomorrah*

It surprises some viewers of this 1963 movie that, contrary to what they might expect, the wicked cities' sins are not just sexual. They are cesspools of deceit, corruption, and exploitation—something approaching hell on earth. Like so many biblical movies, this one was filmed in Italy.

61. *From the Manger to the Cross*

This was probably the first feature-length biblical movie ever made. Its making was a happy accident: director Sidney Olcott was shooting some outdoor films in Egypt when one of his actresses, Gene Gautier, suffered a sunstroke. While recuperating, she wrote the script for a movie on the life of Jesus. Released in 1912, the movie was (naturally) filmed on location in the Middle East. Gautier played the Virgin Mary. Curiously, the extremely reverent movie stirred up controversy, because in those days (when movies were new and still considered a morally questionable form of entertainment), many people considered it blasphemous to depict Christ on the screen. The controversy helped the movie become a commercial success.

62. *The Passover Plot*

Did Jesus actually "fake" His crucifixion? This controversial 1975 movie (based on an equally controversial book) takes that as its premise. Departing from the Gospels in numerous ways, the films depicts Jesus as a leader of the violent, revolutionary Jewish group known as the Zealots. (For the record, the Gospels tell us that one of Jesus' twelve disciples was Simon the Zealot.) In collaboration with His followers, He fakes His death on the cross, then "rises," with the fake resurrection gaining Him even more followers.

63. *The Prodigal*

Who would have thought the brief parable of the prodigal son (Luke 15:11–32) could be turned into a two-hour movie? MGM did this in 1955, starring (of all people) Lana Turner (who played, appropriately, the priestess of a pagan cult). The movie falls in the old Hollywood tradition of turning a familiar Bible story into a lavish costume drama with hints of sexual titillation.

64. *Noah*

This miserable excuse for a TV movie pleased almost no one. Aired in 1999, it purported to tell the Genesis story of Noah, his wife and family, and the ark. But it was hopelessly confused in its storytelling, for it featured the character Lot (who lived several generations after Noah) and a gang of pirates. Hardly inspiring, and viewers and critics alike were displeased, even with respected actor Jon Voight in the role of Noah.

65. *Salome*

The Gospels tell the sad story of the stepdaughter of Herod, whose dancing pleased him so much he offered her anything she wanted. She asked for, and got, the head of John the Baptist on a platter. (Her famous "dance of the seven veils" is from folklore, not the Bible itself.) The Bible never mentions the girl's name, but tradition has named her Salome, and in this 1953 movie she was played by Rita Hayworth. Chubby actor Charles Laughton played the lecherous Herod in this religious epic that wasn't exactly inspiring, though the costumes and sets were attractive.

66. Monty Python and the Bible

The famous British comedy troupe Monty Python was known for its irreverent (and sometimes downright smutty) skits. The group spoofed the life of Christ in the controversial 1979 movie *Life of Brian*, which depicted a Palestinian peasant mistaken for the Jewish Messiah.

67. *Barabbas*

The New Testament doesn't tell us much about Barabbas, the thief and murderer who was freed at the time of Jesus' trial and crucifixion. Swedish author Par Lagerkvist wrote a novel about Barabbas's wild life, which ends with his own redemption—and crucifixion. In the 1962 movie version, actor Anthony Quinn played Barabbas.

68. *David*

TV mogul Ted Turner hasn't exactly been kind to Bible-believing Christians, but that hasn't stopped his cable channels from producing TV movies based on the Bible. These have included the 1997 production *David*, which sticks fairly close to the Bible in telling its story of the shepherd boy who became king of Israel, plus the numerous subplots about his wayward children.

69. *Jacob*

Made for cable TV, this 1994 movie looks at the trickster Jacob (played by Matthew Modine), who is in turn tricked by his wily uncle Laban. The movie is a fairly dignified telling of the Genesis stories of Jacob and his twelve sons.

70. *Joseph*

The follow-up to the 1994 cable movie *Jacob* follows the life of Jacob's favorite son, Joseph, sold into slavery by his envious brothers. He comes to serve in the household of the Egyptian Potiphar (played by Oscar-winner Ben Kingsley) and eventually becomes the chief power next to Pharaoh himself.

71. *King David*

Actor Richard Gere, known for his attachment to Buddhism, played the king of Israel in this 1985 movie, which pleased neither audiences nor critics. Some Christians who saw the movie objected to the fact that at the end of David's life, he has serious doubts about his devotion to God. Otherwise the movie was a fairly faithful retelling of David's fascinating life.

72. *Between Heaven and Hell*

This 1999 documentary aired on the American Movie Classics cable channel. Its subtitle says it all: *Hollywood Looks at the Bible.* The film provided some forgotten history about the Bible in movies—for example, a long period of time when it was considered extremely irreverent to actually show Jesus on film.

73. Donny as Joseph

In April 2000, the Public Broadcasting System aired a bouncy production of *Joseph and the Amazing Technicolor Dreamcoat*, the pop opera by Andrew Lloyd Webber and Tim Rice. The still-popular play is based, of course, on the Genesis stories of Joseph, his eleven brothers, and his father, Jacob. Forty-two-year-old Donny Osmond sang the role of an extremely youthful-looking Joseph, and TV vamp Joan Collins had a cameo role as the randy wife of Potiphar.

74. quote, misquote

Sometimes the secular media are lax about checking Bible facts. One example: in the violent movie *Pulp Fiction*, one of the main characters quotes (several times, in fact) a long passage from Ezekiel. His quote is completely fictional—not only is it not in Ezekiel, it is not in the Bible at all.

75. *The Last Temptation of Christ*

This very controversial movie was based, sort of, on the Gospels, but more on a novel of the same name by Nikos Kazantzakis. The chief point of controversy was that Jesus, dying on the cross, has a sort of dream-vision in which He imagines Himself as a normal family man, married to Mary Magdalene. Also, the Jesus of the film is One who has grave doubts about His divine mission on earth. Many Christians protested the film, and despite the controversy, it did not make much money.

76. *The Robe*

The first movie released in the wide-screen CinemaScope process in 1953, this was based on a popular novel by Lloyd

Douglas. The robe of the title is Jesus' seamless robe, which falls into the possession of a Roman soldier (played by Richard Burton) who eventually becomes a Christian. The sequel made a few years later was *The Big Fisherman* (the apostle Peter, that is), also based on a Douglas novel.

77. Intolerance

D. W. Griffith is generally regarded as the greatest director of silent movies. His 1916 film *Intolerance* was a four-part drama about man's inhumanity to man. One of the four parts is called "Biblical Story," showing how Jesus was persecuted both by the Romans and by His own people, the Jews.

78. *Esther and the King*

The vampish femme fatale Joan Collins as Esther, the virtuous Jewish girl? So it was in this 1960 movie, which gives the Hollywood treatment to the book of Esther, with all the pomp and splendor of the Persian court.

79. the Hays Code

In its early days, Hollywood feared that the public might lash out against some of the violence and sex in movies. So in 1921, studio heads invited Will Hays, a former postmaster general, to become head of the Motion Picture Producers and Distributors of America, serving as the industry spokesman and arbiter of good taste. A devout layman, Hays developed the Production Code (usually called the Hays Code), with fairly strict guidelines about sex, violence, profanity, and how religious figures could be depicted in films. The code required that films never degrade or defame any religion, nor could God or Christ be blasphemed.

Worth noting: the Hays Code was *not* government censorship. It was voluntarily adopted by the movie industry, not forced on the industry by the government or by any religious group.

80. *David and Bathsheba*

One of the most popular films of 1951 was a biblical epic about King David of Israel and his affair (and later marriage) with the beautiful Bathsheba. It starred two attractive screen idols of the time, Gregory Peck and Susan Hayward.

81. *From Jesus to Christ*

The Public Broadcasting System has generally steered clear of religious subjects, but in 1999 it broadcast this multipart series about the life of Jesus. Mostly it consists of scenes of Israel mingled with sound bites of various scholars commenting on the stories told in the Gospels. Not surprisingly for a PBS program, the scholars were mostly liberal, taking a highly skeptical view of the truth of the Bible.

82. Cinemax 2, with a new gospel

In April 1996 the cable channel Cinemax 2 ran a religious program, "The Gospel According to Jesus." Had Cinemax "got religion"? No way. The program was highly skeptical of the Bible. In fact, it was a recording of people reading from an "edited" version of the Gospels by author Stephen Mitchell. He chose to delete most of the miracles and a good many of the statements made by Jesus in the four Gospels (see 40).

4

What the Famous Said

83. *homo unius libri*

John Wesley (1703–1791), founder of the Methodist movement in the 1700s, called himself a *homo unius libri*—"a man of one book." That book, of course, was the Book itself, the Bible. While Wesley read widely in theology and devotional books, he always came back to the Bible as the one sure foundation for belief. Wesley borrowed the phrase *homo unius libri* from Pilgram Marpeck, an Anabaptist preacher in the 1500s.

84. the real Kenobi

English actor Alec Guinness (1914–2000) was probably best known to American audiences for his role as Obi-Wan Kenobi in the original *Star Wars* trilogy. In fact, he was a multitalented actor, famed for playing Shakespeare as well as dozens of modern comic and tragic roles, doing both stage and film. Guinness was a devout Catholic, one who daily quoted this verse: "Cause me to hear thy lovingkindness in the morning; for in thee do I trust" (Ps. 143:8 KJV).

85. warmed-up Wesley

Methodist founder John Wesley had a dramatic conversion experience in 1738, partly brought about by hearing someone read from Martin Luther's commentary on Romans. Wesley wrote in his journal that he felt his heart "strangely warmed," and in the following days found the Bible meaning more to him than ever before: "I scarce remember to have opened the New Testament but upon some precious promise. And I saw more than ever that the gospel is in truth but one great promise."

86. "the night cometh"

John 9:4 records these words of Jesus: "I must work the works of him that sent me, while it is day: the night cometh, when no man can work" (KJV). For some reason these words caught the imagination of two of the greatest British authors. Walter Scott, author of *Ivanhoe* and other classics, had the verse inscribed on his home's sundial, and Dr. Samuel Johnson, literary dictator of England in the late 1700s, had the same verse inscribed on his pocketwatch.

87. Scott's inscription

Sir Walter Scott (1771–1832), author of *Kenilworth*, *Ivanhoe*, and other classic historical novels, wrote this poem inside his own Bible: "Within that awful volume lies / The mystery of mysteries! / Happiest they of human race / To whom God has granted grace / To read, to fear, to hope, to pray, / To lift the latch, and force the way, / And better had they ne'er been born / Who read to doubt or read to scorn."

88. Sir Walter Scott, terminal

Death has a way of focusing people's minds on the divine. Take the example of novelist Sir Walter Scott (see 87). The story goes that Scott on his deathbed asked his son-in-law to bring him "the book" from his huge library. His son-in-law asked, "Which book, sir?" and the great author replied, "There is only one Book," referring, of course, to the Bible.

89. Stanley, I presume?

The man who uttered the famous words, "Dr. Livingstone, I presume?" was Henry Morton Stanley, a journalist-explorer who had gone to seek out the great missionary-explorer David Livingstone. When Stanley began his trek through Africa, he carried seventy-three of his favorite books. He and his crew grew fatigued after their African journey, and eventually most of Stanley's books were cast aside as unnecessary weight—except for one, his Bible, of course. Biblically speaking, Stanley had put his long, fatiguing journey to good use: he had read the Bible three times from Genesis through Revelation.

90. Old Hickory, tamed

Andrew Jackson (1767–1845) was not only a two-term president but also a military hero of the War of 1812, a feared fighter (and conqueror) of the Indians, and a hot-tempered man who fought duels and fought off a would-be assassin with his own cane. Under the influence of his beloved wife, Rachel, the man known as "Old Hickory" came to accept the truths of Christianity. While on his deathbed, he pointed a visitor to the Bible on his bedside table and said, "That Book, sir, is the rock on which our republic rests."

91. "the secret of England's greatness"

England's Queen Victoria gave her name to the entire nineteenth century, a century that saw a burst of worldwide missionary activity. Not deeply religious herself, Victoria was at least aware that the faith of the Bible played a considerable role in England's prominence in the world. Receiving an ambassador from an African prince, she was asked the question "What is the secret of your country's power and success throughout the world?" The queen picked up a Bible and answered, "Tell your prince that this Book is the secret of England's greatness." The National Gallery in London has a famous painting of this scene, with the queen's beloved husband, Prince Albert, smiling with approval.

92. Burke the eloquent

Edmund Burke (1729–1797) was a great British politician, noted for his eloquent writings and speeches in the Parliament. Burke was a highly moral man (a rare thing in the political life of that age) and a practicing Christian. Like many noted public speakers, he salted his speeches with phrases and images from the Bible. When the American colonies rebelled against Great Britain (a rebellion that Burke supported), Burke was horrified to learn that the king, George III, had ordered the churches to hold services in support of England's winning the war with America. Burke wrote that "till our churches are purified from this abominable service, I shall consider them not as temples of the Almighty, but the synagogues of Satan." He took the phrase "synagogues of Satan" from Revelation 2:9 and 3:9. Burke said that before a major speech he liked to read a chapter from Isaiah: "Isaiah possesses both the blaze of eloquence and the light of truth."

93. Sidney the poet

Sir Philip Sidney (1554–1586) was considered the perfect man of his day: a gentleman, soldier, poet, and Christian. This man, an ornament to the court of England's Elizabeth I, wrote much about the art of poetry. According to Sidney, the oldest and best types of poetry "were they that did imitate the inconceivable excellencies of God. Such were David in his Psalms, Solomon, in his Song of Songs, in his Ecclesiastes, and Proverbs, Moses and Deborah in their hymns, and the writer of Job. Against these none will speak that hath the Holy Ghost in due reverence."

94. Bacon and truth

Francis Bacon's *Essays* used to be required reading in school, and it is a pity they have fallen out of use. One of his essays begins with the famous line "'What is truth?' said jesting Pilate, and would not stay for an answer." Bacon took Pilate's words from John 18:38. In another work, Bacon harked back to the Garden of Eden story in Genesis and wrote, "God Almighty first planted a garden, and indeed it is the purest of human pleasures."

95. the Russian's mystery

In his classic novel *The Brothers Karamazov*, Russian author Fyodor Dostoyevsky wrote that "the greatness of the Bible lies just in the fact that it is a mystery—that the passing earthly show and the eternal truth are brought together in it . . . What a book the Bible is, what a miracle, what strength is given with it to man."

96. Bitter Bierce

Ambrose Bierce (1842–1914) was an American journalist and short-story writer known for his sarcasm and bitterness. Author of "The Devil's Dictionary," the man called "Bitter Bierce" was no Christian, but he claimed to have a moral center in his life: "'What in the circumstances would Jesus have done?'—the Jesus of the New Testament, not the Jesus of the commentators, theologians, priests, and parsons."

97. Helen Keller

This amazing woman overcame the obstacles of deafness and blindness and became an inspiration to everyone who knew her. The famous play and movie *The Miracle Worker* depicts her childhood and her amazing teacher, Annie Sullivan. Keller was widely read, and regarding the Bible, she wrote, "How shall I speak of the glories I have since discovered in the Bible? For years I have read it with an ever-broadening sense of joy and inspiration, and I love it as I love no other book."

98. Wilberforce and the slavers

In Britain's Parliament there was no one more committed to ending the slave trade than the passionate William Wilberforce (1759–1825). He was a leading member in the evangelical group known as the Clapham Sect, committed not only to missions and evangelism but to rooting out social evils as well. Wilberforce helped end Britain's role in slave trading. He wrote, "Through all my perplexities and distresses, I seldom read any other book. It has been my hourly study."

99. Prime Minister Gladstone

One of England's greatest statesmen was the devout William E. Gladstone (1809–1898), who tried to combine wisdom and compassion in the political sphere. Gladstone kept a voluminous diary that testifies to his devotion to God and the Bible. One example: "On most occasions of very sharp pressure or trial, some word of Scripture has come home to me as if born on angel's wings."

100. Daniel Webster

One of America's greatest statesmen and orators was the formidable Webster (1782–1852), who perhaps inherited his rhetorical gifts from his father, who would read from the Bible in a beautiful voice. His father could mesmerize tavern guests by reading from the Psalms. Webster said that before delivering a speech in the U.S. Senate he would take "as a tonic the eighth Psalm and the fortieth chapter of Isaiah."

101. TR

This is how historians often refer to Theodore Roosevelt (1858–1919). TR was not religious in the usual sense, but he was a highly moral man who loved, and often quoted from, the Bible. At the 1912 convention of his newly founded Progressive Party, the man who said he felt as "fit as a bull moose" proclaimed, "We stand at Armageddon and battle for the Lord!" The bull moose lost the election to Woodrow Wilson, but his place in American history is assured. On one occasion, TR said that "if a man is not familiar with the Bible, he has suffered a loss which he had better make all possible haste to correct."

102. William Hazlitt

Hazlitt (1778–1830) was an English political radical but is best remembered today as an excellent essayist. One of his highly readable essays bears the title "On Persons One Would Wish to Have Seen." In the essay, he speaks of the desire to meet Judas Iscariot: "I would fain see the face of him who, having dipped his hand in the same dish with the Son of Man, could afterwards betray him."

103. Ralph Waldo Emerson

The essays of Emerson (1803–1882) used to be required reading for every schoolchild, and he is still quite readable. The man known as a Transcendentalist was hardly a Christian in the usual sense, but he did have a deep respect for the Bible. In fact, Emerson noted that mankind would probably never get rid of the Bible, even if it wished to: "Pitch it out the window and bounce it comes back again." He claimed that the Bible was "the most original book in the world," "the alphabet of the nations," and "an engine of education of the first power."

104. James Russell Lowell

One of the great American poets of the 1800s, Lowell (1819–1891) did what so many intelligent people do: start out young as a renegade, then come around later to an appreciation of tradition and religion. At age twenty he wrote that he was unsure whether certain parts of the Bible were truly inspired. At age fifty he wrote that he had learned to take comfort in God, and at fifty-seven he admitted that, in spite of Darwinism and the new science, he wasn't willing to throw away the truths of the Bible. At age sixty-six he wrote that the Bible's moral teachings stand unchanged: "The Ten Commandments will not budge, / And stealing will continue stealing."

105. Thomas Carlyle

Scottish-born Carlyle (1795–1881) was a noted historian and biographer. Carlyle was reared in a devout Presbyterian family, but as an adult he threw aside the religion of his youth. Even so, he had a deep appreciation for the Bible. "In the poorest cottage," he wrote, "are books—is one BOOK, wherein for several thousands of years the spirit of man has found light, and nourishment, and an interpreting response to whatever is deepest in him." Regarding the Jesus of the Gospels, he wrote, "Look on our divinest symbol, on Jesus of Nazareth, and his life, and what followed therefrom. Higher has the human thought not yet reached."

106. Walter Savage Landor

True to his middle name, author Landor (1775–1864) led a wild youth, being thrown out of college because of his radical political ideas. He did write some excellent poetry, along with *Imaginary Conversations*, a series of discussions among historical figures. Regarding the Bible, Landor wrote that the Bible is "a Book which, to say nothing of its holiness or authority, contains more specimens of genius and taste than any other volume in existence."

107. the Brownings' love letters

English poet Robert Browning (1812–1889) exchanged warm (and highly intellectual) love letters with poet Elizabeth Barrett (1806–1861). Browning frequently quoted from or alluded to the Bible, and Barrett responded in kind. They eventually married, and both of them frequently quoted the Bible and wrote on biblical subjects. Robert responded to Darwinism the way many religious people of his day did: he chose to ignore it rather than confront it.

108. Lord Tennyson

The great English poet Alfred, Lord Tennyson (1809–1891) faced a dilemma that most sensitive people faced in his day: Should we accept—or ignore—the findings of science, particularly the theory of evolution? It was never clear just how Tennyson solved the dilemma. His poetry shows the clear influence of the Bible, and he helped organize a Metaphysical Society to help men solve the religion-science problem, yet he practically never took part in the society. Tennyson learned Hebrew late in life for the express purpose of being able to translate the book of Job, then dropped the whole project. While on his deathbed, he asked not for his Bible but for his book of Shakespeare. Tennyson's long and greatest poem, "In Memoriam," contains these famous lines: "Strong Son of God, immortal Love, / Whom we, that have not seen thy face, / By faith, and faith alone, embrace, / Believing where we cannot prove."

109. the Bible-and-pagan curriculum

Thomas Arnold (1795–1842) was a noted preacher and head of England's famous Rugby School who devoted himself to producing "Christian gentlemen." While Arnold was a truly saintly man and great educator, his biographers have noted something curious about what schools in those days taught the "Christian gentlemen": while they studied the Bible and were taught that it was God's guide for life, they also studied the Greek and Roman poets, who celebrated the joys of the flesh (including promiscuity and homosexuality) and saw no life beyond this world. The "great literature" the boys were brought up on had a moral basis that contradicted everything they read in their Bibles. Small wonder that the younger generation—including Thomas Arnold's son, the poet Matthew Arnold—began to seriously doubt the Bible's truths (see 157).

110. the Quaker poet

John Greenleaf Whittier (1807–1892) was one of the best American poets of the 1800s, and also a Bible man from his childhood on. At age seven he could recite whole chapters of the Bible. His father would invite guests to start a familiar Bible chapter, stop midway, and have young John finish it. Whittier had a reputation as a "gentle Quaker," but his pen could grow vicious in denouncing slavery, which he saw as a horrible practice that did not square with the Bible.

111. Garrison the liberator

One of the most outspoken abolitionists in the pre–Civil War days was Bible-quoting William Lloyd Garrison (1805–1879), who published *The Liberator* and never let up in denouncing slavery. Garrison was something very familiar in the 1800s: the social reformer who claimed to base his position on the Bible. "Take away the Bible," he wrote, "and our warfare with oppression and infidelity and intemperance and impurity is removed—we have no authority to speak and no courage to act."

112. Uncle Tom's author

Harriet Beecher Stowe gave the world the popular anti-slavery novel *Uncle Tom's Cabin*, and people often forget that its author was a devout Christian. She credited the Bible not only with giving her a moral foundation but also with stimulating creativity: "I am certain that the constant contact of the Bible with my childish mind was a great mental stimulant, as it certainly was the cause of a singular and vague pleasure."

113. Lincoln's creed

Abraham Lincoln, a great reader of the Bible, frustrated many Christians because he refused to associate with any church in particular. When one visitor to the White House asked Lincoln what his creed was, Lincoln replied with Micah 6:8: "He hath showed thee, O man, what is good; and what doth the LORD require of thee, but to do justly, and to love mercy, and to walk humbly with thy God?" (KJV).

114. Sidney Lanier

Sadly neglected today, Lanier (1842–1881) was a notable Southern poet of his day, famous for "The Marshes of Glynn" and other poems. The former Confederate soldier (and prisoner of war) wrote that "in any wise distribution of your moments, after you have read the Bible and Shakespeare, you have no time to read anything until you have read these."

115. Francis Thompson

Best known for the deeply Christian poem "The Hound of Heaven," Thompson (1859–1907) was a devout Catholic who claimed that the Bible not only aided him spiritually but also creatively. He wrote that "its influence was mystical; it revealed to me a whole scheme of existence, and lit up life like a lantern."

116. Robert Louis Stevenson

Author of *Treasure Island, Dr. Jekyll and Mr. Hyde,* and other classics, Stevenson (1850–1894) was brought up in a religious Scottish home. He wrote that his earliest memories were of "nursery rhymes, the Bible, and Mr. M'Cheyne"—M'Cheyne being the author who developed a much-used system for reading through the Bible in one year (see 926). Concerning the Bible, Stevenson wrote that though the Bible characters were "penned in rude times, they are prized more and more as civilization advances."

117. Hall Caine

Sadly forgotten today, English novelist Caine (1853–1931) admitted that he snatched many of the plots for his novels from the Bible. *The Manxman* is the story of David and Uriah, *The Deemster* is the story of the prodigal son, and so on. Caine could also have borrowed a novel title from the Bible for *The Woman Thou Gavest Me* (see Gen. 3:12 KJV).

118. nature boy Muir

John Muir (1838–1914) was a well-known naturalist, active in helping the U.S. establish national parks. Born in Scotland, he was forced by his father to memorize a certain number of Bible verses each day. By age eleven he knew all the New Testament and three-fourths of the Old, and could recite the Bible from Matthew 1:1 to Revelation 21:21 without a hitch. In spite of this "force-feeding," he still appreciated the Book as an adult.

119. William Collins

Collins (1721–1759) was of a group that the 1700s had a wealth of: talented poets who suffered from mental illness. He wrote a few excellent poems in his short life, and was a friend of the great literary dictator of London, Dr. Samuel Johnson. In his last years he gave away all his books and read only the New Testament, telling Dr. Johnson, "I have only one book, but that Book is the best."

120. Cowper, the stricken deer

William Cowper (1731–1800) was a noted poet, but, like his contemporaries William Collins and Christopher Smart, a sufferer of mental illness. All his life poor Cowper was sensitive and easily depressed, though he often found comfort in the Bible. He recalled suffering from a local bully as a child, but taking comfort in Psalm 118:6: "I will not fear: what can man do unto me?" (KJV). Cowper became friends with the noted pastor John Newton, and the two collaborated in producing a hymnal that is still the source of excellent hymns. Newton is best known for his "Amazing Grace," and Cowper wrote such classics as

"God Moves in a Mysterious Way" and "There Is a Fountain Filled with Blood," all of them filled with phrases and images from the Bible. But in his last years Cowper practically gave up religion altogether, feeling almost constantly depressed, describing himself as a "stricken deer that left the herd."

121. Mrs. Blake's absent husband

Catherine Blake was the wife of poet-artist William Blake (1757–1827), who may have lived his life just this side of insanity. No one doubts Blake's poetic talents today, nor that his mental world was filled with people and images from the Bible. But the poor man was, frankly, delusional, feeling from childhood on that he could see and converse with angels, people from the Bible, even God Himself. His wife lived with him forty-five years, once remarking, "Mr. Blake has been so little with me, for though in body we were never separated, he was incessantly away in Paradise."

122. Hogg the shepherd

Scottish poet James Hogg (1770–1835) was known as the "Ettrick Shepherd" because he was (surprise!) an actual sheepherder from the village of Ettrick. Hogg was largely self-taught, growing up with knowledge of the Bible and his mother's many stories about brownies, kelpies, and other imaginary creatures. Hogg had memorized almost all the Psalms and once said that the Bible was "this herd-boy's only book."

123. William Wordsworth

Wordsworth (1770–1850), who certainly had an appropriate name, was one of England's greatest poets, famous for his nature poems and a leader in what came to be called the Romantic movement in literature. Wordsworth was so "in tune with nature" that we could more accurately call him a nature worshiper than a Christian. Even so, he knew the Bible well. In his book-length poem *The Prelude*, he referred to the Bible as "the voice that roars along the bed of Jewish song," and as "God's pure word by miracle revealed."

124. Patrick Henry

Best known for his famous "Give me liberty or give me death!" speech, Henry (1736–1799) was a master of oratory, peppering his speeches and writings with images from the Bible. His "Give me liberty" speech contains the words "Gentlemen may cry, Peace, peace—but there is no peace," almost a direct quotation from Jeremiah 6:14. Henry was more a man of the spoken word than the written word, but he wrote that "there is a Book worth all other books that were ever printed."

125. "speak as a man of the world"

John Quincy Adams was a president and son of a president. Also a powerful member of the House of Representatives, at the end of his public life he was known as "Old Man Eloquent." Adams said, "The first and almost the only book deserving of universal attention is the Bible. I speak as a man of the world, and I say to you, 'Search the Scriptures.'"

126. hammering the Philistines

Rudyard Kipling (1865–1936), English author, is known for his poems and for such classics as *The Jungle Book* and his *Just So Stories*. Kipling was a world traveler, and in Jerusalem he bought a pen and gave it a name, Jael. He said he was going to use Jael to "hammer the Philistines." Kipling had in mind the story of the Israelite woman Jael, who in Judges 4 kills an enemy captain by hammering a tent peg through his head. Kipling was using "Philistines" to refer to uncultured people—specifically, critics who disliked his writings.

127. Coleridge the Christian

English poet and essayist Samuel Taylor Coleridge (1772–1834) was familiar with the Bible (as were almost all authors of his day) and commented that Paul's Letter to Philemon (one of the shortest "books" of the Bible) was "the most completely sweet and cultured letter ever sent by one gentleman to another."

On a more serious level, Coleridge observed a decline of faith in his day and feared that people were becoming materialists, with no feeling for God or faith. He noted that the words of Genesis 2:7—"And man became a living soul" (KJV)—would always be more comforting than any secular system of thought.

128. Coleridge's list

The great poet Samuel Taylor Coleridge (1772–1834) had a high opinion of the Bible, at least after a youthful spell of agnosticism and doubt. Coleridge wrote that "for more than a thousand years the Bible has gone hand in hand with civilization, science, law—in short, with the moral and intellectual cultivation of the species." Asked by a friend to name the best books to have in a library, Coleridge told him, "I'll give you my list: the Greek plays, Plato, Lord Bacon's works, Shakespeare, Milton, Dante, Petrarch . . . and last, yet first, the Bible."

129. Housman on the KJV

Laurence Housman (1865–1959) was brother of the noted English poet A. E. Housman, and was himself a successful novelist and artist. Commenting on the influence of the King James Version on English writers, Housman stated that "not Shakespeare nor Bacon, nor any great figure in English literature that one could name has had so wide and deep an influence on the form and substance of all the literary and poetic work which followed during the next two centuries as has the King James Version of the Old and New Testaments."

130. Abraham Cowley

Cowley (1618–1667) was a great poet in an age that had so many. Among his many poems was a long (but unfinished) epic poem, *Davideis*, about the life of King David of Israel. Cowley, like his contemporary John Milton, believed strongly that the Bible was an excellent source of plots and ideas for poems.

131. mornings with Hebrew

English master poet John Milton (as all of his readers know) was absolutely saturated with the Bible. From his childhood he formed the habit of reading it every morning—not in English, but in the original Hebrew and Greek. Milton was aware of his own poetic powers and the talents of the great poets of the past, but he thought the words of the Bible were best: "There are no songs to be compared to the songs of Zion, no orations equal to those of the Prophets, no politics equal to those the Scriptures can teach us."

132. *Tetrachordon*

The word is Greek for "four strings," and it was the title that English poet John Milton used for his long essay on divorce. The "four strings" were four key Bible passages on divorce, one passage each from Genesis, Deuteronomy, Matthew, and 1 Corinthians. Milton was married (and widowed) several times and was not an easy man to live with. He wrote *Tetrachordon* in 1645, during a time when he was hoping to justify a divorce from his current wife, who had left him and returned to her parents. Suffice it to say that in his book he maintained that the Bible did not *prohibit* divorce.

133. Daniel Defoe

The author of *Robinson Crusoe* and other classics, Defoe (1669–1731) had very religious Presbyterian parents who made him copy out sections of the Bible and take notes on sermons. Defoe did not always live as a Christian, but he certainly thought like one, and many people are surprised to find how deeply Christian the tale *Robinson Crusoe* really is. Just as some classics have had the sex taken out, so this classic (which is often published in children's editions) has had the religion taken out. In Defoe's original version, the shipwrecked Crusoe, who had not been religious in the past, finds himself more and more dependent on God, and pleased that there is a Bible among the few articles he was stranded with. Crusoe gains much comfort from the Bible, learning a new, God-centered way of life in the wilderness, "Thus I lived mighty comfortably." Meeting a heathen (his "man Friday"), he converts him to Christianity, instructing him in the Bible.

134. Frederick Faber

Faber (1814–1863) was a Church of England minister who, with many others, left that church to become a Catholic priest. Faber's hymns today are sung by Catholics and Protestants alike (the most famous being "Faith of Our Fathers"). Changing from Protestant to Catholic meant that Faber had to give up the King James Version and switch to the Catholic-approved Douai Version. He lamented the loss, saying that the KJV "lives on the ear like a music that can never be forgotten, like the sounds of church bells . . . It is part of the national mind, and the anchor of the national seriousness."

135. Robert Burns's discovery

Burns (1759–1796) was Scotland's most famous poet, but one with a grudge against Christians, most of whom he believed were hypocrites. Nevertheless, at age twenty-eight the loose-living poet made a discovery: the Bible was fascinating. He wrote to a friend, "I have taken tooth and nail to the Bible and got through the five books of Moses and halfway in Joshua. It is really a glorious book."

Burns ordered a new copy from a printer and asked that it be lavishly bound.

136. "The Cotter's Saturday Night"

Scottish poet Robert Burns had many harsh things to say about Christianity, particularly in such poems as "Holy Willie's Prayer" and "The Holy Fair," in which he lashed out at hypocrisy. But Burns wasn't always so antireligion. In his poem "The Cotter's Saturday Night," he pictured the happy home life of a Scottish family, which included the father of the family leading in the singing of psalms: "Compared with these, Italian trills are tame." Apparently Burns did, on occasion, believe that Bible-believing Christians could be both sincere and happy.

137. John Ruskin

Ruskin (1819–1900) was a noted English author and art expert, in large part responsible for the revival of Gothic architecture in England and America. He was also one deeply influenced by the Bible. His mother had him reading aloud from the Bible as soon as he was able: "she began with the first verse of Genesis and went straight through to the last verse of the Apocalypse—hard names, numbers, Levitical law, and all; and began again at Genesis." Ruskin was a brilliant man, widely read in every subject, but in his old age he wrote that his education in the Bible "I count very confidently the most precious, and on the whole the one *essential* part of all my education."

138. "Cursed be Sally!"

Thomas Babington Macaulay (1800–1859) was a noted English statesman, poet, and historian, best known for his popular *History of England*. Macaulay was typical of people of his day, being steeped in the Bible from his early childhood. When only a tot he threw a tantrum because the family maid had moved some of the stones in his play garden. "Cursed be Sally!" he cried, "for it is written, 'Cursed be he that removeth his neighbor's landmark.'" The child was quoting Deuteronomy 27:17.

139. language via the Bible

Thomas Babington Macaulay (see 138), the great English historian, had an amazing memory and an equally amazing ability to learn languages. When he wished to learn a new one, he would begin with the Bible in that language, picking up the language's vocabulary and grammar without having to consult reference books. Macaulay wrote that the Bible was indispensable for literary culture—indeed, it was the one book "which, if everything else in our language should perish, would alone suffice to show its beauty and power."

SKEPTICS AND CRITICS

140. the goddess on God's Word

Glamorous film queen Marlene Dietrich (1902–1992) was (like most Hollywood folk) a skeptic about religion and the Bible. Her daughter claimed that Dietrich said, "The Bible is the best script ever written, but you can't really believe it." Her daughter also noted that her mother, who hated and feared air travel, always carried a cross, a star of David, a St. Christopher medal, and a rabbit's foot whenever she flew. Apparently even people who "can't really believe" the Bible feel an occasional need for some spiritual support. In her old age, Dietrich mentioned to the daughter that Christmas "has something to do with someone being born in a stable, doesn't it?"

141. D. H. Lawrence

The son of an English miner, Lawrence (1885–1930) gained fame as a poet but even more fame as author of some near-pornographic novels, such as *Women in Love* and the notorious *Lady Chatterly's Lover*. Lawrence wrote a short novel, *The Man Who Died*, in which the resurrected Christ does not ascend to heaven but enters into a carnal relationship with an Egyptian priestess, teaching that physical love is more important than spiritual. Lawrence, who had grown up among working-class Christians, noted that they loved the book of Revelation, with its images of the poor and powerless seeing the rich and the mighty brought to destruction; he also called Revelation "the least Christian book in the New Testament."

142. the poet Swine-born

Algernon Charles Swinburne (1837–1909) was one of England's greatest poets in the late 1800s—and also, as he himself put it, "an evangelist for atheism." In one of his poems, Swinburne spoke of "the supreme evil, God," and he enjoyed shocking Christians with his antireligion views. The short, redheaded Swinburne was addicted to drinking and brothels, and even some of his admirers referred to him as "Swine-born." He knew the Bible well even as he despised it. In his poem "Hymn to Man," he compares the religious people of his day to the prophets of Baal who are made to look silly in their confrontation with God's prophet Elijah (1 Kings 18).

143. Samuel Butler

"I hate God and my father" was the theme of novelist Samuel Butler's life. Butler (1835–1902), son of a Church of England minister, is most famous for his auto-biographical novel *The Way of All Flesh*, in which the main character's cold, narrow-minded father is clearly Butler's own father. Butler's hatred of Christianity and the Bible mostly stemmed from hatred of his father. He became convinced that the Gospel authors were con artists and that Jesus had not died on the cross but had been laid in the tomb still alive and later resuscitated. Butler's writings appealed to a whole generation that had turned against whatever their parents believed. For the record: Butler not only tried to demolish Christianity, but also Darwinism, which he saw as being full of contradictions.

144. Voltaire, mistaken

The revered French author Voltaire (1694–1778) claimed to believe in God but was an avowed enemy of traditional Christianity and a severe skeptic where the Bible was concerned. In one of his optimistic (and anti-Christian) moods he wrote these words: "I will go through the forest of the Scriptures and girdle all the trees, so that in one hundred years Christianity will be but a vanishing memory." Well, Voltaire failed to "girdle all the trees," and greater intellectuals than himself have likewise failed to make Christianity a "vanishing memory."

145. "Moses the juggler"

Christopher Marlowe (1564–1593) was a contemporary of William Shakespeare, and also a noted poet and playwright, famed for *Dr. Faustus* and other plays. Marlowe led a fairly wild and unconventional life, and some accused him of "atheistical opinions," meaning that his religious views were unorthodox. Like all educated men of his day, Marlowe read the Bible, but he referred to Moses as a "juggler" of words, and said that if he were to create a new religion, it would be far superior to Christianity. Marlowe died young in a tavern brawl.

146. Gibbon's *Decline and Fall*

One of the great works of history is *The Decline and Fall of the Roman Empire*, the masterpiece of English author Edward Gibbon (1737–1794). Being an extreme skeptic in religion, Gibbon was certain that the main cause of Rome's downfall was Christianity, which he saw as hypocritical and corrupt. When reporting the persecution of Christians under the Roman emperors, Gibbon said it was not as bad as people thought, and besides, Christians had persecuted each other throughout the centuries.

Gibbon's history was widely read, not only in his own day but for the next century, so generations of readers absorbed skepticism about the Bible, miracles, and the worth of Christianity. Without ever writing one direct criticism of the Bible or the church, his masterwork helped to undermine people's faith in both.

147. Aldous Huxley

The English author who created *Brave New World* was a dabbler in drugs and Eastern religions and had little use for

Christianity. He was familiar with the Bible, but had the notion (a very modern one) that the only purpose religion might serve was a revolutionary one: "From Isaiah to Karl Marx, the prophets have spoken with one voice. In the golden age to which they look forward there will be liberty, peace, justice, and brotherly love." One wonders how the great prophet Isaiah would have responded to being lumped together with Communist founder Karl Marx.

148. Thomas Hardy

Hardy (1840–1928) was a great poet and also a novelist who produced such classics as *Tess of the D'Urbervilles* and *The Return of the Native*. Yet he was also a gloomy soul who put no faith in God or the Bible. His poem "God's Funeral" is a sad statement of a godless world. Even so, he knew the Bible well and an amazing number of the characters in his novels have biblical names—the most comical being Cain Ball (whose mother, "not being a Scripture-read woman, made a mistake at his christening, thinking 'twas Abel killed Cain").

149. evangelist in reverse

The English poet James Thomson (1834–1882) had an extremely religious mother, which turned him against Christianity and the Bible, even though he learned it at her knee. Thomson was a talented poet but an angry, depressed, and alcoholic man who considered himself an evangelist for atheism. Choosing an image from the Bible, he referred to himself as "Ishmael in the desert."

150. before Marx, Hegel

Before the influential German philosopher Karl Marx there was the greatest influence on Marx, Georg Wilhelm Friedrich Hegel (1770–1831). Unlike Marx, Hegel was not an atheist, but he was hardly a Christian, either. For Hegel, the Bible and Christianity were a collection of myths, interesting as illustrations of the truths of philosophy. Hegel said Christianity was "the religion of truth," but then immediately added that it was "not historically accurate." From Hegel, Marx took the idea that man was moving toward a heaven on earth, but one that would be achieved without God or religion.

151. Engels and the Bible

Friedrich Engels (1820–1895) stands in the shadow of Karl Marx, his coauthor of the infamous *Communist Manifesto*. Engels did not despise religion quite as much as Marx did, and he noticed that Communists and social reformers in general often took their inspiration from the Bible, even when they rejected Christianity. Engels believed that Christianity in its original form was communistic (see Acts 4:32).

152. *Il Duce,* Antichrist

Throughout history, dictators have always been accused of being the Antichrist—sometimes to their face. Italian fascist dictator Benito Mussolini, *Il Duce*, was told by some Belgian Christians that he was feared to be the Antichrist. Mussolini was fascinated: "Is that really described in the Bible? Where is it found?"

153. Southey vs. Byron

Robert Southey was Britain's Poet Laureate from 1813 until his death in 1843. Southey had harsh things to say about some of the younger poets, many of whom he described as the "satanic school of poetry" because of their immorality and opposition to traditional religion and morality. When King George III died in 1820, Southey wrote a long poem, "Vision of Judgment," in honor of the late monarch. In a preface to the poem he attacked the "satanic school," using words drawn from the Bible (describing their attachment to the false gods Belial and Moloch, for example). Regarding this preface, Southey wrote, "I have sent a stone from my sling which has smitten their Goliath in the forehead." This "Goliath" was talented but immoral Lord Byron (see 154), who countered with his own "Vision of Judgment." In Byron's poem, Satan is suave and genteel, Peter is temperamental, and the archangel Michael is cowardly. Generations of readers have concluded that Byron was a better poet than Southey, but their opposing morals and values are another matter.

154. the wicked lord

Several poets of the early 1800s were loosely referred to as the "satanic school" of poetry because of their contempt for religion and conventional morals. The best-known of these was Lord Byron (1788–1824), whose life was pretty much the opposite of a Bible-guided morality. Even so, Byron was well read in all fields, including the Bible. He wrote, "I am a great reader of these books and had read them through and through before I was eight years old; that is to say, the Old Testament, for the New struck me as a task, but the other as a pleasure." On one occasion a Methodist tried to convert Byron to a better life, but he found that Byron was quite adept at quoting the Bible. Late in his life Byron wrote, "I do not reject the doctrines of Christianity; I only ask a few more proofs to profess them sincerely." Byron died young, before he had the chance to experience enough "proofs."

155. Walt Whitman

American poet Whitman (1819–1892) is best known for his *Leaves of Grass*, a collection of free-verse poetry that readers either love or hate. Whitman was a homosexual, and his writings make clear that he despised Christianity. Even so, late in life he indicated that he had read and admired the Bible: "How many ages and generations have brooded and wept and agonized over this Book! What untellable joys and ecstasies, what support to martyrs at the stake! . . . Translated in all languages, how it has united this diverse world! There is not a verse, not a word, but is thick-studded with human emotion."

156. the Walden Pond man

Famous for *Walden* and other writings, Henry David Thoreau (1817–1862) was a friend and neighbor of Ralph Waldo Emerson (see 103), and both men were part of that broad philosophical movement known as Transcendentalism. Thoreau did not consider himself a Christian and had some harsh things to say about religion in general, but fairly late in life he did learn to appreciate the Bible. Having become fond of the New Testament, he wrote that "I know of no book that has so few readers. To Christians, no less than Greeks and Jews, it is foolishness and a stumbling block." In other words, Thoreau's reading of the Bible made him appreciate the Bible more but Christians even less.

157. Matthew Arnold

A noted poet and critic, Arnold (1822–1888) was the son of the devout Thomas Arnold, headmaster of the elite Rugby School and self-appointed shaper of "Christian gentlemen." Matthew did not have the religious certainty of his father, however (see 109). In his poem "Dover Beach," he lamented the subsiding of the "Sea of Faith" that had once seemed so reliable. As well as his poetry and literary essays, Arnold wrote such books as *God and the Bible*, *St. Paul and Protestantism*, and *Literature and Dogma*. Arnold was one of many people who thought Christianity and the Bible served useful social purposes even if they were not true. He was genuinely sad that, in his day, it was not just the intellectuals who were doubting the Bible but the common people as well.

158. Hearn's observation

American author Lafcadio Hearn (1850–1904) was a curiosity: born of Greek and Irish parents, a world traveler, and, late in life, a citizen of Japan. Hearn had no use for the Bible as a spiritual guide, but, like many authors, he valued it as literature. In fact, he made a wise observation: "It is only since Englishmen ceased to believe in the Bible that they began to discover how beautiful it was." He had a point: when people truly believe that the Bible is the foundation for their thoughts and deeds, they do not waste time praising it as literature.

159. bad boy Shelley

One of England's great poets was Percy Bysshe Shelley (1792–1822), a lifelong radical who enjoyed mocking Christianity and conventional morality. Yet the loose-living Shelley was fascinated with the Bible, and he contemplated writing a long epic poem based on the book of Job. In her diary, his wife, Mary (who wrote the novel *Frankenstein*), recorded that Shelley read the Bible almost every day. This was the same man who in his college days had written a book titled *The Necessity of Atheism*. Like many people of his time—including, across the Atlantic, Thomas Jefferson—Shelley wanted the high morality of the Bible without all the "mythology," yet he was clearly fascinated by those "myths."

5

Customs of Christians

160. the four Advent candles

There are four Sundays in the pre-Christmas season of Advent, and traditionally the Advent wreath has four purple candles, lit on the successive Sundays. Many people don't know that the candles have symbolic—and biblical—meanings: (1) The first is the *prophecy* candle, reminding us that Jesus' birth was foretold in the Old Testament. (2) Next is the *Bethlehem* candle, recalling Micah's prophecy that Jesus would be born in Bethlehem. (3) The *shepherds'* candle is a reminder of the first people who worshiped the baby Jesus. (4) The *angels'* candle recalls the angel Gabriel, who announced the birth of Jesus to the Virgin Mary, and also recalls the angels who announced the birth to the shepherds.

161. holly

The spiky leaves and red berries of holly are so much a part of Christmas that few people ever think of their Christian connections. In times past, the leaves reminded people of the crown of thorns placed upon the head of Jesus, while the red berries were (obviously) a reminder of the drops of blood that the thorns caused.

162. Christmas wreaths

Holly (see 161) is a plant loaded with Christian symbolism. In general, Christmas wreaths, whether they are made of holly or some other plant, are a reminder of the crown of thorns worn by Jesus on His way to crucifixion. In olden days the wreath was a reminder, during the festive season of Christmas, that the infant Jesus would grow into the suffering Savior of the world.

163. Xmas and Christmas

Some Christians are offended at using "Xmas" as a kind of shorthand for Christmas, since it leaves the "Christ" out of the word. For what it is worth, the *X* is actually the Greek letter *chi*, the first letter in the Greek word *Christos*. So, in a sense, the *X* is actually Christ's initial, and was often used that way in the past.

164. New Year's Day, and circumcision

New Year's Eve has turned into an extremely secular holiday, with New Year's Day becoming "Recovery from the Night Before." Even so, some churches hold services on both the eve and the day itself, reminding believers that God watches over the new year. But there is an even older connection with January 1 and the church: according to the New Testament, Jesus was, as a member of a faithful Jewish family, circumcised on the eighth day—that is, if He was born on December 25, the circumcision would be celebrated January 1. In times past Christians celebrated the Feast of the Circumcision, ignoring the pagan holiday that happened to fall on the same day.

165. pastors and shepherds

We get our word *pastor* from the Latin word meaning "shepherd." (It's the reason that the word *pastoral* can mean "relating to a church minister" but also "relating to the rural life.") The earliest Christians often spoke of their ministers as pastors—that is, spiritual shepherds of the congregation. The image is from Jesus Himself, who described Himself as the "good shepherd," who lays down His life for His sheep (John 10:11).

166. "the call"

In Christian history, many of the most effective pastors and missionaries have been called by God—believing that against their own impulses, God spoke to them directly and summoned them to His service. The most dramatic incident was that of Paul, related in Acts 9. Writing to the first generation of Christians, Paul spoke several times of his "call" to be an evangelist (see Gal. 1:15), and God calls others to be pastors, evangelists, and teachers (Eph. 4:11). In a wider sense, all Christians are called to be Christ's ambassadors on earth (Rom. 1:6).

167. aids to confession

In the Middle Ages, before Christians went to the priest to confess their sins, they were urged to think through the Ten Commandments and recall if they had violated any of them. If so, they would then confess to the priest. If not, they were urged to think of any lesser sins they might have committed.

168. "primitive Christians"

Is "primitive" better when it comes to Christianity? Several denominations have thought so, which is why there have been "Primitive Baptists," "Primitive Methodists," and so forth. For the record, they didn't take *primitive* to mean "backward" or "crude." They used it in the old sense, meaning "as it was originally" or "as it was at the beginning." Thus a "primitive" group of Christians were those trying to imitate the beliefs and practices of the original Christians of the New Testament—an attempt to get "back to our roots."

169. the beatific vision

Beatific means simply "blessed," but the beatific vision refers to actually beholding God—if not with the eyes, then inwardly and intimately. The Roman Catholic Church officially teaches that the beatific vision is the ultimate destiny of the saved person. Catholic theologians believe that of the people in the Bible, the vision was granted to Moses (see Ex. 34:28–35) and Paul (see 2 Cor. 12:2–4).

170. give up chocolate—or read the Bible?

Many people make some kind of sacrifice for Lent—such as giving up a favorite food, or using it as a good excuse to give up smoking or drinking. In recent years many Christians have shifted to a new emphasis: instead of giving up something, they spend more time reading the Bible during the forty-day Lenten period.

171. nails and Good Friday

For obvious reasons, there is a connection between nails and Good Friday: Jesus was nailed to the cross, the nails penetrating His wrists and feet. This remembrance has led to some curious customs. For instance, in the distant past some blacksmiths would not shoe horses on Good Friday, since doing so required using nails. In Puritan New England in the 1600s, some people walked barefoot that day, so the nails in the soles of their shoes would leave no marks on the ground.

172. Good and Great Friday

What Protestants and Catholics call Good Friday, the Eastern Orthodox Christians call "Great and Holy Friday." Christian tradition has it that Jesus' crucifixion was, although a tragedy, also the saving act that delivers people from their sins. This is a good thing, or, as the Orthodox have it, a *great* thing.

173. Good Friday kites

On the island of Bermuda a custom began in the 1950s of schoolchildren flying kites on Good Friday. A teacher started the custom as a way of teaching the story of Jesus' resurrection and ascension. The students would let the kites sail higher and higher, then let them go, a reminder that the risen Jesus ascended into the highest heaven.

174. Via Dolorosa

People did, and still do, flock to Jerusalem during Holy Week to retrace some of the steps of Jesus, particularly the dramatic events of Good Friday. This retracing has long been referred to by the Latin phrase *Via Dolorosa*—"the way of grief."

175. the bread tabernacle

In the Old Testament, the Tabernacle was the "Tent of Meeting," Israel's center of worship until the Jerusalem Temple was completed. For some reason Catholic churches apply the name "tabernacle" to a small compartment on the church altar that holds the consecrated bread used in Communion.

176. beeswax candles

Christ, according to the New Testament, was pure and sinless. For this reason, church tradition mandated that candles used in church had to be made of beeswax, not of some cheaper material like tallow. Beeswax (so folk wisdom had it) was the purest of materials, and since candles symbolized Jesus, the Light of the World, they had to be as pure as He Himself was.

177. the aspergillum

Catholics and Episcopalians probably know what this is: a sort of water-holding wand that a priest uses to sprinkle people or objects with holy water. The name aspergillum comes from the Latin version of Psalm 51: *Asperges me, Domine*—"Sprinkle me, Lord."

178. salt and holy water

"Holy water" is water that has been blessed for use in Christian rituals. It is ordinary tap water, to which a pinch of salt has been added, that has had a blessing pronounced over it by a priest. The Bible says nothing whatsoever about the practice, but the use of salt in the water has a biblical origin: Jesus told His followers they were to be the "salt of the earth" (Matt. 5:13), and salt has long symbolized purity and preservation.

179. tonsures

In the past, members of Catholic monastic orders were easy to spot: not only did they wear a distinctive frock, but the men often were tonsured, that is, the crown of the head was shaved, with the remaining hair making a sort of ring around the head. In the distant past the tonsure was also the first step toward the priesthood. Why this distinctive look for monks and priests? Aside from the fact that it was just that (a distinctive look), it reminded the monks, so they said, of the crown of thorns that the suffering Jesus wore. Most monks today are not tonsured.

180. shoes of the fisherman

Peter was, according to Catholic tradition, the first bishop of Rome, and thus the first pope. It was believed for many centuries that a special pair of shoes worn by the popes had actually belonged to Peter himself. Since Peter had been a fisherman when Jesus called him, the special shoes of the pope were known as the "shoes of the fisherman."

181. red-letter days

Curiously enough, this practice began with the Church of England's Book of Common Prayer. Centuries ago, the book listed the various days on which saints were remembered. The most important saints—specifically, the saints from the Bible, such as the apostles, Mary, and so forth—were listed in red letters, while the less important saints were listed in plain black letters. Thus the first red-letter days were the days celebrating the saints of the New Testament. The phrase "red-letter day" has, of course, become part of our language.

182. the Thirty-nine Articles, Article 6

The Church of England's faith is summarized in its Thirty-nine Articles, which are also used by the world's other Anglican churches (including the Episcopal Church in the United States). Article 6 concerns "The Sufficiency of the Holy Scriptures for Salvation" and reads thus: "Holy Scripture containeth all things necessary to salvation: so that whatsoever is not read therein, nor may be proved thereby, is not to be required of any man." Put another way, the Bible tells us all we need to know for our own salvation, and any belief not founded on Scripture is not required.

183. the Thirty-nine Articles, Article 7

What do Christians do with the Old Testament Law? Obviously its many regulations about animal sacrifices are not binding on us, but what about its moral laws (such as, obviously, the Ten Commandments)? Article 7 of the Church of England's Thirty-nine Articles sums it up nicely: the Old Testament laws regarding ceremonies and rites are not necessary for Christians to keep, "yet notwithstanding, no Christian man whatsoever is free from the obedience of the Commandments which are called moral." A nice summary of Christian belief about the Old Testament's many rules.

184. closed Communion

In many churches, Communion is "open"—that is, anyone in the church may receive the bread and wine that are offered. The New Testament itself had a much stricter standard. The apostle Paul told the Corinthian Christians that "whoever eats this bread or drinks this cup of the Lord in an unworthy manner will be guilty of the body and blood of the Lord. But let a man examine himself . . . For he who eats and drinks in an unworthy manner eats and drinks judgment to himself . . ." (1 Cor. 11:27–29). In other words, Christians needed to be right with God and their neighbor before taking Communion. Paul may also have meant that Communion was only for those people who understood its meaning; thus nonbelievers should not take Communion. In times past pastors sometimes met with their parishioners before Communion to determine if they were spiritually ready to receive it. This was "closed Communion," which can also refer to denominations that insist that you be a member of their group before taking Communion.

185. the offering

From the very beginning Christians have made an offering part of their worship service. Consider the apostle Paul's words: "On the first day of every week, each one of you should set aside a sum of money in keeping with his income" (1 Cor. 16:2 NIV). The early Christians took care to support their needy brothers and sisters, a practice that deeply impressed many nonbelievers.

186. praying for those in power

"Honor all people. Love the brotherhood. Fear God. Honor the king" (1 Peter 2:17). The phrase "honor the king" suggested to the early Christians that they should pray for those in authority, a practice that still continues. One example: the Episcopalians' Book of Common Prayer includes a weekly prayer for the U.S. president. In colonial days, many churches offered a regular prayer for the king. In Civil War days, Southern churches prayed for Confederate president Jefferson Davis while Northern churches prayed for Abraham Lincoln. The basic idea: pray that authorities will do what God intended, punishing evil and maintaining order in society.

187. hats or not?

Hats are not the essential part of dress that they once were for men and woman. Even so, for many years it was considered essential that women wear hats in church. Why so? It's rooted in the words of Paul: "Every man praying or prophesying, having his head covered, dishonors his head. But every woman who prays or prophesies with her head uncovered dishonors her head, for that is one and the same as if her head were shaved" (1 Cor. 11:4–5).

188. worship times seven

Part of the monastic life was worship several times a day. In fact, in many monasteries and convents there was regular worship at seven scheduled times: lauds (dawn), prime (beginning of the day's work), terce (nine in the morning), sext (noon), none (three in the afternoon), vespers (at close of day), and finally compline (before bedtime). The practice was rooted in Psalm 119:164: "Seven times a day I praise You."

189. praying in Jesus' name

Most Christians end their prayer with "in Jesus' name, amen," or some similar phrase. While most people probably don't give these often-repeated words much thought, they are full of meaning. To pray in someone's name means "on their behalf," that is, praying as if you were that person. So to pray "in Jesus' name" is like saying "in the character of Jesus." The practice is rooted in the words of Jesus Himself: "Whatever you ask the Father in My name He will give you" (John 16:23).

190. meatless Fridays

"Fish every Friday" was rooted in the old custom of never eating meat (beef, pork, etc.) on Fridays. Centuries ago Christians began the practice of denying themselves meat on

Friday as a way of remembering Good Friday, the day of Jesus' crucifixion and death. The small sacrifice of abstaining from meat was a reminder of Jesus' supreme sacrifice on the cross. For many years the Catholic Church made the practice mandatory. It no longer is, but many people do it voluntarily.

191. "three to get married"

Fulton Sheen, the noted Catholic bishop famed for his *Life Is Worth Living* TV series in the 1950s, claimed that at every Christian wedding there was a third party: Christ. Sheen coined the phrase "three to get married," claiming that a proper wedding had a groom, a bride, and Christ. He based this on the words of Paul: "Husbands, love your wives, just as Christ also loved the church and gave Himself for her . . . For no one ever hated his own flesh, but nourishes and cherishes it, just as the Lord does the church" (Eph. 5:25, 29).

192. the "obey" vow

The traditional marriage vow taken by the bride reads thus: "Wilt thou have this man to be thy wedded husband, to live together after God's ordinance in the holy estate of matrimony? Wilt thou obey him and serve him, love, honor, and keep him . . . ?" (The proper answer is, "I will.") In modern times the vow to *obey* has raised a few eyebrows, and many couples omit any such vow from the ceremony. For what it's worth, on two occasions the apostle Paul instructed wives to be subject to their husbands (Eph. 5:22–24; Col. 3:18).

193. the bridal veil

Many cultures embrace the custom of having the bride wear some sort of veil or other covering to the wedding. We know that in the Bible a veil was once used to play a nasty trick on the groom: poor Jacob labored for seven years to gain the hand of the beautiful Rachel, then, the morning after the wedding, found that his crafty father-in-law had substituted her less-than-stunning sister, Leah (Gen. 29). Jacob had to labor another seven years to finally win his Rachel. We can't be sure, but the traditional lifting of the bride's veil during the wedding may hark back to the Jacob story, the groom's last chance to ensure that he does indeed have the right bride.

194. "no longer two but one"

Jesus was not, so far as we know, married, yet He held marriage in high esteem. Speaking of husband and wife, He said, "They are no longer two but one flesh" (Matt. 19:6). This belief is at the root of the wedding custom of the groom and bride each bringing a lighted candle, which they carry to an unlighted candle in the front of the church. The minister may read the words of Jesus just quoted, then the man and woman light the single candle with their individual candles, which they then extinguish. It is a symbol that what were formerly two lives are now one.

195. Pauline privilege

The Bible takes a dim view of divorce . . . usually. One exception is what is sometimes called the "Pauline privilege." (*"Pauline"* means "relating to the apostle Paul.") Paul told the early Christians that a marriage between a believer and an unbeliever could be dissolved with no guilt on the believer's part (1 Cor. 7:12–16). However, it can only be dissolved if the unbeliever chooses to get out. If the unbelieving spouse is willing to stay in the marriage, the Christian is bound to stay also. Paul held out the hope that an unsaved spouse might eventually be won to the faith by the believing spouse.

196. forty-day fasting

Forty is a good biblical number, and it occurs several times in connection with fasting. Moses fasted forty days on Mount Sinai prior to receiving the Ten Commandments (Exod. 34), Elijah fasted for forty days on his journey to Horeb (1 Kings 19), and Jesus fasted forty days before His temptation by Satan (Matt. 4). These biblical fasts are part of the reason that the season of Lent, the "give up something" season before Easter, has forty days.

197. flowing rivers

It isn't nearly as common as it once was, but in times past many churches insisted on performing baptisms in flowing rivers or streams. Does the Bible command this? No, but the great role model for baptisms was John the Baptist, who baptized people (including Jesus) in the Jordan River. Many rural churches in the South liked to continue this tradition—weather permitting, of course—as a kind of baptism "New-Testament style." As the country has grown more urbanized, river baptisms are fewer and fewer, although some churches settle for second best: a painting of a river on the wall behind the church's baptismal pool.

198. "In remembrance of Me"

These words are carved on many churches' Communion tables. They are from 1 Corinthians 11:23–26, which quotes Jesus' words to His disciples at the Last Supper: "This do . . . in remembrance of me" (KJV). Many Christians believe the Lord's Supper is just that—a remembrance of the original Last Supper, a kind of memorial meal. For centuries Christians fought over this issue, some believing it is just a memorial (called *consubstantiation*), others believing that in the ritual the bread and wine literally become the body and blood of Christ (called *transubstantiation*).

199. Sundays and Constantine

The first Christians observed Sunday as their special day of worship and fellowship. For nonbelievers, including Jews, it was simply the first day of the week, nothing more, a workday just like Monday. The change came with the Roman Empire's first Christian emperor. He established Sunday—the Lord's Day, as it is sometimes called in the New Testament—as a day of rest for everyone except farmers. (They, we assume, might be busy with harvest and not able to take the day off.) Constantine's decree on behalf of the "Lord's Day" has affected business and leisure ever since.

200. brother and sister Christians

The earliest Christians saw one another as newborn children of God the Father. Hence they often called each other "brother" and "sister." We see the old word *brethren* used many times in the New Testament. "Brother" and "sister" are still used today, particularly in some close-knit country churches.

201. graded lessons

Wealthy laymen are a neglected element in Christian history. One of the most influential was B. F. Jacobs, a Chicago produce broker and devoted friend of evangelist D. L. Moody. Jacobs had a lot to do with injecting life into

America's Sunday schools, notably through an agency called the Sunday School Union. In 1872 Jacobs was able to get the Union to adapt the "uniform lesson plan," which meant that all grade levels in a Sunday school would be studying the same basic lesson (and Bible passages) at the same time—the idea being that parents and children would be all attuned to the same ideas at the same time. Some publishers of Sunday school literature still follow this sensible approach.

202. latitudinarians

This cumbersome words refers to Christians in England and America in the 1700s who had a broad-minded view of their faith. Generally speaking, they were willing to downplay doctrine, miracles, and the Bible and emphasize man's ability to carve out his own destiny. English philosopher John Locke was willing to compress Christianity into two basic rules: believe in Jesus as Lord, and lead a virtuous life.

203. restorationism

This refers to "restoring" Christianity to the purity it had in the New Testament. One problem: as we see from the New Testament itself, Christianity was torn by divisions from its very beginning, divisions over doctrine, authority, church customs, etc. Even so, the desire to "get back to the book of Acts" has been an important motivation in

Christian history. *Restorationism* is often used to specifically refer to the denominations (such as the Churches of Christ) traced back to the followers of Thomas and Alexander Campbell in the 1800s.

204. Quaker meetings

The Society of Friends, better known as Quakers, began in England in the 1600s and quickly spread to America. Reacting against the dryness and spiritual laziness of the Church of England, Quakers chose not to call their own congregations churches (since "church" suggested the dull, state-supported Church of England) but rather "meetings." Whether they knew it or not, this term was a fairly close translation of the New Testament Greek word *ekklesia*, which in most Bibles is translated "church" but is more accurately "assembling together" or "congregation," or even "meeting together."

205. nine Christian rites

In colonial America, there were numerous Baptist groups, none of which believed in sacraments (as Catholics did and do) but which claimed that in the New Testament there were "nine Christian rites," all instituted by Jesus or His apostles. These are: baptism, the Lord's Supper, the love feast, laying on of hands, footwashing, anointing the sick, extending the right hand of fellowship, the kiss of peace, and dedicating children to the Lord.

206. the sand dollar

Some things that have become Christian symbols are perfectly understandable—the cross, for example, or the dove. But how did the sand dollar become associated with Christianity? Why are the dried, hardened sand dollars found in Christian gift stores? A leap of imagination: the sand dollar has five holes, or slits, in its body. Sometime in the past some devout person made a connection between those five holes and the five wounds on the crucified Jesus (one each on the hands, one each on the feet, plus the wound in His side made by the Roman soldier's spear).

207. apostle spoons

There was a time when people took seriously their role as godparents. It was a custom in the 1500s and later to present one's godchild with a set of "apostle spoons," twelve spoons engraved with images of the twelve apostles. These were probably the forerunners of modern souvenir spoons.

208. the seven cardinal virtues

Most people have heard of the "seven deadly sins," but there are also "seven cardinal virtues." During the Middle Ages some of the theologians decided that the three things that abide—faith, hope, and love, as described by Paul in 1 Corinthians 13—are the three "theological virtues," while prudence, courage, temperance, and justice are the four "natural virtues" taught by Greek and Roman philosophy. Collectively, these are the seven chief virtues that people should pursue.

209. priests and presbyters

We get our word *priest* from the Greek word *presbyteros*, found in the New Testament and meaning "elder." That Greek word is, obviously, also the source of "presbyterian," referring to a form of church government involving elders. Most Protestant churches do not call their ministers "priests," since the New Testament (particularly the Letter to the Hebrews) indicates that Christ alone is our High Priest.

210. ordination

The commissioning of Christian ministers and missionaries was fairly simple in the New Testament. Jesus' twelve apostles had already been chosen by Him (thus their ordination was obvious), and Acts 6 relates how seven "deacons" were chosen for being "full of the Holy Spirit and wisdom" (Acts 6:3), and these seven were "set before the apostles; and when they had prayed, they laid hands on them" (Acts 6:6). A similar act is seen in Acts 13:1–3, where Paul and Barnabas are ordained as missionaries, and, again, there is the laying on of hands. Ordination rituals became more complex with the centuries, but part of all of them is the traditional laying on of hands, symbolizing a passing on of authority.

211. churching of women

This refers to a ritual of thanksgiving after the birth of a child, and it is traced back to the purification ritual found in Leviticus 12:6. It used to be performed on the fortieth day after childbirth, but later became part of the infant baptismal service. Christians shifted the emphasis from purification (which is the idea in Leviticus) to thanksgiving for the child.

212. friars

Catholic men belonging to such monastic orders as the Franciscans, Dominicans, and Carmelites are known as *friars*, meaning simply "brothers." The name harks back to the New Testament, which refers to members of Christ's community as "brethren" or "brothers."

213. Old Testament saints

According to the New Testament, all Christians are "saints." In Catholic usage, a "saint" is someone in heaven, and of course, many of the great figures from the

New Testament are there: Jesus' apostles (St. Peter, St. John, etc.), Paul, Barnabas, Mary Magdalene, Timothy, Stephen, etc. But since only Christians can (in theory) be in heaven, there are no Old Testament saints, since they lived before Christ.

However, the Eastern Orthodox churches have a different view of saints, one that includes worthy figures from the Old Testament. Thus there is a St. Moses, St. Isaiah, St. Job, St. Amos, and St. Elijah.

214. roman and Latin

The type of letters you are now reading on this page are known in the printing trade as roman type. The old "fancy" letters you find sometimes in old books (such as the original Gutenberg Bible, printed in the 1400s) are known as Black Letters. Here's a tidbit from the early days of Bible printing: books written in Latin (the international scholars' language in those days) were set in roman type, while books written in the vernacular languages (the people's spoken languages—English, French, etc.) were set in Black Letter type. Naturally the roman type is much easier to read. The Geneva Bible, printed in 1560 and extremely popular in England for many years, was the first English Bible to be printed in the readable roman type.

6

The Joys (and Woes) of Translating

215. *Traduttore traditore*

This melodious Italian phrase means "The translator is a traitor." It is similar to a saying used by many Jewish translators: "All translators are liars." The gist of both sayings is this: whenever you translate words, something important is lost. But in regard to the Bible, what are the alternatives to translating? Is it reasonable to make every Bible-reader learn Greek and Hebrew? We can be thankful that through the centuries there have been some extremely good, faithful translators—not all of them traitors or liars.

216. dynamic equivalence

Translating the Bible involves taking two ancient languages (Hebrew and Greek) and trying to make them understandable to modern people speaking entirely different languages. One common question for translators is this: Do we try to make the translation's *words* follow the same pattern as in Greek and Hebrew, or do we try to make the *ideas* the same? When translators strive to make the words and sentences as much like the original languages as possible, this is known as *formal equivalence*. When the translators strive to communicate the ideas, it is known as *dynamic equivalence*. Translators argue often about what is the "best" method, but the truth is that all translations end up being some form of compromise between formal equivalence and dynamic equivalence.

217. "concordant consistency"

A mouthful, isn't it? What it refers to is a principle sometimes used by Bible translators. It works this way: a particular word or phrase in the Hebrew or Greek original is always translated by the same English word or phrase. Some tidy-minded people like the idea of consistency, but most Bible translators today agree that it usually makes for very unreadable Bibles. A basic fact of translation: it is very rare that a word in language *A* is the exact equivalent of a corresponding word in language *B*.

218. "stumbling" with the eye and hand

Word-for-word translations always run into a problem:

there are times when word-for-word just doesn't make sense. Take Matthew 5:29–30, which, if translated literally, would read "If your right eye causes you to stumble" and "If your right hand causes you to stumble." The Greek word here literally means "stumble," but it is obviously referring not to stumbling (as in "falling down") but sinning, committing a moral lapse, etc. Good translations today read "causes you to sin" or something similar.

219. useless footnotes?

Most contemporary translations of the Bible have at least a few footnotes, which explain the meaning of certain words and also explain that variant readings are possible. Not everyone likes these, and in the past footnotes were often criticized as a distraction and burden. When the English Revised Version was published in 1881, one critic claimed that footnoting was "for the devout reader of Scripture, the reverse of edifying; it is never helpful; it is always bewildering."

220. why italics?

Did you ever wonder why some Bibles have certain words in italics? The practice began with the Geneva Bible in 1560, and was intended to tell the reader that the italicized words are not found in the original Greek and Hebrew, but are supplied by the translators to complete the sense. Take one example from the King James Version of Matthew 5:5: "Blessed *are* the meek: for they shall inherit the earth." The "are" is in italics because, strictly speaking, it is not in the Greek original. In other words, if the Greek was followed slavishly, the translation would read "Blessed the meek, for they shall inherit the earth." Very few modern Bibles use italics for this purpose today.

221. why update?

One reason that Bible translation is an ongoing process is that we are continually learning more and more about the ancient languages. God's truth in the Bible never changes, but our understanding of words certainly does. The translators of the King James Version admitted that the meanings of many Hebrew words eluded them, particularly seldom-used words referring to birds, animals, gems, etc. With every passing year Bible scholars gather new data about the meanings of Greek and Hebrew, and the newer translations reflect these findings.

222. the fall of Constantinople

In 1453, three years before Johann Gutenberg printed his Bible, another event got even more attention: Constantinople, capital of the Byzantine Empire, fell to the Muslim Turks. Politically, it meant that the Byzantine Empire, a bastion of Christian culture, was now under a foreign power with a different religion. In regard to the Bible, the event meant something else: scholars skilled in Greek (the language of the Byzantine Empire) fled the Turks and sought refuge in western Europe. There, as it happened, their skills in Greek were put to good use in translating the Greek New Testament into the various languages of Europe. A curious chain of events: Greek scholars leaving their homeland for western Europe; the invention of printing; the Protestant Reformation, leading Christians to produce readable Bible translations from the original Greek and Hebrew. Historical coincidence, or the hand of God?

223. what is translated most?

Missionaries are certain that a key part of their work is getting the Bible translated into the language of the people they are evangelizing. Since this can be extremely time-consuming, missionaries do not wait until the whole Bible is translated but, rather, they begin with the New Testament (usually the Gospels) and make the various parts available when they are finished. The most widely translated book (so far) is the Gospel of Mark, which is available in over 900 different languages and dialects.

224. "crocodiles in human form"

Translating the Bible isn't easy. For the first Christians, Jesus' reference to "wolves in sheep's clothing" made perfect sense, because most of His hearers were familiar with sheep, wolves, and shepherds. But not all cultures are. One example: in an Indonesian version of the Bible, the translators opted for "crocodiles in human form"—since the Indonesians are unfamiliar with wolves preying on sheep, but very familiar with crocodiles.

225. translators anonymous

One version of the Bible that was popular for years with evangelical pastors and seminary students was the New American Standard Bible, sponsored by the Lockman Foundation of La Habra, California. Essentially the NASB was a revision of the American Standard Version of 1901, with some modernizing and simplifying of language. The NASB has had a special appeal to readers who want a "literal" translation, one as close as possible to the original Hebrew and Greek. The NASB has never had wide use as a "pulpit Bible," for it is not, frankly, a pleasure to read it aloud.

One curious note: for a long time the Lockman Foundation did not reveal the name of the NASB translators. The idea was that the value of the translation should be judged on its own merits, not the reputation of those who prepared it.

226. Webster's blue-light special

Noah Webster of dictionary fame produced his own "edited" version of the King James Version of the Bible.

While his dictionary was a smashing success, his Bible wasn't, and Webster was forced to drop the price of it from $3.00 to $2.00 and finally to $1.50. The city schools of New Haven, Connecticut, liked the bargain price and purchased a set for school use . . . back in those days when Bibles in public schools were not frowned upon.

227. from "thou" to "you"

We all know that the venerable King James Version has "thee" and "thou," for that was the standard usage of the 1600s. But which version was the first to modernize the pronouns, changing "thou" to "you," and so forth? The first we know of was a translation of the Gospels by scholar Andrews Norton, published in 1855, two years after Norton's death. Norton's translation was issued in two volumes—one containing the four Gospels, the other containing Norton's notes on how he translated. It was a long, long time after 1855 that most Bible readers felt comfortable with "you" instead of "thou."

IN MERRY OLDE ENGLAND

228. Aelfric (c. 955–c. 1020)

He was a clergyman and author, who wrote many sermons in Latin and in Old English (Anglo-Saxon). He also produced the Heptateuch, an Anglo-Saxon translation of the first seven books of the Bible. He was thus one of the first to attempt to bring the Bible to the English in their own tongue.

229. the Constitutions of Oxford

The English translation circulated by the followers of the great John Wycliffe had made a deep impression: some people loved it, some (mostly the church officials) hated it. In 1408 a church council met in Oxford, England, and issued the "Constitutions of Oxford," which prohibited anyone from translating the Bible, in whole or in part, into English—unless, that is, they had the approval of a bishop, which was practically impossible to obtain. The Constitutions were designed to halt heretical movements. They didn't, nor did they stop the Wycliffe version from circulating widely. However, the Constitutions remained in effect until the Protestant Reformation in the 1500s.

230. More vs. Wycliffe

Sir Thomas More, a saintly man and chancellor of England under King Henry VIII, was not always kind to Bible translators. In 1528 More published *A Dialogue Concerning Heresies*, in which he railed against "the great arch-heretic Wycliffe," referring to John Wycliffe, who had translated the Bible in the late 1300s. Wycliffe, More said, undertook his translation "for a malicious purpose" and "purposely corrupted the holy text." More did not go so far as to say that the Bible should not be translated into English, only that Wycliffe's was "heretical." History has sided with Wycliffe.

231. John Cheke, and basic English

The brilliant John Cheke (1514–1557) was a clergyman and tutor to Prince Edward, son of King Henry VIII. Like most scholars of his day, Cheke spoke and wrote Latin, but he wanted the Bible written in a readable English. He composed a thoroughly English Bible version that threw out any words that had Latin roots: thus "lunatic" became "mooned," "captivity" became "outpeopled," "parables" became "bywords," "converts" became "freshmen," "crucified" became "crossed," and (here's an odd one) "foreigners" became "Welshmen."

232. "diversity of translations"

"Diversity" is considered a virtue today, but in the 1500s it was not so highly valued. Neither was religious tolerance. One rare example of a tolerant Christian who valued diversity was Matthew Parker, archbishop of Canterbury under Queen Elizabeth I. As head of the Church of England, Parker was official sponsor of the version known as the Bishops' Bible. Yet he read and liked other English versions, including the Geneva Bible, which was so popular with the laity. Parker thought it was fine for more than one version to be in circulation, and he wrote that it would "do much good to have diversity of translations and readings."

233. skip the genealogies

The whole Bible is inspired, but is the whole Bible *interesting*? Most people are bored stiff by the long genealogies found in Matthew 1, 1 Chronicles 1–9, etc. The Bishops' Bible of 1568 was designed so that the genealogies "or other such places not edifying" were specially marked so they could be left out in public reading.

234. Whittingham without Paul

Who wrote the Letter to the Hebrews? No one knows for sure, for no name is attached to it. For many years it was referred to as "Paul's Epistle to the Hebrews," even though scholars seriously doubted that Paul wrote it. William Whittingham, an Englishman living in Switzerland, did his own translation of the New Testament, published in 1557. It was the first English Bible to leave Paul's name off the Epistle to the Hebrews. Whittingham included a note, explaining to the reader that "seeing the Spirit of God is the author thereof, it diminishes nothing the authority, although we know not with what pen he wrote it." In other words, if the Spirit inspired the epistle, the identity of the human author is not so important.

TYNDALE AND COVERDALE,
FATHERS OF THE ENGLISH BIBLE

235. Bishop Gardiner vs. clarity

In the 1500s, William Tyndale's translation of the New
Testament caused a lot of controversy, so much so that
Tyndale himself was eventually executed by the king. But
most people loved Tyndale's readable, dynamic translation. One who objected was the high-ranking bishop,
Stephen Gardiner, a staunch Catholic who held to the old
practice of having the Bible in Latin, not in the original
language of the Bible. One of Gardiner's chief objections
to Tyndale's version: it was too clear, thus any person
might actually read it and understand it—which was
exactly Tyndale's aim.

236. Tunstall's book burning

In 1526 Cuthbert Tunstall, bishop of London, staged a
book burning. Specifically, he was out to exterminate
William Tyndale's translation of the New Testament
within the diocese of London, so he ordered all possessors
of Tyndale's translation to hand over the book or face
excommunication—or worse. He staged a burning at a
public area known as St. Paul's Cross (an ironic name for
a place where Bibles were burned). The burning was not
quite as effective as Tunstall wished (see 237 [Tunstall vs.
Tyndale]). An interesting footnote: a few years earlier,

Tyndale had visited Tunstall and asked his aid in producing an English New Testament. Tunstall declined.

237. Tunstall vs. Tyndale

William Tyndale had his translation of the New Testament printed in Europe, not in England, where such translations were banned. However, his version made its way to England anyway, which aroused church authorities such as Cuthbert Tunstall, bishop of London, who ordered the book burned. Living in Europe, Tyndale learned of Tunstall's action—and was mightily pleased. He confided to a friend that Tunstall was aiding him immensely: he was buying up copies of the book (which made money for Tyndale) and by burning it in London was giving it free publicity. Tyndale used the money to produce even more copies of his New Testament. God moves in mysterious ways.

238. More vs. Tyndale

Sad that great men sometimes oppose each other. Sir Thomas More, lord chancellor of England under Henry VIII, published a *Dialogue* in 1529, addressing, among other matters, "the pestilent sect of Luther and Tyndale"—in other words, the Protestant movement. More attacked William Tyndale's translation of the New Testament into English, among other "heretical things."

Tyndale replied with his *Answer unto Sir Thomas More's Dialogue*, which More followed up with his *Confutation of Tyndale*. An ironic footnote: both More and Tyndale ended up being executed by order of Henry VIII.

239. "crafty, false, and untrue"

Henry VIII had an interesting religious journey: a staunch Catholic, then a Protestant who supported the people reading the Bible in English, then, in his old age, a semi-Catholic who discouraged laypeople from reading the Bible. In 1543 he had Parliament pass a law forbidding any "unlicensed" person to read or interpret the Bible for others, and forbidding the lower classes of society from reading the Bible at all. The act of Parliament specifically mentioned that the translation of William Tyndale was forbidden, for it was a "crafty, false, and untrue" translation.

240. Tyndale's "churchless" New Testament

Sir Thomas More complained loudly about William Tyndale's English New Testament—and mostly because of certain words Tyndale chose to use. Tyndale chose to translate the Greek *ekklesia* as "congregation," not "church," *presbuteros* as "elder" instead of "priest," and so forth. In short, his translation didn't seem "churchy" enough for the church authorities. Ironically, Thomas

More's friend Erasmus had translated the Greek New Testament into Latin and followed the same path as Tyndale did, translating *ekklesia* as *congregatio* and *presbuteros* as (big change) *presbyter*. Yet More lauded Erasmus's translation but condemned Tyndale's.

241. Queen Anne and Tyndale

Henry VIII's ill-fated second wife, Anne Boleyn (the first of his wives to be beheaded), was presented with an elegantly bound copy of William Tyndale's New Testament, bound in vellum with gold edges. The words *Anna Regina Angliae* ("Anne, Queen of the English") can still be seen on the edges of the book, which is in the British Museum in London.

242. Anne Boleyn and Coverdale

Queen Anne Boleyn, Henry VIII's second wife, was an intelligent woman who took a great interest in the Protestant movement. Her influence may have been the reason that Henry took such a tolerant view of Miles Coverdale's Bible translation of 1535. Henry's church advisers were not fond of Coverdale's Bible, but Anne liked it and urged Henry to tolerate it. It is quite possible that Coverdale's Bible would have become the officially approved English Bible had not Anne displeased the king so much that in 1536 he had her beheaded.

243. Bonner the burner

In his old age, Henry VIII struck out harshly at certain Bible translations, notably those of William Tyndale and Miles Coverdale. In 1546 he ordered that no person could possess a Tyndale or Coverdale Bible. Some of his bishops followed out his order by staging Bible burnings. One of the most notable was staged in London by its bishop, Edmund Bonner. Odd that being a faithful bishop included the role of Bible-burner. Later the bishop took to burning more than Bibles: he burned many Protestant martyrs at the stake, and came to be known as "Bloody Bonner."

244. Henry VIII and Coverdale

England's King Henry VIII had had William Tyndale executed for translating the New Testament and part of the Old into English. Yet within a few years, Miles Coverdale was publishing—legally—Tyndale's work and the rest of the Bible, the first complete printed Bible in English. Henry asked his counselors what they thought of Coverdale's Bible, and generally they approved of it. Then Henry asked an obvious question: "Are there any heresies maintained thereby?" They admitted that they knew of none. Henry replied, "If there be no heresies, then in God's name let it go abroad among the people." Appropriately, Coverdale's Bible includes an extremely flattering dedication to the king.

245. "the author thereof"

Who wrote the Bible? Lots of different human authors, yes, but Christians also believe that the Spirit of God guided those authors to write their inspired words. In the Coverdale Bible of 1535, Coverdale added an appendix, "The Translator unto the Reader," which includes these words: "Let the plain text be thy guide, and the Spirit of God (which is the author thereof) shall lead thee in all truth."

246. "Salomons Balettes"

Miles Coverdale was an excellent writer, and the Coverdale Bible of 1535 is in many ways a superb translation. Sometimes Coverdale got carried away with the text, however. In one case, he even changed the usual title of one of the books of the Bible: the Song of Songs, also known as the Song of Solomon. Coverdale gave the book the title "Salomons Balettes," that is, "Solomon's Ballads."

SOME NOTABLE TRANSLATORS

247. the NET

It had to happen: the Bible via Internet. In the case of the New English Translation—the NET—the new version was available on the Internet before it was ever published in book form. The project was the brainchild of Joe Head, a wealthy Christian businessman who wanted a fresh translation for the new millennium. Using a team of respected evangelical scholars, the NET was for a long time "in process," with Internet users able to send E-mail comments and suggestions about the new version. The production team bypassed bookstores and wholesalers and sold the printed version of the NET through (big surprise!) the Internet.

248. CSB and SBC

It had to happen: the nation's largest Protestant denomination has its own version of the Bible. The Holman Christian Standard Bible (CSB) has been scheduled for completion in 2004. If the name "Holman" rings a bell, it is because Holman Bible Publishers is the Bible-selling division of the Southern Baptist Convention. Holman has for years marketed various Bible translations, but with the CSB there is at last a Southern Baptist Bible. However, Holman took steps to ensure that the project was not *just* Southern Baptist, and the translation team is interdenominational (though about half the translators are, to no one's surprise, Southern Baptists).

249. "the most difficult thing . . ."

Of all the Bible translations done by an individual, probably the best-known and most respected was that done by Edgar J. Goodspeed, a scholar at the University of Chicago.

Goodspeed's *The New Testament: An American Translation*, published in 1923, was based on a simple principle: the Koine Greek of the New Testament was a fairly simple, straightforward language of its day, so the original New Testament was an "everyday" book, not a "monument of prose." Goodspeed tried to produce a contemporary English version that would match the liveliness of the original.

In his autobiography, Goodspeed admitted that he labored in the shadow of previous versions, including (of course) the wonderful King James Version: "The most difficult thing, I found, was to forget the old translations."

As a Greek scholar, Goodspeed did not, of course, translate the Hebrew Old Testament. That task was completed by J. M. Powis Smith of the same university. He completed his Old Testament in 1927, and his work, with Goodspeed's, was published as the complete *American Bible* in 1931.

250. Laubach and literacy

Frank Laubach (1884–1970) had a dual career as a missionary and literacy expert. His famous "Laubach method" for literacy was expressed as "each one teach one," meaning that each newly literate person teaches another the language. He and his associates developed literacy primers for some 300 languages and dialects worldwide. Inevitably Laubach developed his own New Testament, or a portion of it, *Inspired Letters of the New Testament*, intended for people new to English. Laubach claimed that his "elementary" version would (once the person was a better reader) be replaced by one of the standard translations.

251. for the Christian counselor

Jay Adams has been for years one of the big names in Christian psychological counseling. Adams translated the New Testament (published in 1977), in which passages particularly relevant to counselors are highlighted in yellow, as well as marginal notes.

252. Verkuyl and Berkeley

By a curious coincidence, Gerrit Verkuyl produced a New Testament with a name similar to his own, *The Berkeley Version*, named for the city where it was first published in 1945. *The Berkeley Version* is one of many attempts at a "modern-language" text, and, some say, one of the better efforts. Zondervan Publishing merged his New Testament with a new Old Testament translation, which was published as *The Modern Language Bible*.

253. basic English

A group called the Orthographical Institute claimed that with only 850 words anyone could communicate anything of value in English. In the 1940s a group collaborated with the Institute in producing a Basic English Bible, limited to the 850 words, plus about one hundred special "Bible words." It was especially pitched toward people newly literate in English, including immigrants.

254. knocked down, not out

Charles B. Williams's *New Testament in the Language of the People* was published in 1937 and still has some admirers. Consider Williams's wording of 2 Corinthians 4:9, where Paul is talking about his woes: "always being persecuted, but not deserted; always getting a knock-down, but never a knock-out." That last phrase is one of the reasons many people enjoy one-man translations: a freshness and directness that "committee" Bibles usually lack. (For purposes of comparison: the New King James Version has "struck down, but not destroyed"—a perfectly fine translation, but lacking the power of "getting a knock-down, but never a knock-out.")

255. *The Amplified Bible*

No, not louder, but perhaps clearer. Bible translators have long struggled with a serious problem: it isn't possible to do a word-for-word translation from the Greek and Hebrew originals. Too many of the ancient words and phrases are, well, difficult to explain in just a few contemporary English words. So in 1965 the public could buy *The Amplified Bible*, which features expanded meanings for thousands of words and phrases. Take, as an example, this version's Matthew 5:3, the first of Jesus' Beatitudes: "Blessed (happy, to be envied, and spiritually prosperous with life-joy and satisfaction in God's favor and salvation, regardless of their outward conditions are the poor in spirit (the humble, who rate themselves insignificant), for theirs is the kingdom of heaven!" Pretty clear, yes—but obviously not a good Bible for reading aloud in church. Simply put, *The Amplified Bible* puts, in its main text, the same information that most other versions put in the footnotes.

256. from the Odyssey to Revelation

Richmond Lattimore (1906–1984) was well known in his day as a Greek scholar, one who translated such ancient masterpieces as Homer's *Odyssey* and the great dramas of Aeschylus and Sophocles. As it happened, Lattimore, almost as a joke, tried translating the book of Revelation from Greek into English. He claimed that he was "struck by the natural ease with which Revelation turned itself into English," so he decided to do the entire New Testament. Alas, Lattimore's aim (to reflect the word order and style of the original Greek) did not yield the most readable New Testament.

257. the trench Bible

An unexpectedly popular Bible—or portion of the Bible—was *St. Paul from the Trenches*, a translation of some of

Paul's epistles by Gerald W. Cornish. He was killed in action in World War I, and among his effects was a stained notebook containing the translation he had been working on. It was published in 1937, and became popular (not surprisingly) with servicemen.

258. Phillips the electrician

Among the most popular one-man translations was the New Testament version of J. B. Phillips, completed in 1958 as *The New Testament in Modern Speech*. One of Phillips's first cheerleaders was C. S. Lewis, who wrote that "it would have saved me a great deal of labor if this book had come into my hands when I first seriously began to try to discover what Christianity was." Phillips walked that thin line between translation and paraphrase—and readers loved it. But it wasn't an easy task: he wrote that he "felt like an electrician rewiring an ancient house without being able to 'turn the mains off.'" He claimed he had to forget (so far as possible) the beauty and majesty of the King James Version and to translate the Greek as one would translate any foreign document. Incidentally, Phillips's work was published piecemeal, with the epistles published first as *Letters to Young Churches*.

259. compressing the family trees

Most people are rather bored by the Bible's genealogies, including the ones of Jesus found in Matthew 1 and Luke 3.

In J. B. Phillips's translation of the four Gospels, he did a shocking thing: he compressed them, leaving out all the men who "begat" and mentioning only the key people—Abraham, David, and Joseph, in Matthew's gospel, and Abraham, Adam, and God, in Luke's gospel. Not many readers protested.

260. the Bible's author?

One of the best one-man translations ever made was that by Scotsman James Moffatt, whose readable version of the Bible was published in 1924. Moffatt frequently lectured on the Bible, and after his translation was published, one lecture hall billed him on the marquee as "Author of Bible Lecture Tonight."

261. "the Eternal"

The Hebrew name of God, YHWH, gives translators problems, mostly because they don't wish to use *Yahweh* (which may be the way it is pronounced, though we aren't sure), since Yahweh sounds a bit strange in most people's ears. Usually translators settle for "the LORD" (with a note that the small caps mean it is a translation of YHWH). French versions of the Bible often use *L'Eternal*, meaning (of course) "the Eternal." The Scottish translator James Moffatt chose to use "the Eternal" in his 1924 version. It is probably as valid a translation as "the LORD."

262. Justin Perkins

The country we today call Iran was for centuries known as Persia, and one of the most active missionaries to Persia was Justin Perkins (1805–1869). Born in Massachusetts, Perkins went to Persia in 1833. He not only translated the Bible into the native language but also established Christian schools and a publishing house.

263. Henry Obookiah

He was born on the island of Hawaii (the "big island") and saw his parents slain in a local war. Taking refuge in America, Obookiah (1792–1818) became a Christian after reading through the Gospel of John. He wanted to return to the Hawaiian Islands and preach the gospel. Though he died before he could do so, he did inspire the first missionaries to the islands.

SOME OF THE MORE CURIOUS VERSIONS

264. John the Immerser

One of the most colorful characters in the Bible is Jesus' kinsman, the wilderness prophet-preacher John the Baptist, who baptized repentant people in the river. Did John merely sprinkle them with water, or were they totally immersed? Tradition says that they were totally immersed. In the 1850s some American churches felt so strongly about this that they insisted that John be referred to in new Bible translations as "John the Immerser" instead of "John the Baptist."

265. the immersion version

Since its founding, the American Bible Society has worked to get the Bible into as many people's hands as possible. One thing the Society would *not* do, however, was publish an "immersion version" of the Bible. One of its officers, Spencer Cone, was so put out with the ABS's refusal that he left to form his own American and Foreign Bible Society. But then *they* would not publish an "immersion version," so in 1850 Cone founded the American Bible Union, and with William Wyckoff, he hastily prepared an "immersion version" of the King James Version. The upshot was this: Cone and others who believed strongly in baptism by immersion wanted the Bible to make it clear that *baptism was by immersion only.* So in Cone's immersion version (and there were many others), the words *immerse* and *immersion* were substituted for the King James Version's words *baptize* and *baptism.*

266. omitting the troublesome parts

The Bible has been many times "adapted" for use, meaning that some editor chose to toss out parts that were "offensive" for some reason or other. In 1783 in England some gentlemen published *The Holy Bible Adapted to the Use of Schools and Private Families*. This edition threw out the entire book of Revelation, along with most of Paul's epistles. The publishers felt that Revelation, and some sections from Paul, might give readers "revolutionary" ideas.

267. Hanson's edited New Testament

In 1885, John Wesley Hanson published his own edited version of the English Revised Version. It had several distinctives: for one thing, it was an "immersion version" (see 265). For another, Hanson took the four Gospels and merged them into one continuous narrative (and he was neither the first nor last to do this). Hanson also arranged the New Testament books in what he thought was their chronological order. Oh, and one more unique trait: Hanson was a Universalist—that is, he believed everyone would eventually be saved—and he wrote notes for the New Testament reflecting his Universalist beliefs. (An obvious question: If everyone will eventually be saved, why bother publishing the Bible at all?)

268. another "simple" version

Give translators an *A* for good intentions: so many of them have tried to translate the Bible into simple, readable language (while, incidentally, accurately reflecting the original). One recent effort was published by Julian G. Anderson in

1984, *New Testament into Simple, Everyday American English*. Anderson's translation is fairly readable, but his version has its quirks: for example, he arranged the epistles in what he thought was their chronological order, beginning with James and ending with 3 John. One other oddity: he designated 2 Corinthians 1–9 as "3 Corinthians."

269. the concordance man

Robert Young, a Scottish bookseller, is remembered today for his still-used *Analytical Concordance to the Bible*. Young also was a master of several ancient languages, and he produced his own *Literal Translation of the Bible* in 1862. Like many word-for-word translations of the past, it is tedious to read, as seen in this example from 2 Kings 5:18: "For this thing Jehovah be propitious to thy servant, in the coming in of my lord into the house of Rimmon to bow himself there."

270. "anointed" New Testament

The word *Christos* in Greek means "anointed one." Most New Testaments in English translate it in the traditional way: Christ. But in 1958, James Tomanek published his New Testament translation, aiming for "a clearer rendering" of some parts of the New Testament. One of these "clearer renderings" was that he consistently used "Anointed" instead of "Christ," and also used "It" (instead of "He") to refer to the Holy Spirit.

271. *The Word Made Flesh*

That very popular version *The Living Bible* was often criticized because it is a paraphrase, not a true translation.
Some paraphrases depart even further from real translation. Andrew Edington published *The Word Made Flesh* in
1976, and he took quite a few liberties with the original
text. Examples: the judge Othniel is "Mack the Knife,"
and in Judges 6 the Lord's sign to Gideon is that "fire
came out and cooked the TV dinner as if by laser beam."
Hmmm.

272. EFV (Early Feminist Version)

We tend to think of feminism as a twentieth-century phenomenon, but it was already rearing its head in the 1800s.
By 1898 there was already *The Woman's Bible*, a version
produced by twenty feminists (all women, of course),
headed by noted feminist leader Elizabeth Cady Stanton.
Her group wrote commentaries on several sections of the
Bible, aiming to show that rather than being a source of
oppression for women, the Bible could be a liberating force.

273. Sawyer's innovation

The Bible's chapter divisions have existed since the 1200s,
and its verse divisions since Robert Estienne of France cre-

ated them for his 1551 edition of the New Testament. The chapters and verses have pretty much stayed the same over the centuries, but a few radicals have attempted to improve the divisions, creating their own system. One of the "improvers" was Leicester Ambrose Sawyer, who published a pretty readable translation of the New Testament in 1891. While his translation work was fine, his renumbering of chapters and verses (for example, Matthew 13:44 is Matthew 11:7 in Sawyer's version) stood no chance at all of ever being accepted by Bible readers. In Sawyer's final edition of his translation he did the obvious thing: he reverted to the traditional chapter and verse numbers.

274. simple enough for twelve-year-olds

Edward Vernon believed that some books of the Bible, such as Mark's gospel, should be simple enough for a twelve-year-old to understand. So in 1951 he published his *Gospel of St. Mark: A New Translation in Simple English*. Like many one-man translations, it has its odd moments. Consider Mark 5:20, concerning the Gadarene demoniac, who "turned away and went off; and all over Ten-Town-Land he spread the story of what Jesus had done for him. What a sensation it caused!" And consider Mark 6:25, with Herodias's daughter making this request to Herod: "Please, I'd like the head of John the Baptizer on a plate; and please can I have it now?"

275. Harwood's oddity

One of the odder Bible versions published in the past was the 1768 version done by Edward Harwood of England. He called it the *Liberal Translation of the New Testament*, but most readers would probably describe it as the "Pompous Bible." Consider Harwood's rendition of the Lord's Prayer, the familiar "Our Father which art in heaven": "O Thou great governor and parent of universal nature—who manifest thy glory to the blessed inhabitants of heaven—may all thy rational creatures in all the parts of thy boundless dominion be happy in the knowledge of thy existence and providence."

276. the curious Fenton Genesis

English businessman Ferrar Fenton took a great interest in the Bible and in 1895 published his own *Holy Bible in Modern English*. Fenton knew the ancient languages well, and was convinced that as a competent amateur he could create a more readable translation than professional Bible scholars. Did he succeed? Consider his wording of the familiar opening words of Genesis: "By periods God created that which produced the solar systems; then that which produced the earth." Is that better than "In the beginning God created the heavens and the earth"?

277. "joyfully agitated"

Most modern translations are done by committees, not by individuals. While some outstanding versions have been produced by individuals (Martin Luther's German version, for example), individual labors can be, well, somewhat awkward. Take the New Testament translation done by Rodolphus Dickinson, an Episcopal minister. In 1833 he published his translation, with a preface stating that "the lapse of centuries has produced a revolution in the English language, requiring a correspondent change in the version of the Scriptures." Well, he was right about that—the language had changed a lot since the King James Version was published in 1611. But Dickinson himself was not really up to the task of producing a readable Bible. Take his translation of Luke 1:41: "When Elizabeth heard the salutation of Mary, the embryo was joyfully agitated." Or consider Luke 12:29: "Be not therefore inquisitive, what you shall eat, or what you shall drink; nor be in unquiet suspense." Also, his sentences could get overlong: Ephesians 1:3–14 was rendered as one sentence of 268 words.

278. "impossible English"

Several translators have tried to do their work using the principle of "concordant consistency" (see 217). One of these was Adolph Ernst Knoch (1874–1965), who published, as individual pamphlets, the books of the Bible in what he called his Concordant Version. He pretty much proved that concordant consistency makes for a very unreadable Bible, but he stood by his method, even if (as he admitted) it involved using "impossible English." Take an example, his version of Genesis 12:2: "And make you will I into a great nation, and bless you I will and make your name great and become must you a blessing." Try this one, Luke 19:11: "Now at their hearing these things, He spoke, adding a parable because He is near Jerusalem, and they are supposing that the kingdom of God is about to be looming up instantly."

And Some Notable Errors

279. the Murderers' Bible

Printers' errors can make for amusing Bibles. Consider an edition of the Bible published in England in 1795. Mark 7:27 should read, "Let the children first be filled," but in this misprinted version it read, "Let the children first be killed." This misprinted Bible (which is eagerly sought by book collectors) has been referred to as the Murderers' Bible.

280. persecuting printers

In the King James Version, Psalm 119:161 reads, "Princes have persecuted me without a cause." Sometime in the 1600s a printer who was not doing his job properly produced a Bible that had the verse as "Printers have persecuted me without cause."

A Few Translation Stumbling Blocks

281. the Jehovah Bible and the Yahweh Bible

Many Bible readers know that in the Hebrew Old Testament, the name of God is "YHWH" (that's right— no vowels), usually written as "Yahweh" or, in the past, as "Jehovah." But almost all English Bibles have chosen to translate the Hebrew YHWH as "the LORD" (note the small caps in LORD). One notable departure from this was the American Standard Version, issued in 1901 and intended as an updating/revision of the King James Version. Because the ASV used "Jehovah" instead of "the LORD," some people referred to it as the "Jehovah Bible." There is also a "Yahweh Bible," the Jerusalem Bible, first published in the 1960s. The translators chose not to use "the LORD," but used the Hebrew name itself, Yahweh. Not all readers have been pleased with this, though in a sense the "Yahweh Bible" is true to its Hebrew roots.

282. translating "cherubim"

A Hebrew word that gives translators fits is "cherubim," plural of "cherub," but referring to majestic winged crea- tures (or angels)—definitely *not* the cute, chubby babies we call "cherubs." The *-im* on the word indicates it is plural, although most modern readers don't know that, and it isn't appropriate to use the plural "cherubs" (the fat baby problem again), although several translations do so. Today's English Version has "living creatures," which doesn't communicate much—but then, neither does "cherubim" or "cherubs." It is one of many cases where the Bible reader definitely needs an explanatory footnote.

283. *almah*

Here's a Hebrew word that has made translators' hair turn gray: it means "young woman," and its most notable occurrence is in Isaiah 7:14, in which the prophet predicts that the *almah* will conceive and bear a son. It so happens that this verse is quoted by Matthew (1:23), who connects the prophecy to the Virgin Mary giving birth to Jesus. Matthew, writing in Greek, used the word *parthenos*, which means "virgin." Matthew probably knew the Isaiah prophecy in a Greek version, which uses *parthenos*. Christian translators face a problem: obviously Matthew took Isaiah 7:14 to be a prophecy of the virgin birth of Jesus. Knowing that, should they translate Isaiah's word *almah* as "virgin" or (more accurately) "young woman"? The King James Version, the favorite for centuries, had "virgin" in Isaiah 7:14, and when the Revised Standard Version was first published, a storm erupted because the RSV used "young woman" in that verse. Most likely this was one of the chief reasons the RSV met with such resistance at the beginning.

284. *pericope adulterae*

This is the name that Bible scholars use to refer to John
7:53–8:12, the story of the woman about to be stoned for
adultery. The story puzzles the scholars, not because they
don't believe it is authentic, but because the oldest Greek
manuscripts of the New Testament show it in different
locations. Those who study Greek closely agree that it
doesn't seem to fit in John's gospel, for its wording makes
it read more like Matthew, Mark, and Luke. Worth doing:
read John 7, ending at verse 52, then start reading again
at John 8:13. It seems to flow perfectly, doesn't it?
Scholars have also noticed that verses 7:53 through 8:12
are an "interruption," but nobody knows just where the
"interruption" really belongs.

285. *doulos*

Here's a Greek word translators argue about: Do we
translate it "servant" or "slave"? Strictly speaking, it
means "slave," and many translations present it that way.
The difference is meaningful, for in the ancient world
there was a definite difference in status between a servant
and a slave. There are other Greek words that mean "servant," and one wonders if translators simply don't like to
use "slave," even in such phrases as "slave of Jesus
Christ."

286. "overcome" or "understood"?

All languages have words with double meanings, and sometimes Bible translators can't be sure if the authors intended a double meaning or not. The classic case is John 1:5, which in the New King James Version reads, "And the light shines in the darkness, and the darkness did not comprehend it." The Greek word translated "comprehend" here is *katelaben*, which could also mean "overpower." Thus various modern translations have something like "comprehend" or "understand," while others tilt toward the other meaning and have "over-power" or "overcome." Usually a footnote explains that the other meaning is possible. The New English Bible of 1970 came up with an attractive alternative: "mastered," which itself has the double meaning of "understood" and "overcome" (as in "I finally mastered algebra"). The New English Translation, available via Internet, also has "mastered."

287. Isaac, Izhak, and Isahac

Bible translators face a problem when translating names from the Hebrew and Greek: Should they use the familiar English form of the name (if there is one), or should they literally translate the name as it appears in the original? Some examples: the Greek text of Acts has *Stephanos*, but we usually use the familiar name "Stephen," just as we use "Jesus" instead of the Greek name *Iesous*. Some early translations into English tried too hard to follow the Hebrew and Greek: for example, using *Izhak* or *Isahac* instead of the familiar name "Isaac." The King James Version was the first to try to use the familiar names instead of the sometimes bizarre-sounding Greek and Hebrew names.

THE CATHOLIC FACTOR

288. *Dei Verbum*

It's Latin for "Word of God," and of course it refers to the Bible. In the early 1960s the Catholic Church's Vatican II Council made some major changes in the Catholic view of Bible translations. For centuries, all Catholic Bibles were required to be translated from the Latin version known as the Vulgate (done in the 400s), while Protestants insisted that the best translations were done from the original Hebrew and Greek. Also, for centuries the Catholic Church would not allow its Bible scholars to collaborate on translation projects (since Protestants were, technically, heretics). The Vatican II document *Dei Verbum* stated that, yes, new translations should be done from Hebrew and Greek, and since the Bible was the common heritage of both Catholics and Protestants, it was fine for Catholics and Protestants to labor together on translations. Several of these projects have been done.

289. "official approval"

Nothing prevents any person today from translating the Bible—assuming that person knows Hebrew and Greek. Any individual or group can, in theory, publish its own version of the Bible. This was not always so. For centuries the Catholic Church was extremely strict regarding translations. In 1564, Pope Pius IV decreed that no translations could be made without approval of a bishop or (gulp!) inquisitor. The Latin Vulgate Bible (published around 400) was the Catholic Church's official Bible, and all translations had to be made from it, not from the original Hebrew and Greek. Needless to say, Catholics were absolutely prohibited from reading any translations made by Protestants. Things have changed over the centuries, and today Catholics and Protestants collaborate often on translations.

7

Some Curious Beliefs and Practices

290. the Rastafarians

This offbeat messianic movement began in Jamaica in 1930, when some Jamaicans decided that Ras Tafari, who was crowned as Haile Selassie of Ethiopia, was the fulfillment of prophecies. He assumed the biblical titles "King of kings" and "Conquering Lion of the Tribe of Judah," both from Revelation 19:16. The Jamaican group believed he was the "Black King" and "Redeemer"—in fact, that he was God Himself. The group is probably more famous for such practices as wearing their hair in dreadlocks and for smoking marijuana, which they call "ganja."

291. Adamites

Before they sinned, Adam and Eve were naked and unashamed. Afterward, they felt compelled to cover themselves (Gen. 3). Throughout history there have been various groups on the fringes of Christianity that have tried to "get back to Eden" by making nakedness a part of their lives. There was a group of so-called Adamites as early as the year 300, and there have been many since. Some of the groups have practiced sexual promiscuity, some have not. (Even when they didn't, it is understandable that they would be accused of such.) Most Christians have been rightly critical of such dubious activity.

292. Cainites

Cain, the first murderer, is hardly an admirable character, yet there was once a group calling itself the Cainites. Active around the year 200, the group said that God was evil, and that rebels against Him (such as Cain) were the real heroes. The group even made a hero of Judas Iscariot and circulated a "Gospel of Judas."

293. Apollonius of Tyana

Jesus was a genuine miracle-worker, but during His lifetime there were various other phony wonder-workers, one of the most famous being Apollonius, a wandering philosopher whose life was recorded about the year 200 in the *Life of Apollonius*. Several anti-Christian writers tried to prove that Apollonius was the genuine article while Christ's miracles had been invented by the Gospel authors. Some of the Roman emperors honored him, and Emperor Caracalla had a private chapel with images of Abraham, Christ, and Apollonius. Historians think that devotion to Apollonius was a kind of pagan reaction to the spread of Christianity.

294. Lindbergh's widow

Anne Morrow Lindbergh, widow of American aviator Charles Lindbergh, became a celebrity in her own right with such books as *Gift from the Sea* (1955). Mrs. Lindbergh was a sign of something new in America: a kind of mystical blending of Christianity, pagan thought, and the vague new religion of self-help and "looking inward." In her books she would use such phrases from the Bible as "kingdom of heaven" but invest them with "me-centered" meanings that readers of the 1950s and 1960s responded to.

295. *Cosmic Consciousness*

The New Age movement is quite old, actually, though the New Age name is still fairly recent. As far back as 1901, a self-styled "seer" named Richard Maurice Bucke published *Cosmic Consciousness*, in which he drew on the insights of Jesus and Paul—and also Buddha, various Christian heretics, and many anonymous Americans who testified to living on "a new plane of existence," having

been "illuminated." Two of the "illuminated," Walter and
Lao Russell, put Bucke's ideas into practice at their
University of Science and Philosophy, founded in Virginia
in 1957. Needless to say, the university's curriculum was
only loosely connected to the beliefs taught in the Bible.

296. baptism by Bible

The Bogomiles were a group of Christian heretics who
lived in the Balkans in the eleventh century. Though
Christian in some ways, they threw out the Old Testament,
saying it was the work of Satan, not God. Satan, they said,
made the material world, so all matter is evil. Because matter is evil, they did not practice the traditional rituals of
water baptism and the Lord's Supper. Both were turned
into entirely "spiritual" acts. In baptism, a copy of John's
gospel was placed on the head of the person being baptized while the Lord's Prayer was recited.

297. "corrected by the spirits"

Spiritualism—the practice of trying to communicate with
the dead—was popular in America in the late 1800s.
Inevitably there was a "spiritualist" Bible, or at least a New
Testament. In 1861, Leonard Thorn published *The New
Testament, as Revised and Corrected by the Spirits.*
According to Thorn, Jesus and His apostles came "in spirit"
and revised and corrected the New Testament. The spirits

apparently liked to shorten things, for the "revised" edition has a Romans with only seven chapters, a Revelation with only three, and is entirely missing Hebrews. Thorn also added an appendix for his fellow spiritualists.

298. one spirit, or several?

There have been several versions of the Bible published by and for spiritualists (people who attempt to communicate with the dead—even though the Bible itself forbids doing so). In 1937 Johannes Greber, a former Catholic priest who became a spiritualist, published his New Testament with several "corrections" given by spirits. Consider his translation of John 4:24: "God is a spirit, and those who worship Him must therefore be under the guidance of a spirit of God and of the divine truth when they come to do Him homage." (Here's the wording of John 4:24 in the King James Version: "God is a Spirit: and they that worship him must worship him in spirit and in truth.")

299. vegetarian Christians

Among the more curious versions of the Bible ever published was one done by American vegetarianism advocate Olive Pell. Her version of the Bible, published in 1852, "cleaned up" the King James Version, not only by taking out all the sex and violence (a major deletion) but also by removing all references to eating meat. Miss Pell believed that true believers would (like herself) frown on anything but pure vegetarianism.

300. the Ebionites

From the very beginning, various groups split off from Christianity, preserving some Christian beliefs but adding some distinctive features of their own. The group known as the Ebionites used the "Gospel According to the Hebrews," which apparently was an altered version of Matthew's gospel, leaving out the parts about the virgin birth. They believed that Jesus was the son of Mary and Joseph, and that He "became" the Son of God at His baptism. Generally they regarded Jesus more as teacher than Savior, and they rejected the authority of Paul's epistles.

301. the Paulicians

This sect, which started sometime around 650 in the Middle East, may have named itself after the apostle Paul, or after some other Paul that they honored. The Paulicians threw out the Old Testament altogether but studied Paul's epistles and the gospel of Luke. They were adoptionists, believing that Jesus "became" the Son of God at His baptism. In their Communion service they used water instead of wine. Most of them were celibate, and quite a few were vegetarians.

302. adoptionism

Was Jesus always the Son of God, or did He "become" the Son at His baptism? Many early Christians taught that Jesus of Nazareth, fully human, became God's Son at His baptism, basing this belief on the voice of God declaring "This is My beloved Son" at the baptism (Matt. 3:17). Christian theologians have generally taught that this view—called adoptionism, because it seems to hold that the man Jesus was "adopted" by God at the baptism—is a heresy.

303. the Albury Conferences

In the 1800s in England, many noted ministers, along with several members of Parliament, set up the Albury Conferences. These had one main theme: examining the Bible to determine if the Lord's coming was at hand. The conferences decided that at the French Revolution, which began in 1789, the "vials of wrath" from the book of Revelation had begun to be poured out on mankind. Considering the bloodshed of the Revolution, it was easy to see how people might connect it with the end of time.

304. the Buchanites

There have been many sad and deluded people misled by their reading of the book of Revelation. One of these was Elspeth Buchan, a woman of the village of Irvine,

Scotland. In the 1780s she claimed to be the third person of the Godhead and the "woman clothed with the sun" of Revelation 12:1. She and Hugh White, a young minister who believed her, led a band of followers who awaited their rapture into heaven. The event was delayed time after time, until finally one follower remained, keeping watch over the corpse of Elspeth Buchan and expecting her resurrection.

305. Christian communism

No, not an attempt to combine Christianity and Marxism (although that has been tried, unsuccessfully), but the attempt by various Christian groups over the centuries to do what the Christian community in Jerusalem did: share property. "All the believers were together and had everything in common. Selling their possessions and goods, they gave to anyone as he had need" (Acts 2:44–45 NIV). Just how long this happy situation lasted among the Jerusalem Christians we are not told. Suffice it to say that when it has been tried in later generations, it has inevitably failed. Worth noting, however: Christian communes have generally lasted longer than secular ones (see 306).

306. the Rappites

Christian communism is an interesting idea, based on Acts 2:41–47, which describes how the Jerusalem Christians shared all their property in common. This has been tried many times in history, and it inevitably fails. One attempt at it, which lasted quite a while, was the Harmony Society, a German group also known as the Rappites after their leader George Rapp. The group founded a Christian commune in New Harmony, Indiana, in 1816, then relocated to Pennsylvania, where their commune survived until 1916. Like many other Christian communes, the Rappites were industrious, well organized, and devout. Their commitment to celibacy probably had something to do with their decline.

307. the first Muslim

The Jews consider Abraham their physical and spiritual ancestor—and so do the Muslims. While the Jews trace their descent from Abraham's son Isaac, Muslims trace theirs from Abraham's other son, Ishmael (called Ismail in the Muslim holy book, the Koran). According to the Koran, God revealed the true religion to Abraham, and with his son Ismail, he built the holy site known as the Kaaba. Jews and Christians, the Muslims believe, have distorted the pure religion that God gave to Abraham.

308. "Two Seed" predestination

Many Christians have held to the doctrine of predestination, and they can quote Bible passages to support their position.

One extreme form of the teaching has no basis in the Bible, however. This was the "Two Seed" theology, taught by American frontier preacher Daniel Parker in the 1800s. According to Parker, mankind fell into two groups, depending on whether they were descended from Eve's good seed or bad seed. Parker said that the good seed was planted by God, the bad seed by Satan. This, Parker said, explained why some people accepted the gospel and others did not.

309. Landmarkism

Some Baptists have taken baptism by immersion *very* seriously—so much so, they believe that any other form of baptism is simply wrong, not Christian at all. "Landmarkers" were Baptists who taught that since the New Testament period, true believers passed on the belief and practice in baptism by immersion. Only where this was done was Christianity truly present. Thus the Middle Ages, when almost all baptism was by sprinkling, was a time of spiritual darkness. Likewise for any Protestant churches that advocated baptism by sprinkling. Any church that practices immersion is a true church, any that does not is a false church.

THE SECTS

310. the Smith revision

Joseph Smith (1805–1844) was, of course, founder of the Church of Jesus Christ of Latter-day Saints—that is, the

Mormons. Smith claimed to be a faithful Christian and follower of the Bible (which in his day meant the King James Version of it). But Smith claimed he received a "direct revelation" of the Bible in 1830, and this led to his revision of the Bible. This was, Smith said, necessary because "ignorant translators, careless transcribers, or designing and corrupt priests have committed many errors." Curiously, Smith's "corrected" Bible contains numerous references to Jesus Christ—in the *Old* Testament. One example: Noah's call to repentance (Gen. 8:11) includes a challenge to "be baptized in the name of Jesus Christ"—centuries before Christ had even been born. In all, Smith made changes to more than three thousand verses of the King James Bible. His revision is often called the Inspired Version. The Mormons officially teach that Smith was a "translator," even though he worked from the English Bible, not the original Hebrew and Greek.

311. "The Standard Works"

Most Christians claim the Bible alone as the basis of belief and morality. The Mormons count the Bible as only one of their "Standard Works," the others being the Book of Mormon, the Doctrine and Covenants, and the Pearl of Great Price.

312. Brigham Young (1801–1877)

Young succeeded Joseph Smith as leader of the Mormon Church, and it was Young who led the Mormon settlers on their long trek to Utah. Young, like Smith, claimed to have a high view of the Bible. He wrote that "they who observe the precepts contained in the Scriptures will be just and true and virtuous and peaceable at home and abroad. Follow out the doctrines of the Bible, and men will make splendid husbands, women excellent wives, and children will be obedient; they will make families happy and the nations wealthy and happy and lifted up above the things of this life."

313. the LDS Bible

The Mormon movement began in the 1800s, and like most religious groups of that period, they used *the* Bible, the old and honored King James Version. In 1979 the Mormons published for the first time their own Bible, a King James Version with notes and study helps that give the Bible a distinctive Mormon slant.

314. Nebuchadnezzar and Lehi

According to the Old Testament, the mighty Nebuchadnezzar, king of Babylon, conquered Jerusalem and carried off many of its people to Babylon (see 2 Kings 24–25). The Book of Mormon carries the story far beyond the Bible: a prophet named Lehi was instructed by God to take his family and a few others and leave Jerusalem for a new home in . . . America. The Book of Mormon claims to contain the record of Lehi's people from the time of Nebuchadnezzar until the fifth century after Christ.

315. three Testaments?

Our Bibles contain the Old and New Testaments. Most Christians believe that though Christ is not mentioned by name in the Old Testament, His life and work were predicted there, so in a sense both Old and New Testaments are "Christian" books. The Mormons believe there is a "third Testament," their own Book of Mormon, which actually has the subtitle "Another Testament of Jesus Christ." Mormons believe that the New Testament does not contain "the fullness of the gospel," and so the Book of Mormon is necessary for right belief.

316. The Pearl of Great Price

One of the sacred books valued by Mormons is The Pearl of Great Price, which takes its name from Jesus' parable of the man finding a valuable pearl (Matt. 13:45–46). The Mormons' Pearl contains several sections in which Mormon founder Joseph Smith elaborates on stories found in the Bible.

317. the order of Jacob

This phrase is what the Mormons used to refer to their practice of polygamy. As the patriarch Jacob (and so many other wealthy men in the Old Testament) had multiple wives and concubines, so men today might have the same. The first Mormons were aware that both Christians and non-Christians reacted with horror at this, and for a time it was kept secret. Worth remembering: various Christian (or semi-Christian) sects and cults throughout history have attempted to reinstitute Old Testament polygamy.

318. the no-testament Bible

The Jehovah's Witnesses publish their New World Translation of the Bible. Curiously, this version has no Old Testament or New Testament. Rather, the Bible is divided into the "Hebrew-Aramaic Scriptures" (that is, the Old Testament) and the "Christian Greek Scriptures" (the New, of course).

A few other tidbits about the New World Translation: the word *church* (*ekklesia* in the Greek) is not used but instead, "congregation." As might be expected from a group that calls itself Jehovah's Witnesses, the name of God ("Yahweh," which is translated "the LORD" in most English versions) is "Jehovah." Likewise in the New Testament, when "Lord" (Greek *kyrios*) refers to God, the New World Translation uses "Jehovah" instead of "Lord."

319. the Witnesses' second Bible

Here's a curiosity: in 1972, the Watchtower Bible and Tract Society, the publishing arm of the Jehovah's Witnesses, published *The Bible in Living English*, translated by Steve Byington—even though Byington was in no way affiliated with the Witnesses. Perhaps one thing that attracted the Witnesses to Byington's version is that he used the divine name "Jehovah" in his Old Testament.

320. "impaled" on a cross

The New World Translation, the version used by the Jehovah's Witnesses, has some curious readings. The cross is a "torture stake" (Matt. 10:38; 27:32) on which Jesus was "impaled" instead of crucified (Luke 23:21). A footnote beneath the text explains that, yes, Jesus was nailed to a piece of wood, but it was an upright pole, not a cross.

321. the Christian Science "pastor"

We think of a pastor as a human being, but one American religious sect has the Bible as its "pastor": Christian Science. In 1895, Mary Baker Eddy, founder of Christian Science, officially "ordained" as "pastors" of her church the Bible, along with her own book, *Science and Health, with Key to the Scriptures*.

322. Bible sermons

Most Christian sermons quote the Bible at some point, but in Christian Science sermons, fully half the time or more is devoted to readings from the Bible. However, the Christian Science service also devotes time and authority to their own distinctive book, *Science and Health, with Key to the Scriptures.*

8

Back in the U.S.A.

323. Moses and the Supreme Court

In the U.S. Supreme Court Building stands a statue of Moses holding the Ten Commandments. The statue symbolizes the law's dependence on the laws of God. Given the trend of the courts in recent years, it is a miracle that someone hasn't protested the statue as indicating "establishment of religion." Stand by.

324. Indiana and the Decalogue

In spring of 2000, the state of Indiana passed a law allowing public buildings to display the Ten Commandments. The law was an obvious slap at the American Civil Liberties Union and its continuing (and effective) efforts

159

to strip all evidences of the Bible and Christianity from public life.

325. give 'em heck

Harry S. Truman (1884–1972), America's thirty-third president, will forever be remembered in the phrase "Give 'em hell, Harry." Truman was noted for his outspokenness, temper, and frequent profanity, but the Missouri-born Baptist nonetheless loved and honored the Bible and tried to live by it. He met his beloved wife, Bess, in Sunday school. His speeches, like those of many past presidents, were seasoned with allusions to the Bible.

Criticized for sacking General Douglas MacArthur, Truman watched as his popularity declined in opinion polls. In typical Truman fashion, he responded by asking, "I wonder how far Moses would have gone if he had had taken a poll in Egypt? What would Jesus Christ have preached if He had taken a poll in the land of Israel?"

A staunch supporter of the new nation of Israel, Truman promised American aid, hoping that the Middle Eastern deserts would be as fruitful "as the Garden of Eden."

326. Sonny and Cher and the Bible

In the 1960s, the American Bible Society ran a series of magazine ads in which various pop stars claimed they read the Bible. Among them were Sonny and Cher (married, at that time) and a briefly popular rock group known as Moby Grape.

327. manna for breakfast

The cereal that later became well known as Post Toasties first had the very biblical name Elijah's Manna (which is slightly wrong, since Elijah the prophet was fed by ravens in the wilderness, but it was not manna they brought him, manna being the miracle food provided for the Israelites in the days of Moses).

328. naming the presidents

The Bible has been a fertile source of names for children, even in today's less Bible-conscious days. Consider how many American presidents have been named for people in the Bible: John (Adams, Quincy Adams, Tyler, Kennedy), Thomas (Jefferson, and also the first name of Woodrow Wilson), James (Madison, Monroe, Polk, Buchanan, Garfield, Carter), Andrew (Jackson, Johnson), Zechariah (actually Zachary—a form of the name Zechariah—for Taylor), Abraham (Lincoln), Stephen (first name of Grover Cleveland), Benjamin (Harrison), Gamaliel (the middle name of Warren G. Harding), David (middle name of Dwight Eisenhower). Of the nation's first seventeen presidents, twelve had biblical names.

329. bestsellers, so long as they aren't religious

The *New York Times* best-seller list is considered the ultimate authority regarding which books are "hot" in
America. But the list has never been totally scientific, as
seen by the fact that it never listed *The Living Bible*, even
though it was the best-selling nonfiction book in both
1972 and 1973. In recent years the list has become a bit
more accurate, as in the late 1990s when it listed (at the
No. 1 spot, even!) some of the popular end-time novels
by Tim LaHaye and Jerry Jenkins.

330. onward, Christian soldiers

Washington (Episcopal) Cathedral in D.C. is, like many
grand churches, "a Bible in stone," with innumerable statues and paintings of biblical people and sayings. These
include a symbolic representation of the "whole armor of
God" (Eph. 6). This is part of a memorial to two
Christian soldiers, the Confederate generals Robert E.
Lee and Thomas "Stonewall" Jackson.

331. Senate approval

Since 1904, people elected to the U.S. Senate have been
presented by Congress with a copy of the Bible . . . sort
of. In fact, they are given a copy of Thomas Jefferson's
Life and Morals of Jesus of Nazareth, Jefferson's

"edited" Gospels, in which he throws out all the miracles and references to Jesus as the Son of God. (For Jefferson, Jesus was a great moral teacher, nothing more.) Congress had decided in 1904, when Jefferson's book was first published, to print 3,000 copies for the Senate and 6,000 copies for the House. Perhaps it is appropriate that Jefferson, the man given credit for the doctrine of "separation of church and state," should have his "de-miracled" Gospels given as a gift to government officials.

332. David Koresh and company

Vernon Howell had, at a tender age, memorized long passages from the Bible. He took the Bible prophecies seriously and expected the millennium to come in his generation. Howell joined a community called the Branch Davidians, believing that they were a righteous remnant destined to play a part in the final Armageddon. Howell changed his name to David Koresh, and the group hailed him as the Lamb destined to open the seven seals of Revelation and explain their meaning. Before they shared in Christ's victory at Armageddon, they believed they had to survive the coming Tribulation and the reign of Antichrist, which is why the group stocked provisions and weapons. In April 1993, after a fifty-one-day siege, Koresh and seventy-three men, women, and children were killed by federal agents acting under orders of Attorney General Janet Reno.

333. seeking out the Jewish view

Jews today like to point out that anti-Semitism was and is alive and well in America. They overlook something important: Christians in America have often sought out the Jewish view on various subjects, because many Christian scholars see the Jews as God's chosen people. Thus Christian seminaries sought Jews to be teachers of Hebrew, and Christians wanted to know the Jewish views on moral questions such as slavery, temperance, capital punishment. Jewish books on biblical subjects received respectful attention from Christian scholars.

334. "Bible Reading"

Note the capital *R* in "Reading." In the late 1800s and early 1900s, many Christians (particularly in the Holiness Movement) sponsored Bible conferences throughout America. An important part of any Bible conference was the "Bible Reading," which involved stringing together a series of Bible passages on a given topic—say, marriage, or the Holy Spirit, or money. The idea was simple: the Bible passages on a particular topic were never all together in one place in the Bible, so the Bible Reader did people a service by presenting them with all the Bible had to say about that topic. Many people actually preferred Bible Readings to sermons.

335. the synthetic method

In 1904, James M. Gray, who had taught at Chicago's Moody Bible Institute, published his *How to Master the English Bible*. Gray's book was published in the period when many Bible scholars were becoming extremely skeptical about the truths of the Bible. What was called "higher criticism" was causing many people to lose faith in the Scriptures, and many sensitive Christians claimed that the scholars were "taking apart" the Bible. Gray had another aim: to get people to see the Bible as a whole, as one amazing piece of revelation from God. So in his book he explained his five-part method to understanding the Bible: (1) Read the Bible book by book, starting with Genesis, and try to read the entire book at one sitting; (2) read it through without any regard for the chapter and verse divisions; (3) read it repeatedly until one has a feel for the flow of the book; (4) read it without consulting any outside aid or authority; (5) read it prayerfully. After doing this, getting a view of the whole Bible, then the reader could focus on the details.

336. swearing in Johnson

A mere matter of hours after the shooting and death of John F. Kennedy in 1963, his legislative liaison, Larry O'Brien, secured the president's own leather-bound Bible to use for the swearing in of the new president, Lyndon Johnson. Interestingly, Judge Sarah Hughes, who swore in Johnson, hesitated at using Kennedy's Bible because (since Kennedy was Catholic) she feared it might be a "Catholic Bible," not the King James Version that she preferred.

337. Bible college #1

The first Bible college in America was the Nyack Missionary College, founded in New York in 1882 by A. B. Simpson, who started the Christian and Missionary Alliance. There have been many Bible colleges founded since then, and all have served to fill a need that regular colleges and theological seminaries do not fill: providing skilled, knowledgeable laymen with Bible training and sending them out as teachers, missionaries, and sometimes pastors. In America they have their own accrediting association. Moody Bible Institute in Chicago is probably one of the most famous Bible colleges.

338. Hal Lindsey, and the end

The *New York Times,* no friend of Christianity or the Bible, described Hal Lindsey as the best-selling author of the 1970s. He certainly had a string of successes, beginning with *The Late Great Planet Earth*, which sold twenty million copies worldwide. People were fascinated by Lindsey's prediction of the fulfillment of the Bible's prophecies of the end times. Lindsey followed up with *The Liberation of*

Planet Earth, a study of what the Bible says about human sin, and *Satan Is Alive and Well on Planet Earth*.

339. William James

A philosopher and psychologist, James (1842–1910) was brother of noted novelist Henry James. William was fascinated by religion, as seen in his classic book *The Varieties of Religious Experience* (1902). What James actually believed about God has always been a puzzle. He did read the Bible to his children, but he inherited from his father the tendency to "dabble" in religion without ever committing himself to any definite beliefs.

340. *The Power of Positive Thinking*

Published in 1952, this was only one of many best-sellers by Norman Vincent Peale, pastor of the Marble Collegiate Church in New York. Peale was an orthodox Christian, but some critics—and he had many, though he had millions of admirers—said he was more of an "inspirationist" than a Christian prophet. In his many popular books, he used (some might say *abused*) Bible passages by turning them into feel-good thoughts-for-the-day. Example: in one book he made much of Paul's words "If God be for us, who can be against us?" (Rom. 8:31 KJV). Peale individualized it—"If God be for me, who can be against me?" Critics pointed out that turning such verses into "feel-goodisms" leaves out the moral demands of the Bible. Critics also noted that Peale's books seemed to emphasize self-help and worldly success more than God-centered living.

341. *The Man Nobody Knows*

The most popular book of the 1920s was this book by Bruce Barton, who presented Jesus not only as Savior and Lord, but as . . . an incredibly shrewd businessman. Barton, an advertising executive and devout Christian, was typical of many Christian businessmen of his day, emphasizing Jesus' dynamism and charisma. While some criticized the concept of "Jesus as businessman," Barton and other laymen did try to remind Christian business-men that Christian morals did apply to the workplace.

SOME INTERESTING PLACES

342. the Great White Throne, in America

Zion National Park in Utah is home to a site with a bibli-cal name: the Great White Throne. The name is taken from John's vision of God in Revelation 20:11: "I saw a great white throne, and him that sat on it, from whose face the earth and the heaven fled away" (KJV).

343. South, Bible, art

People often connect the South and the Bible, but not the South and art. Yet there is an excellent art museum at the very conservative Bob Jones University in Greenville, South Carolina. Most of the paintings—and many of them are masterpieces by some of the great artists of Europe—are images from the Bible. Officially the collection is known as the Art Gallery and Biblical Museum.

344. finding Jesus' tomb

There is in Israel a tomb that may be (though we can't be sure) the actual tomb where Jesus was laid. But without leaving the United States one can visit Jesus' tomb, the hill Golgotha where He was crucified, Herod's palace, and the temple of Jerusalem. Replicas of all these and more are found in the Shekinah Bible Gardens near St. Cloud, Minnesota.

345. Bible on parade

Where would you see a parade in which all the floats tell a story from the Bible? In Humboldt, Kansas, with its annual Biblesta Parade. (The name is a combination of "Bible" and "fiesta.") All people on the floats must wear biblical costumes.

346. Forest Lawn Cemetery

The famous cemetery in Glendale, California, is the resting place of many celebrities. It is also home of the largest biblical painting in the world of the Crucifixion.

347. the Dead Sea, Pittsburgh

Pittsburgh has the Rodef Shalom Biblical Botanical Garden, in which visitors may see replicas (not actual size, of course) of the Dead Sea, the Jordan River, and the Sea of Galilee.

COLONIALS AND REVOLUTIONARIES

348. the Southwark sermon

In 1609, at St. Savior's church in Southwark, just across the river from London, William Symonds preached a sermon to a group who were readying to settle in the new colony of Virginia. Symonds's Bible text for the sermon that day was Genesis 12:1–3, in which God told Abraham to leave his native country and kindred and journey to a new land, where God would make his descendants into a great nation. This, and a hundred similar sermons of that era, repeated a common theme: the New World was a place where many of God's promises in the Bible would be fulfilled.

349. a Bible Commonwealth

The original Puritan settlers of Massachusetts declared that the colony was to be a "Bible Commonwealth," with laws and standards based strictly on the Bible. Several of the other colonies made similar declarations.

350. Bradford and the Pilgrims

One of America's early heroes, both as politician and religious leader, was William Bradford, governor of the Plymouth Colony and leader of the Pilgrims who settled it. Bradford wrote a history of the colony, in which he explained that the Pilgrims came to America for "the right worship of God, and the discipline of Christ, according to the simplicities of the Gospel, and to be ruled by the laws of God's Word." Life in the colony was to be, Bradford said, "according to the Scriptures."

351. Cotton in Boston

One of the most powerful leaders in the early days of Massachusetts was John Cotton, an English Puritan who immigrated to Boston in 1633. Cotton was both a minister and political force, and for every law he proposed, he wrote in its margins Bible texts that he believed supported that law.

352. constitutional Bible

The Puritans who settled Massachusetts in the early 1600s stated that the Bible itself would serve as their constitution "until they had time to frame a better one." When they did begin to write their own laws, they inevitably based them on the Bible. Not only were laws based on the Bible, but there were laws against those who denied the Bible's authority. For denying that the Bible was the infallible Word of God, a person might be whipped forty lashes and fined thirty pounds. A second offense might lead to banishment or death.

353. "peculiar" Puritans

The world *Puritan* has fallen upon hard times, but history tells us that the Puritans who settled New England in the 1600s were pretty good people—not only good, but also tough in mind and body. So were their leaders. While still on board the ship *Arbella*, Governor John Winthrop preached a sermon, reminding the settlers that they (like the Israelites of old) had been singled out by God for a special purpose. Borrowing a phrase from Titus 2:14 and 1 Peter 2:9, Winthrop called the Puritans a "peculiar people"—not "peculiar" as in "weird," but "distinctive," or "set aside for a special purpose." He said they were to build in the New World a "city upon a hill," a phrase borrowed from Jesus' Sermon on the Mount (see Matt. 5:14).

354. the first table

Traditionally, the Ten Commandments have been seen as "two tables"—the "first table" concerned with honoring God and one's parents, the "second table" concerned with treating our neighbors properly. Christians have always believed that the secular government has the duty of helping enforce the commandments of the "second table"—that is, laws against stealing, murder, perjury, etc. The Puritans who settled New England believed that the government should go further and enforce the "first table"—meaning that taking God's name in vain or working on the Sabbath could be punishable by a fine or imprisonment. This did occur many times, a reminder that our conception of government has changed much since colonial days.

355. Crown Copyright

In colonial America, still ruled by England, the Bible could only be printed by royal permission. This meant not only that English-language Bibles could not be printed in America, but that Bibles shipped from England had to be published by the official King's Printer or by the universities at Oxford and Cambridge. This was referred to as Crown Copyright, and it ended (obviously) when America broke from England in the 1770s.

356. "we have no price"

Because of Crown Copyright (see 355), no English-language Bibles were printed in America until the American Revolution. But Bibles could be printed in other languages in America, and in 1743 Christopher Sauer published a German Bible in Pennsylvania. Sauer was a deeply religious printer who wanted to distribute the Bible for charitable reasons, not for profit. He sold his Bibles cheaply, but also gave them away when necessary: "to the poor and needy we have no price."

357. Yale, originally

Harvard, America's oldest college, started out very Christian and very Puritan, but very quickly became neither. Yale, founded in 1701, remained both a few years longer. In its early days, the Connecticut school emphasized (like all American colleges, originally) the Bible's truth, and as a guide to those truths, the Westminster Catechism (a favorite manual of faith for Puritans) and William Ames's *Marrow of Sacred Theology*. It has been a long, long time since Yale or any of the Ivy League schools have held the Bible to be a source of truth.

358. "glorious work of God"

Many of America's early settlers were convinced of one thing: God was doing something amazing in the New World. Noted colonial preacher Jonathan Edwards wrote of "that glorious work of God so often foretold in Scripture, which in the progress and issue of it shall renew the world of mankind." He and many others believed that what the Bible foretold—the kingdom of God on earth—was beginning in America. It did not happen quite as they expected, but the story is not yet finished.

359. Chauncy and his *Seasonable Thoughts*

The Great Awakening was an amazing Christian revival movement of the 1700s, but not one that pleased all ministers. Some thought the Awakening aroused too much "enthusiasm," and that Christianity should be more rational and calm. One critic of the Awakening was Boston minister Charles Chauncy, who in 1743 published his *Seasonable Thoughts*, condemning the "enthusiasm" of some Christians. To ministers like Chauncy, a sermon was not an explanation of a passage from the Bible, but an academic-style lecture, presenting general moral truths in as calm (some would say *boring*) a manner as possible. Chauncy's book indicated a shift from the Puritan sermon ("The Bible tells us . . .") to the "sensible" sermon ("The light of reason tells us . . .").

360. Tennent's lament

One of the leaders in the spiritual upheaval known as the Great Awakening was colonial New Jersey pastor Gilbert Tennent. Like other authors of the time, Tennent's words were practically saturated with images and phrases from the Bible. Lamenting the lack of good pastors in colonial America, Tennent wrote that "we should mourn over those that are destitute of faithful ministers, as sheep having no shepherd." The "sheep having no shepherd" echoes Jesus' lament over the crowds (see Matt. 9:36).

361. Salem, Massachusetts

America is packed with places with biblical names, including several cities named Salem. None is more famous than Salem, Massachusetts, or perhaps *in*famous (for the 1692 witch trials) might be more appropriate. The city was settled by Puritans in 1628, and they took the name from Psalm 76:2: "In Salem also is his tabernacle, and his dwelling place in Zion" (KJV). Aside from this, and from Salem being a pleasant-sounding name, the word in Hebrew means "peace."

362. doubting Thomas Paine

The great pamphleteer of the American Revolution, Thomas Paine (1737–1809) wrote *The Crisis, Common*

Sense, and other political propaganda that nudged the colonies on their way to independence from Britain. A few years later, Paine also lent his writing skills to the French Revolution, and he fully supported its anti-Christian tilt. In fact, Paine was a confirmed skeptic in religious matters, and his skeptical book *The Age of Reason* had to be published in France, since no publisher in Britain or even America would touch it. By the time Paine died, his radical religious and political ideas had alienated almost all his former friends.

THE FOUNDING FATHERS

363. Franklin and the Psalms

The amazing Benjamin Franklin was a statesman, inventor, and wise man—and also a deist, not a Christian in the usual sense. Even so, Franklin managed to bring the Bible into the founding of America. At the 1787 Constitutional Convention in Philadelphia, it appeared that the thirteen colonies' delegates would never agree on a form of national government. Franklin, eighty-one years old at the time, announced that he had always believed in the psalm that said, "Except the LORD build the house, they labor in vain that build it" (Ps. 127:1 KJV). He moved that the next day's meeting begin with a prayer. Apparently this improved things, for the meetings went much more smoothly afterward. Some say that Franklin's motion is the reason Congress still begins its sessions with prayer.

364. Franklin and Moses

The great Benjamin Franklin was, like his friend Thomas Jefferson, a deist, not a Christian. Still, Franklin read and loved the Bible, and he could see associations between events in the Bible and events in the new nation of America. In 1776, Franklin proposed to the Continental Congress that the new nation's national seal should show Moses leading Israel to safety through the Red Sea. Jefferson wanted a different Exodus image: Israel led by the pillar of cloud and fire through the wilderness. Both men saw the American Revolution as a kind of "Exodus," a liberation from the old nation of Great Britain.

365. Franklin on deeds, not thoughts

The great American thinker Benjamin Franklin was a deist, not a traditional Christian, and he had more respect for virtuous living than for correct belief. Though Franklin read and admired the Bible, he believed morality was more important than thinking the right thoughts about religion. Consider this quote: "I think vital religion has always suffered when orthodoxy is more regarded than virtue; and the Scriptures assure me that at the last day we shall be examined not on what we *thought* but on what we *did*, and our recommendation will be that we did good to our fellow creatures."

366. "the corruptions of Christianity"

Thomas Jefferson, politician and philosopher, was often criticized for his religious beliefs. Most people perceived (correctly) that Jefferson was not a Christian but a deist. Jefferson did not like being criticized, and he claimed that his critics "know nothing of my opinions." To a friend he wrote, "To the corruptions of Christianity I am opposed, but not to the genuine precepts of Jesus himself." Like many intellectuals of his day, Jefferson liked to think of Jesus as a good and moral man, but not as the Savior or Son of God.

367. Jefferson and charity

Thomas Jefferson was hardly a believing Christian; in fact, he probably was a deist, believing in a Creator God who established a moral law and pretty much left mankind to run its own affairs. Jefferson was often criticized because he did not believe in the divinity of Christ or in the miracles in the Bible. Even so, Jefferson the skeptic saw the value in people possessing and reading the Bible. It is a matter of record that in 1814 Jefferson, after his retirement from political life, sent a $50 contribution to one of the many Bible societies of the day.

368. "for the use of the Indians"

In the early 1800s, Americans faced an ongoing problem: what to do with the Indians. One obvious answer was to "civilize" them, which most people thought involved converting them to Christianity and teaching them the other ways of the white man. Thomas Jefferson, president from 1801 to 1809, was hardly a Christian himself, and he frowned on the missionaries' efforts to make the Indians into "good Christians." So Jefferson began working on his "edited" Gospels, a project he called "The Philosophy of Jesus." Essentially he took the Gospels and removed all miracles and all references to Jesus as the Savior or as the Son of God—leaving Jesus as, basically, a moral teacher. He wrote on his manuscript of the "Philosophy" that it was "an abridgement of the New Testament for the use of the Indians," a New Testament they could understand and appreciate. Jefferson hoped that the Indians could be "civilized" without in any sense being made into Christians.

369. Mr. Adams and Mr. Jefferson

America's second and third presidents could not have been more different—pudgy, combative John Adams and tall, soft-spoken Thomas Jefferson. The two men had major political differences while they served in government, but in their retirement years they corresponded frequently, becoming "friends by letter," discussing political theories and the state of the nation. One thing they had in common: neither was a practicing Christian (Adams was a Unitarian, Jefferson a deist), though both admired Jesus as a moral teacher, but not the Savior of man. Adams knew that Jefferson had edited the miracles out of the Gospels, and he wrote to Jefferson, "I admire your employment in selecting the philosophy and divinity of Jesus, and separating it from all mixtures." Like Jefferson, Adams believed that the Gospel authors had taken the simple teachings of Jesus and complicated His story by adding miracles and their belief that He was the Son of God.

THE EARLY REPUBLIC

370. Resurrection Pills

In the 1840s in America, the followers of William Miller (they later evolved into the Adventist churches) were predicting the second coming of Christ, and some entrepreneurs began to advertise Resurrection Pills and even muslin for ascension robes. Since the Second Coming did not occur as Miller foretold, we can assume these products ceased to sell well.

371. Congressional approval

"Separation of church and state" is an issue that gets many people riled today. It was not such a sticky issue in the early days of the United States, and here is an example: In 1782 Robert Aitken published an American edition of the

Bible, which contained, of all things, an endorsement from the Continental Congress. We can imagine the outcry today if the U.S. Congress dared to give its official approval to any religious publication.

372. American-made, American-illustrated

In the 1790s, the distinguished printer Isaiah Thomas produced the first American Bible with illustrations—fifty full-page copperplate illustrations, all by American artists of the day. These were large "luxury" Bibles, the new republic's version of the lavish Gutenberg Bibles of the 1400s.

373. using the census

Do you think census forms today ask too many questions? In earlier days they could be even nosier. For example, an 1824 census in Monroe County, New York, asked residents if they owned a copy of the Bible. When the data was recorded, the local Bible society responded in the obvious way: giving a Bible to each of the 1,200 households that did not possess one.

374. "applications to the heart"

Back in the old days, America's Ivy League colleges were downright Christian. They had such leaders as the notable

Timothy Dwight, president of Yale until his death in 1817. Dwight was a renowned Christian poet and hymn writer, and a strong believer that the Bible not only contained Christian beliefs but also a deep appeal to the human heart: "The Scriptures are filled everywhere with persuasion. Instead of being a cold compilation of philosophical dogmas, they are filled with real life, with facts, with persons, with forcible appeal to the imagination, and with powerful applications to the heart."

375. the ABS in its early days

Founded in 1816, the American Bible Society had some distinguished men at its first meeting, including novelist James Fenimore Cooper, author of the *Leatherstocking Tales* and other classics. In its early days the ABS had an amazing outreach, distributing free Bibles to prisoners, seamen, canal workers, soldiers and sailors, and Sunday schools. The society distributed not only Bibles in English but also, for new immigrants, Bibles in their own languages.

376. Cooper before breakfast

James Fenimore Cooper (1789–1851) practically created the American historical novel, and he will be forever remembered for his five Leatherstocking Tales. Cooper and his wife had the habit of reading a hundred verses from the Bible before breakfast every morning. Cooper was especially fond of the Psalms, Job, Isaiah, Hebrews, James, and Revelation.

377. Nat Turner, preacher and murderer

In the tense years before the American Civil War, many American slave owners feared a bloody uprising of the slaves. The fears seemed to come to gory life in the person of Nat Turner, a preacher and ex-slave who led a slave revolt in Virginia in 1831. More than fifty whites were murdered, and Turner was caught and hanged. Turner knew the Bible well, but chose to neglect its teachings on forgiveness and compassion. He did not neglect such Bible verses as this one from Exodus: "And he that stealeth a man, and selleth him, or if he be found in his hand, he shall surely be put to death" (21:16 KJV). In Turner's opinion, the passage justified the murder of slaveholders. (Worth mentioning: in the county where Turner went on his rampage, the county seat was named Jerusalem.)

378. Lyman Beecher

Patriarch of the amazing Beecher clan (author Harriet Beecher Stowe was his daughter), Lyman Beecher (1775–1863) was a noted preacher and social reformer, a man who saw the new nation of America as (he hoped) the closest thing to the kingdom of God on earth. But

Beecher knew that this kingdom would need major reforming before Christ would come to claim it. He was on the vanguard of many reform movements of his day, including temperance, profanity, and Sabbath-breaking. Note these last two: it was still possible in the 1800s to create a social movement around breaking the Ten Commandments (one regarding the Sabbath, another regarding taking God's name in vain).

379. "enemies of the Bible"

Catholics were a fairly small minority in early America, but beginning in the early 1800s came a new wave of immigrants, many of them from Catholic countries. Many Protestant Americans reacted in horror to this "invasion," and many books and tracts were distributed, telling of the hypocrisies and depravities of the new Catholic Americans. One typical tract of the times referred to the Catholic Church as "Romanism, the bitterest and most successful of all the enemies of the Bible." By 1963, America had changed its attitude so radically that a Catholic (John F. Kennedy) could be elected president.

NORTH AND SOUTH, DIVIDED

380. under a flag of truce

Technically, North could not trade with South during America's Civil War. But a few exceptions could be made, notably the sending of Bibles to the South—under a flag of truce. The Confederacy had its own Bible societies, but as the war progressed and paper and supplies were hard to come by in the South, Southerners looked North for aid in meeting the needs of religious publishing. Foreign aid sometimes came, as in 1864, when sixty thousand New Testaments were imported from England.

381. paper shortages, but still Bibles

Even though it was on its last legs in 1864 and 1865, the Confederacy still managed to print a few books—but only the Bible and some religious tracts. The South had such a serious paper shortage—particularly of *good* paper—that it became almost impossible to print decent-looking books. Some of the Bibles and tracts printed in the Confederacy's last days are almost pathetic in their appearance and paper quality. But then, the message is more important than the container, isn't it?

382. Rehoboam and Lincoln

Before and during the Civil War, the South had a long tradition of biblical preaching. After the war began, many preachers noted a parallel between the events of the day and the events in the Old Testament. Just as Israel had split into two kingdoms after the death of Solomon, so the United States had split into two nations. Solomon's son Rehoboam was unacceptable to a large part of Israel, so it formed a separate nation (see 1 Kings 12). Likewise after the election of Abraham Lincoln a large part of the Union chose to go its own way. One notable difference, though: the split of Israel was permanent, and the Union-Confederacy split lasted a mere four years.

383. Ham and Southern slavery

The book of Genesis tells the strange story of Noah, who approved of his two sons Shem and Japheth but placed a curse on his son Ham and all his descendants (Gen. 9). Ham's progeny were doomed to be slaves to other men. Attempting to justify slavery, Bible-reading Southerners reached the obvious conclusion: Africans were the descendants, so it was right (and biblical) for them to be slaves. Not all Christians agreed with this interpretation of the Bible, and it took the Civil War to settle the matter once and for all.

384. "Father Abraham"

To the Jews of past and present, the patriarch Abraham in the book of Genesis holds a special place as "father of the faithful," the physical and spiritual ancestors of the Jews. In Jesus' parable of the rich man and the beggar, the rich man in hell cries out for some mercy from "Father Abraham" in heaven (see Luke 16:24). During the Civil War, Abraham

Lincoln had numerous critics (not just in the South, but in the North as well), but also many defenders, some who lovingly referred to him as "Father Abraham." The phrase was used even more after Lincoln issued his Emancipation Proclamation, freeing the black slaves.

385. a gift for Lincoln

Black Americans had a major reason to adore President Abraham Lincoln: he had issued the Emancipation Proclamation, smack in the middle of the Civil War. Blacks and liberal-minded whites showered Lincoln with praise and gifts. Among the many gifts he received was, in September 1864, a stunning (and costly) pulpit Bible, bound in purple-tinted velvet, trimmed in gold. A few critics said that this Bible cost far more than the average per capita income of most white Americans at that time.

386. Good Friday, 1865

A sometimes loony actor named John Wilkes Booth hatched a wild scheme in 1865: assassinate the American president and his cabinet. The plot mostly fell through, except that Booth himself did fire one fateful shot, the one that killed Abraham Lincoln. Lincoln's admirers could not help noticing that the president breathed his last on a red-letter day on the calendar: Good Friday, the day Jesus died on the cross.

THE FRONTIER

387. cowboy sedatives

Part of American folklore is the singing cowboy, and it isn't all legend. The real cowboys of the past did sing a lot, partly to pass the time, partly to calm themselves and the cattle, which were easily spooked by sudden noises. Many cowboys reported that they sang hymns to calm the livestock, and one of the favorites was "Old Hundred," better known to us today as the "Doxology," a versified form of Psalm 100.

388. Bible Express

Considering that the Pony Express ran only a few years, it has a secure place in American history. Intrepid young riders made the trek carrying mail from St. Joseph, Missouri, to Sacramento, California, more than 1,900 miles, most of it wild frontier. The managers of the Pony Express presented each rider with his own Pony Express Bible, part of their regular gear (and perhaps a form of protection, since the riders carried no rifles).

389. Sequoyah, also known as George Guess

The Cherokees in the southeastern United States impressed American settlers, one reason being that the Cherokees, an intelligent and civilized people, seemed open to evangelism. Good evangelism requires a Bible in the people's language, and one reason a Cherokee Bible could be produced was that a part-Cherokee named Sequoyah (also known as George Guess) created a Cherokee alphabet of eighty-six letters. The Cherokee chiefs approved Sequoyah's creation, and by 1857 there was an entire New Testament in the Cherokee language, printed in northern Georgia.

390. bypassing mortal man

Alexander Campbell (1788–1866), born in Ireland, is one of America's most interesting religious figures. Like many preachers on the American frontier, Campbell wanted to practice a Bible-based Christianity and get rid of (as far as possible) the peculiar practices of the many denominations. Inevitably, Campbell started his own denomination, known simply as the Disciples (but often called Campbellites). Campbell urged people to forget the denominations and their interpretations of the Bible, and, instead, "Open the New Testament as if mortal man had never seen it before."

391. where the Scriptures speak . . .

Ever heard this maxim: "Where the Scriptures speak, we speak; where the Scriptures are silent, we are silent"? It was first used by the followers of American frontier preachers Thomas and Alexander Campbell, a father-son duo who were looking to establish a nondenominational (or interdenominational) Christianity but ended up founding their own denomination. The maxim is still used sometimes by the Disciples of Christ and the Churches of Christ, which are the present-day descendants of the "Campbellites." The maxim was, by the way, the Campbells' guiding principle, an effort to get past denominational differences and get back to the basics of the Bible.

392. "no creed but the Bible"

On the American frontier, many churches and individual Christians held to the principle "No creed but the Bible." This was a key Protestant belief: the Bible alone is the Christian's foundation for belief and practice. Some frontier churches would not allow any creeds, even the centuries-old Apostles' Creed, to be recited, for these were "man-made" creeds, while the Bible alone had a divine origin. Abraham Lincoln's family belonged to a separatist Baptist church that held to "no creed but the Bible." Historians believe this may be one reason why Lincoln always read and loved the Bible but would never formally associate with any organized church.

9

Words and Phrases

393. raising Cain

People use the phrase so often that they forget its origin. Obviously Cain was the bad son of Adam and Eve, the murderer of his righteous brother, Abel. As the Bible's first human villain, Cain became a kind of symbol of evil (see 1 John 3:12), his name being almost a synonym for *Satan*. So "raising Cain" came to be a polite way of saying "raising hell" or "raising the devil."

394. go the extra mile

We often speak of "going the extra mile" or "second mile," forgetting that the phrase originated with Jesus Himself. "Whoever compels you to go one mile, go with him two. Give to him who asks you, and from him who wants to borrow from you do not turn away" (Matt.

5:41–42). These words follow Jesus' command to "turn the other cheek," a reminder that His followers were to turn the selfish values of the world upside down.

395. "heart's desire"

Some phrases are so common that we can't believe they originated in the King James Version of the Bible. Take for example "heart's desire," still commonly used. It is found in Psalm 21:2: "You have given him his heart's desire."

396. Adam's ale

Presumably the first man had only water to drink, so "Adam's ale" was a quaint way of referring to water. Consider this exchange: "Got anything to drink?" "Nothing but Adam's ale, buddy."

397. flesh and blood

This phrase is so much a part of our language that we forget it comes from the Bible, specifically, from the New Testament. It occurs five times there, usually (in the Greek original) as *sarx kai haima*, meaning, literally, "flesh and blood." As used in the New Testament, it can mean "human nature," "man's physical nature," "man's sinful nature," "man's finite nature," etc. Nowhere in the Bible does "flesh and blood" refer to one's family connections (as in "I'm close to my son; he's my own flesh and blood").

398. kingdom come

We use this old familiar phrase to mean "the hereafter," and it usually occurs in such violent contexts as "We'll blow them to kingdom come!" The phrase comes from the Lord's Prayer, which begins "Our Father in heaven, hallowed be Your name. Your kingdom come" (Matt. 6:9–10).

399. land o' Goshen!

Here's another way of saying, "Oh, my goodness!" Not heard much anymore, this was a common exclamation of surprise and dismay, particularly in the South. Since Goshen was where the Israelite slaves lived in Egypt, we can assume some kind of connection between Goshen and lamentation (see Ex. 8:22; 9:26).

400. the whole megillah

This bit of Jewish slang refers to a long, involved story, one with more details than we care to hear. It comes from the Hebrew *megillah*, meaning "scroll," and refers specifically to the scroll for the book of Esther, which is read aloud at the Feast of Purim.

401. the patience of Job

The Letter of James reminds suffering Christians of the "patience of Job," and the phrase is part of our language (James 5:11 KJV). But "patience" in the King James Version doesn't really communicate what James meant, nor what poor Job actually exhibited. In the book of Job, Job clearly loses patience with his friends, who try to "comfort" him by assuring him that he must have brought all his calamities on himself. The quality of Job that James referred to is better translated "perseverance," having the fortitude (and reliance on God) to endure tough times—something that the word *patience* doesn't really communicate today.

402. fruit of the loom/womb

People are familiar with Fruit of the Loom underwear, forgetting that the brand name is actually a takeoff on a much older phrase, "fruit of the womb" (which means, of course, "children"). The phrase occurs several times in the Bible, notably in Psalm 127:3 and Luke 1:42.

403. "when kings go out to battle"

Those familiar with military history know that winter is a time for settling into encampment, while in spring armies gear up for battle, having better weather at their disposal. We see this even in the Bible: "It happened in the spring of the year, at the time when kings go out to battle . . ." (2 Sam. 11:1). For some reason the phrase has caught the fancy of many authors, and it crops up often in English and American literature.

404. "God save the king"?

As wonderful as the King James Version was, it always was, well, *English*. This shows up in the phrase "God save the king," which occurs many times in the Old Testament (see 1 Sam. 10:24; 2 Sam. 16:16; 1 Kings 1:25; 2 Kings 11:12). The English must love the phrase, for "God Save the King" has been their national anthem for many years. But the Hebrew original means something more like "Let the king live," with no actual mention of God or saving. The New King James Version's "Long live the king" is pretty accurate, certainly more so than "God save the king."

405. "how are the mighty fallen"

This familiar phrase, often quoted with a hint of sarcasm, is from David's sad lament over the battle deaths of King

Saul and Jonathan, Saul's son and David's closest friend. "The beauty of Israel is slain upon thy high places . . . How are the mighty fallen, and the weapons of war perished!" (2 Sam. 1:19, 27 KJV).

406. lazaretto

In times past the word *lazaretto* referred to a leper colony, that is, a home for people suffering from leprosy. The word originated with the parable of the rich man and the beggar Lazarus, told in Luke 16:19–31. Jesus' parable records that Lazarus was "full of sores," which the dogs came and licked. So people have assumed—wrongly—that Lazarus was a leper, and his name passed into *lazaretto, lazar house*, and many other words connected with leprosy. But in fact, Lazarus could not have been a leper, for in Jesus' parable he sat at the gate of the rich man's house, and lepers were not allowed to loiter around houses in this way. They lived a sad life, separated from most other humans, forced to call out "Unclean" if they approached anyone—which is clearly not the case with Lazarus the beggar.

407. fleshpots

The phrase "fleshpots of Egypt" occurs in the King James Version at Exodus 16, where the ungrateful Israelites grumble about their life in the wilderness, wishing they were back in slavery in Egypt, with its "fleshpots." Somehow "fleshpots" has come to suggest sensual pleasures (perhaps because of its similarity to "sexpot"). In fact, *fleshpots* simply meant "pots of meat," as the New King James Version has it. The Israelites were complaining that, though they were slaves in Egypt, they did have meat to eat.

408. onanism

The word means, frankly, masturbation. It is based on Genesis 38, which tells of the man Onan who "spilled out his seed on the ground" (Gen. 38:8–9). But this passage is definitely not speaking of masturbation. Rather, it refers to Onan refusing to father a child by his brother's widow (a standard practice of the time). That is, Onan practiced what we might call *coitus interruptus*, doing so, the text indicates, because he knew the child he produced with his brother's widow would not be his, legally speaking, but his dead brother's. Onan's shirking of his family duty so displeased God that God killed him.

409. strait is the gate

The words *strait* and *straight* are homonyms, pronounced the same, but with very different meanings. In Matthew 7:14, in the King James Version, Jesus taught that "strait is the gate, and narrow is the way, which leadeth unto life." "Strait" here has the usual meaning of the word: "narrow" or "tight," as in such phrases as "dire straits" or "straitjacket," not in any way connected with "straightness." How many church signs have we seen announcing the pastor's sermon on "Straight Is the Gate"?

410. "fight the good fight"

One of the most famous phrases from Paul's letters had to be made into a song: "Fight the good fight of faith, lay hold on eternal life" (1 Tim. 6:12). J. S. B. Monsell, a minister in the Church of Ireland, worked several images from Paul's letters into this popular hymn.

411. fed with St. Stephen's bread

The eloquent and saintly Stephen was stoned by the Jews, becoming the first Christian martyr (Acts 7). The phrase "fed with St. Stephen's bread" referred to being stoned to death, particularly if one died as a martyr for the faith as Stephen did.

412. rob Peter to pay Paul

This old phrase refers to taking money from one person to pay off another—in other words, shifting a debt, paying one debt off only to incur another one. Those who study word and phrase origins have tried to connect the phrase to the Bible in some way, or to an instance in history where the funds for a St. Peter's church were shifted to a St. Paul's church. In fact, no one is quite sure where the phrase came from, only that it uses the name of two prominent New Testament apostles (which suggests that neither one should be robbed, but should be given what they are both due).

413. St. Peter's fingers

The Gospels relate that Jesus' disciple Peter caught a fish with a coin in its mouth (Matt. 17:27). This led to the phrase "St. Peter's fingers"—the idea being that thieves have a "fish hook" on every finger, eager to steal things such as coins. Thus a person with "St. Peter's fingers" is a thief.

414. hocus-pocus

This is one of those meaningless phrases that magicians use in their acts. It originated in the Latin celebration of the Mass: when the priest held up the Communion bread, he intoned the famous words Jesus spoke at the Last Supper: "This is My body." Those words in Latin (the language of the Mass for many centuries) are *Hoc est corpus meum*. Many people believed the priest's words had a sort of magical effect: when he said them, the bread literally became the body of Christ. Since the words had a kind of "presto change-o" effect, *Hoc est corpus meum* evolved into "hocus-pocus."

415. "harvesttime"

Evangelists throughout history have often spoken of "harvesttime," the time of "gathering in" people committed to God. The image is from the words of Jesus Himself: "The harvest truly is plentiful, but the laborers are few" (Matt. 9:37); "Lift up your eyes and look at the fields, for they are already white for harvest!" (John 4:35).

416. "shaking among the dry bones"

This phrase was commonly used in the 1800s to describe American revivals. Preachers drew the image from Ezekiel's famous vision of a valley filled with dry bones, which come to life when they hear the word of the Lord (Ezek. 37).

417. "at ease in Zion"

This phrase is from Amos 6:1, in which the prophet warned people who were lazy and complacent about their religion. It was a phrase frequently used by the Puritans in the Church of England, who saw the state-supported church as spiritually drowsy. They wished to reform the church, purify it (hence their name), and some so despaired of it ever happening in England that they made their way to America for a new beginning.

418. the "Grapes of Wrath" lady

"The Battle Hymn of the Republic" is so familiar that we forget its author, Julia Ward Howe, wrote it as an antislavery song. Howe's anthem is saturated with images from the Bible. The phrase "grapes of wrath" is probably borrowed from Revelation, with such phrases as "the wine of the wrath of God" (14:10) and "the winepress of the fierceness and wrath of Almighty God" (19:15). Howe recommended to people wishing to educate themselves, "If you can command only fifteen or twenty minutes a day, read the Bible with the best commentaries, and a verse or two of the best poetry."

419. "crystal clear"

We use this phrase often yet forget it originated in the King James Bible. Consider Revelation 22:1: "And he showed me a pure river of water of life, clear as crystal, proceeding out of the throne of God and of the Lamb."

420. "talented"

Jesus' parable of the talents (Matt. 25:14–30) used "talent" in the old sense: a unit of money. The parable speaks of the need to use one's talents wisely and in the service of God. Because the word was used in the popular King James Version, "talent" passed into the language, and eventually it came to refer not just to money but to any of a person's resources, including one's character and abilities.

421. the land of Nod

"And Cain went out from the presence of the LORD, and dwelt in the land of Nod, on the east of Eden" (Gen. 4:16 KJV). This verse, not exactly the most important one in the Bible, added a phrase to our language: "the land of Nod." Nod was, we assume, a proper place-name, but through a leap of imagination it came to refer to "Slumberland," that is, the place where we nod off to sleep.

422. stiff-necked

Bowing to one's superiors was, in Bible times, an expected practice. Since God was the ultimate Superior, the highest Authority, not to bow to Him was a sin. This is what lies behind the term "stiff-necked," used many times in the Bible to describe proud, disobedient people who will not accept God's authority. Exodus 32:9 is the first mention of God's anger against the stiff-necked people of Israel.

423. town and gown conflicts

In Germany in the 1600s, university students had a high opinion of themselves—and a low opinion of the residents of the university towns. Students saw the locals as stupid, uncultured brutes. And to describe them they picked a name from the Bible: *Philistines*, the name of a coastal people that were a constant thorn in the side of the Israelites. The term passed from Germany into English and is still sometimes used.

424. diner lingo

The old-fashioned short-order diner has made a come-back in recent years, but the old diner slang has not. An older generation may recall the many biblical names that served as the quickie names for food: Adam and Eve on a raft (two fried eggs on toast), Eve with the lid on (apple pie), Noah's boy (ham), forbidden fruit (pork), yesterday, today, and tomorrow (hash), Lord's supper (bread and water), Adam's ale (water). Someone who never ordered meat would likely be a Nebuchadnezzar (vegetarian, based on Dan. 4:33).

425. patter

It can refer to slang, to empty chatter, to an entertainer's monologue, etc. Curiously, the word has a connection with the Lord's Prayer, which begins "Our Father," or, in its old Latin form, "Pater Noster." In old days people would refer to the Lord's Prayer as the Pater Noster, and in time "patter" came to refer to something repeated mindlessly.

426. Balaam's box

Newspapers and magazines have often used corny jokes ("groaners") as fillers. In times past many newspapers would have a "Balaam's box," a kind of backlog of asinine jokes. (Since *asinine* means "relating to donkeys," the box recalled the Old Testament character Balaam, whose donkey spoke to him.)

427. Solomon's seal

This name is applied to several ornamental plants, but more particularly it refers to two interlocking triangles that form a six-pointed star—exactly the same figure as what people ordinarily call the "star of David" (see 888). There is one difference between Solomon's seal and the star of David: in Solomon's seal, one triangle is dark while the other is light. Solomon was Israel's wisest king, according to the Bible, and later Jewish legend associated him with all kinds of mystical powers, including healing and power over demons. Solomon's seal was sometimes worn as a kind of protective emblem, something to ward off disease and other evils.

428. burning candles on jesse

A "jesse" was, in times past, a branched candelabra. The image comes from the "Jesse windows" in churches, which showed Jesse, the father of King David, with a literal family tree growing from his loins. The "Jesse tree" included all the great kings of Israel and, more important, Jesus Himself.

429. Pharaoh's serpents

Exodus tells the story of Moses at the court of Pharaoh, with Moses miraculously transforming his staff into a serpent, then reversing the process. Pharaoh's court magicians duplicated this amazing feat (Ex. 7). Long ago the term "Pharaoh's serpents" was applied to some fireworks (the large ones that also went by the name of "Roman candles"). Perhaps the name was applied because the fireworks, lying on the ground like mere sticks, came to life in a frightening way when their fuses were lit.

430. Punch and Judy and the Bible

England's children have for years enjoyed the silliness of the Punch and Judy puppet shows. No one is absolutely certain how these goofy husband-and-wife characters developed, but historians have hit on one possibility: the characters grew out of the biblical plays staged in the

Middle Ages—plays that grew so silly and irreverent that
church authorities began to frown on them. It's actually
possible that Punch may have grown out of the character
Pontius Pilate (who, in the old plays, always spoke with a
squeaky voice), and Judy may have been (surprise!) the
nasty character Judas Iscariot. Note the similarity between
"Pontius" and "Punch," and between "Judas" and "Judy."

431. marionettes

It is hard for most Protestants today to appreciate how
Catholics in ages past adored the Virgin Mary. It was not
uncommon in the Middle Ages for girls to name their
dolls "Little Maries," and likewise the name came to be
applied to puppets. Our word *marionette* (meaning
"Little Mary") had just such an origin.

432. strike a Lucifer

The first matches that man used for starting fires were
quite vile-smelling. Their sulfurous fumes reminded
people of something hellish—like Satan himself. So the
first matches were often called Lucifers, an alternate name
for Satan in the Bible.

433. Joseph's coat

Several popular garden plants are called by this name, a name based on Jacob's favorite son, Joseph, being given a "coat of many colors" (see Gen. 37). One of these is *Amaranthus tricolor*. All the various plants called "Joseph's coat" have, not surprisingly, leaves showing a mixture of colors.

434. stormy petrels

These are tiny dark seabirds that flit just above the water's edge. This has reminded people of the apostle Peter trying to walk on water as Jesus did. The name petrel is derived from Peter.

10

Back to Nature

435. ostriches

In Bible times, ostriches lived not only in Africa but in the Middle East as well. The Bible depicts ostriches as stupid (because they lay their eggs right on the ground, unconcerned that something might crush them). The Bible also mentions their amazing speed, able to outrun a horse: "She scorns the horse and its rider" (Job 39:13–18).

436. bird clocks and calendars

Some things never change: people in Bible times used the rooster as an alarm clock just as people have for centuries (Mark 13:35). Likewise the migrations of certain birds marked off seasons: for example a signal of spring

211

was the migration of storks along the Jordan River valley (Jer. 8:7).

437. "a little bird told me"

How many people know that this expression—or at least the idea behind it—comes from the Bible? Consider Ecclesiastes 10:20: "Do not curse the king, even in your thought; do not curse the rich, even in your bedroom; for a bird of the air may carry your voice, and a bird in flight may tell the matter."

438. a companion of owls

Poor Job, beset by so many calamities, lamented that he had become "a companion of owls" (Job 30:29 KJV). Owls, being creatures of the night and possessing spooky voices, were symbols of sadness and desolation (see Ps. 102:6; Isa. 13:21). They were also listed among the "unclean" birds that the Israelites were forbidden to eat (Lev. 11:16).

439. eagles

These large hawks are such majestic birds that legends have grown up around them. It appears, judging from Psalm 103:5, that people in Bible times believed that the eagle could actually renew its youth and strength as it aged.

440. the talking eagle

The Bible never mentions parrots or mynah birds, but one bird is mentioned as having the power of speech: the eagle in Revelation 8:13, which flies overhead crying, "Woe! Woe!" The bird's lament is over the horrors that are about to befall the earth. Worth noting: although eagles are beautiful and majestic, they are also known as scavengers, just as vultures are, feeding on the dead. The image of the eagle in Revelation is an obvious sign that there are about to be a lot of dead bodies around.

441. birds of prey

The Hebrew word *ayit* referred to hawks, falcons, and kites, all of them hook-beaked birds with strong talons made for catching and devouring live prey. Abraham had to drive such birds away from his sacrifice (Gen. 15:11). Like other flesh-eating birds, these were on the Israelites' list of nonkosher items.

442. cuckoo

The King James Version has "cuckow," but it is the same bird, noted for its selfish habit of laying its eggs in other birds' nests (and, of course, noted for its familiar call, just like the clock). Modern translations don't mention the cuckoo at all, substituting "gull" or "seagull."

443. dove's dung

The actual item, or the name for some kind of edible plant? According to 2 King 6:25 (in the KJV), the famished people of Samaria were reduced to eating dove's dung. If this was literally true, perhaps they thought they derived some food value from it. But translators think the original Hebrew may be referring to seed pods, carob pods, locust beans, or wild onions.

444. fowl

In earlier times, people used "fowl" as a general term meaning the same as "birds." Generally speaking, "birds" suggested smaller species while "fowl" suggested larger ones, particularly ground-dwelling birds that might be used for food. "Fowlers" were men who set snares to catch wild fowl for eating.

445. partridges

These are short, stocky-built game birds, similar to quail and grouse. David, pursued by Saul, compared himself to a partridge being hunted (1 Sam. 26:20). It was believed that partridges stole eggs from other birds and hatched them out, which Jeremiah used as a symbol of getting wealth unfairly (Jer. 17:11).

446. pelicans

They live worldwide, wherever their favorite diet (fish) can be found. The familiar species of Palestine would have been the white pelican, with a wingspan of up to ten feet. The psalmist compared himself to a pelican in the wilderness (Ps. 102:6).

447. sparrows

Small, brown, active, and gregarious, these are found worldwide. The Bible mentions that they nested in the temple precincts (Ps. 84:3). As small and common as they were, they symbolized insignificance. Jesus stated that His Father looked after the sparrows, insignificant as they were, and certainly the Father looked after human beings, who were far more valuable than sparrows (Matt. 10:29–31).

448. swallows

Several species live in Palestine, including two that are familiar to Americans, the barn swallow (with the deeply forked tail) and the swallow. Their agility in catching insects in flight is amazing. They seem to spend their entire lives in the air, a fact noted by the author of Proverbs (26:2).

449. swifts

If any bird deserves its name, this one does. Like swallows, swifts seem to spend their entire lives in the air, catching their basic food, insects. Also like swallows, their voices are hyperactive twitters, which is why the same Hebrew word is "swift" in some translations and "swallow" in others. The prophet Jeremiah spoke of how the swift and the swallow know the time of the seasons (Jer. 8:7).

450. vultures

Two distinguishing features: they're ugly and they eat dead things. In Bible lands, some of them were also huge, such as the cinereous vulture, with a wingspan of nine feet. Smaller but familiar to the Israelites would have been the Egyptian vulture, also called "Pharaoh's chicken." (The Egyptians thought more highly of the vulture than most nations did: they incorporated a vulture head into the pharaoh's crown.) The vulture, not surprisingly, is among the birds that Israelites were prohibited from eating (Deut. 14:12). Jesus spoke of vultures gathering around a carcass (Matt. 24:28).

CREEPY THINGS

451. five golden rats

The Israelites had no higher opinion of rodents than we do, and, not surprisingly, rats and mice are on the list of "unclean" animals that could not be eaten (Lev. 11:29).

When the Philistines captured the ark of the covenant from the Israelites, a horrible illness befell them, and their pagan priests insisted that the ark be returned to the Israelites . . . along with a "trespass offering" of images of five golden tumors and five golden rats. (Apparently the plague had some connection with rats—which, scientifically, makes perfect sense.) The ark was returned as ordered. Supposedly the five rats represented the five "lords of the Philistines" (see 1 Sam. 5–6).

452. bat as bird

Scientifically speaking, the bat is definitely a mammal, not a bird. (As a mammal, it has hair and gives milk to its young.) The writer of Leviticus was not a modern scientist, so the bat is listed as a bird—specifically, one of the unclean birds the Israelites were prohibited from eating. (We can assume that it was no loss to the Israelites to give up eating bats.)

453. lizards

None of the lizards of the Middle East are venomous, but some are pretty darn intimidating, particularly the Nile monitor, which can reach six feet in length. Various lizards live in the region, including the color-changing chameleons, harmless little skinks, and many others. Like all reptiles, lizards are on the "unclean" list, prohibited as food (Lev. 11:29–30).

454. scorpions

These nasty little creatures with their poisonous tail stingers were fairly common in ancient Israel. The only times the Bible mentions them are, it appears, figurative. Solomon's arrogant son Rehoboam caused the kingdom of Israel to split by warning the people that while his father had used whips on the people, he himself would use scorpions (1 Kings 12:11–14), which, we assume, was not meant to be taken literally. Speaking of God's care for His children, Jesus asked earthly fathers if they would give their children a scorpion if they asked for an egg (Luke 11:12). Jesus told His followers that they were given authority to "trample on serpents and scorpions" (Luke 10:19).

455. snails and slugs

Alas for those who love to eat *escargot:* snails and slugs are on the kosher law's "unclean" list (Lev. 11:30). Outside the food laws, these land-dwelling mollusks are not mentioned in the Bible, except in Psalm 58:8, which speaks of "a snail which melts away as it goes." Perhaps the ancient peoples believed that the slimy trail these creatures left behind indicated that they were literally melting away as they moved.

The dye used to make garments purple came from a snail (scientifically, the *Murex* snail). For only a small amount of dye, thousands of snails were needed. No wonder that purple became the color of the wealthy, particularly rulers. The Christian woman Lydia, a "seller of purple," was a dealer in the dye (Acts 16:11–15).

456. serpents and snakes and such

The ancient Israelites feared snakes, particularly venomous ones. The various Hebrew and Greek words that refer to snakes don't enable us to pinpoint any specific species. There are various venomous snakes, usually called "viper" or "adder" or "cobra" in English translations (see 457). On one occasion God sent venomous snakes among the Israelites because of their constant complaining against God and Moses (Num. 21:6–9).

Snakes were listed as "unclean" animals, forbidden as food, though Peter's famous vision of the sheet filled with unclean animals indicates that Christians are free to eat any animal (Acts 10:12).

457. the asp

Cleopatra was known as the "serpent of the Nile," but she used a real serpent to commit suicide, namely the asp, or Egyptian cobra. It is said that snake charmers, who use the asp in their street performances, can make the snake rigid

like a stick by a pressure on its neck. Some biblical scholars believe this might be the trick played by Pharaoh's
magicians at the time of Moses (Ex. 7). The asp lived in
Israel and was widely feared.

458. leeches

In the bad old days, slimy, bloodsucking leeches were
used for medicinal purposes. (This was back in the days
when it was considered wise to "bleed" a patient to help
rid the body of whatever was ailing it—a stupid idea, and
using leeches was just as stupid.) Leeches are mentioned
only once in the Bible, in Proverbs 30:15, which speaks of
their insatiable appetite for blood.

459. frogs

In the Bible they are mentioned in only two situations,
both of them repulsive: the plague on Egypt and spewing
from the mouth of the dragon (Rev. 16:13). In Exodus 8
we read of Aaron summoning frogs from their natural
habitat of streams and ponds, creating a loathsome plague
on the Egyptians. Since the Egyptians revered frogs (and
many other animals as well), the plague was not only a
nuisance and a health hazard, but also a slap at their idola-
trous religion. John's vision of the frogs spewing from the
dragon's mouth in Revelation probably reminded his
readers of the plague of frogs on Egypt.

SEA THINGS

460. manatees

Were the ancient Israelites familiar with manatees? Possibly. In the New International Version, the hides of sea cows (the same as manatees, also called dugongs) are used in the sacred items in the Lord's sanctuary (Ex. 25:5; 26:14; 35:7; 36:19). As often happens with the Hebrew Old Testament, we aren't totally sure which animals are referred to by certain Hebrew words. Where the NIV has "sea cows," the New King James Version has "badgers" and the RSV has "goatskins."

461. whales

We learn very early in the Bible that "God created great whales" (Gen. 1:21 KJV). They are mentioned only a few times in the Bible, though we can assume that when the book of Jonah says that the prophet was swallowed by a "great fish," what actually swallowed Jonah was a whale (which is, technically, a mammal). In fact, though a "great fish" swallowed Jonah, when Jesus spoke of the incident He referred to the "whale" that swallowed him (Matt. 12:40). (For the record: yes, large whales like the sperm whale can swallow a man, and, yes, men have been swallowed and lived to tell it.)

There is a possibility that the water monster Leviathan (see 484) may have been a whale instead of a mythical monster.

462. fish

Fish are mentioned many times in the Bible, and they were probably a more common food than what we today call "red meat." Apparently the Israelites liked fish, for in their years in the wilderness they complained to Moses that they missed the fish they had in Egypt (Num. 11:5). Jesus used two fish in His miracle of feeding the five thousand (Matt. 14:17), and He ate a meal of fish with His disciples after the Resurrection (John 21). There were, of course, several fishermen among Jesus' disciples.

The Bible relates that a "great fish" swallowed Jonah, but Bible scholars and scientists agree that "whale" was the proper meaning.

463. pearls

Though they come from the insides of oysters, they are and were prized for their delicate beauty. Jesus spoke in one of His parables of a pearl so precious that a merchant sold everything he had to buy it (Matt. 13:45). Jesus also told His followers to (figuratively speaking, of course) avoid casting their pearls before swine (Matt. 7:6). Undoubtedly the Bible's most famous pearls are the twelve that form the gates of the heavenly city (Rev. 21:21).

464. coral

Is it animal or mineral? Both, actually. Coral consists of the hardened skeletons of sea polyps. Man has used it for centuries as a mineral, specifically for the making of jewelry. The red coral of the eastern Mediterranean Sea is mentioned in Job 28:18 and Ezekiel 27:16.

465. sponges

We are so accustomed to the artificial type, we forget that for centuries sponges were, well, real sponges, the dried bodies of an aquatic creature. The one mention of a sponge in the Bible is, of course, the sponge the Romans used to hold the wine that was offered to Jesus on the cross (John 19:29).

BEASTS GREAT AND SMALL

466. foxes

They were common enough in ancient Israel, sleeping in burrows and feeding on small animals and fruits. Jesus referred to Herod as a "fox," perhaps alluding to the fox's craftiness (Luke 13:32). Tobiah the Ammonite sneered at the Jews' rebuilding of Jerusalem's walls, saying that the walls would break down if a fox walked on them (Neh. 4:3).

It's possible that some of the Bible's references to foxes are actually referring to jackals. This is probably true of Song of Solomon 2:15 ("the little foxes that spoil the vines") and of the story of Samson catching three hundred foxes (or jackals, which are easier to catch), tying torches to their tails, and setting them loose in the Philistines' grain fields (Judg. 15:4–5).

467. wolves

"Wolves in sheep's clothing" is one of the Bible's most familiar phrases. Jesus applied this term to false prophets (Matt. 7:15), and there is no doubt that in a land where sheep were constantly threatened by ravening wolves, the image would have had an impact. Running in packs (unlike coyotes, which are solitary), wolves are a problem wherever domestic livestock is kept. The prophet Isaiah spoke of an idyllic future time when all would be at peace, symbolized by the wolf lying down with the lamb (Isa. 11:6; 65:25).

468. leopards

While lions have a reputation for being the ferocious "king of the beasts," leopards are actually more dangerous to man. Though these large spotted cats no longer live in the Bible lands, they did in ancient times, as evidenced by Jeremiah's oft-quoted question about whether a leopard could change its spots (Jer. 13:23). Isaiah spoke, figuratively, of a time of peace when the leopard would lie down with the goat (Isa. 11:6). The prophet Habakkuk paid tribute to the leopard's swiftness. In one of Daniel's visions, he saw a creature that looked like a leopard, but with four wings and four heads (Dan. 7:6). In a similar vision, John saw an evil leopard-like beast with feet like a bear's (Rev. 13:2).

469. pigs

Pork is popular, and for a while the potbellied pig was a trendy pet, but let's face it: pigs still have an image problem. This was even more true in Bible times, where pigs were on the list of animals the Israelites could not eat (Lev. 11:7). That nonkosher list is a long one, but since it mostly lists things no one would eat anyway (such as bats and owls), people seem to remember that the one popular food that is forbidden is pork. Pork in those days possibly carried various intestinal parasites, so God may have been protecting the Israelites from illness. Also, pigs may have had some association with pagan gods. At any rate, pigs were detested, as seen in the story of Jesus sending a herd of demons into a herd of pigs, which then plunged themselves over a cliff (Matt. 8:30–32). The degradation of the prodigal son is complete when he is reduced to tending hogs (Luke 15:15). However, the New Testament makes it clear that the old laws of kosher do not apply to Christians (Mark 7:19; Acts 10). Even so, some groups, such as the Seventh-Day Adventists, still choose to observe the prohibition on pork.

470. lions

Lions today live in Africa and some isolated parts of India, but in Bible times they lived throughout the Middle East. They must have been fairly familiar to the Bible authors, for lions are mentioned about 130 times, more than any other wild beast. As it has been throughout history, the lion symbolized strength and royalty. Perhaps the most famous lions were the one slaughtered by the strongman Samson, leading to his famous riddle (Judg. 14), the one killed by the shepherd boy David (1 Sam. 17:36), and, of course, those that could have (but didn't) devour the saintly man Daniel (Dan. 6).

471. camels

They are mentioned many times in the Bible, particularly in connection with the rapacious Midianites, the world's original "camel jockeys." These desert raiders were notorious for their swift and violent attacks on the Israelites. Apparently the raids paid off, for Judges 8:26 mentions that some of the camels actually wore gold chains around their necks.

472. a sheepish Bible

Not surprisingly, the most-mentioned animal in the Bible is the sheep, mentioned more than seven hundred times.

The sheep was the most common grazing animal, a source of both meat and wool. Sheep are, generally speaking, rather stupid, wayward animals, very much dependent on their human protectors, so it is not surprising that the Bible many times compares humans to sheep, with God as the wise, protective Shepherd.

473. lambs

Yes, they're the same animal as the sheep, but there was always something special about the young ones. Their meat was prized more than the meat of adult sheep (mutton, that is), and, of course, from the earliest times lambs were used in sacrifices (Gen. 4:4; 22:7). Probably the most famous lamb in the Bible (other than, figuratively speaking, Christ, the Lamb of God) was the one mentioned in the prophet Nathan's parable, the adored pet lamb that belonged to the poor man but was selfishly taken by the rich man who had sheep to spare (2 Sam. 12).

474. cattle

We use "cattle" only to refer to domestic cows, but in the King James Version it has a wider use, something like our word *livestock,* or even "animals" in general. In the Old Testament, the number of cattle a man owned was a measure of his wealth. Cows figured prominently in Pharaoh's dream interpreted by Joseph (Gen. 41:1–7). Beef was a favorite food, but apparently veal was even more valued, as seen in the order to "kill the fatted calf" to welcome home the prodigal son (Luke 15:23). As we know from Exodus, worship of calf idols was a temptation to the people (Exod. 32:19). Cattle of all types figured prominently in Israel's system of animal sacrifices, a system that is no longer necessary in the lives of Christians (Heb. 9:13).

475. deer

These are mentioned many times in the Bible, and that includes references to the "hart" (a male deer, that is, what we call a stag or buck) and to the "hind" (a female deer, a doe). In Psalm 42, David compared his thirst for God to the thirst a hart feels for cooling streams. Proverbs 5:19 compares a man's wife to a loving doe. The prophet Isaiah predicted a time when the lame would leap like a deer (Isa. 35:6). Deer were approved eating for the Israelites, and apparently Solomon valued their meat highly (1 Kings 4:23).

476. dogs

Much as people love dogs today, we are surprised to learn that they were despised in Bible times. Their habit of vomiting up their food and returning to it is mentioned in Proverbs 26:11. Twice the phrase "dead dog" is used to mean "worthless person" (2 Sam. 9:8; 16:9). Most dogs of this era were strays and usually seen as nuisances. In one of Jesus' parables, dogs licked the sores of the beggar Lazarus (Luke 16:21). The woman who pleaded for Jesus' aid mentioned that "even the dogs" eat the crumbs from the master's table (Matt. 15:26–27). Ecclesiastes 9:4 claims that a live dog is better than a dead lion.

The only breed specifically mentioned is the greyhound, which the Egyptians had bred for centuries, both for racing and as pets. Proverbs 30:31 speaks of their swiftness.

477. gazelles

These graceful, swift-moving antelopes lived in wilderness areas, and they were hunted with falcons and greyhounds. Their meat was highly valued (Deut. 12:15), and Solomon had gazelle meat as part of his fare (1 Kings 4:23). In the New Testament, the kindhearted woman Dorcas's name means "gazelle" (Acts 9:36).

478. hyenas

Distantly related to dogs, these vicious, repulsive creatures are nothing to laugh about. The Bible mentions them only a few times, always as symbols of desolation and wildness, as in Isaiah's prophecy against Babylon: "The hyenas will howl in their citadels" (Isa. 13:22). Some Bible versions use "wild beast" instead of hyenas.

479. rabbits and hares

The surprising thing about the kosher law is that it prohibits eating rabbits and hares (Lev. 11:6), which most people do not consider "unclean" animals. The law forbids eating them because, though they chew the cud, they do not have a split hoof. (Obviously they have no hoof at all.) Common as rabbits and hares are throughout the world, they are not mentioned in the Bible except in the law that forbids eating them.

480. pairs of animals

When we think of Noah and the ark, we picture him leading one pair each of every animal into the ark. But in fact the ark contained *seven* pairs of every bird and animal—the "clean" ones, anyway. The "unclean" animals (such as the pig) and birds were those that could not be eaten according to the kosher laws (which came *after* Noah, by the way). There was only one pair each of the unclean birds and animals (Gen. 7:1–4).

BEASTS OF LEGEND

481. unicorns

Unicorns really do exist . . . in that wonderful place called Fantasyland. Oddly enough, they are in the Bible, too—or at least in the King James Version, which mentions them several times (Num. 23:22; Deut. 33:17; Job 39:9; Ps. 22:21; 92:10; Isa. 34:7). The King James translators were sure of one thing: the Hebrew word was referring to something with horns (or *one* horn, at least). Did they really believe that the unicorn existed—or that it had existed in the days of the Old Testament? Hard to say. Modern translations have taken a more down-to-earth approach: for example, the New King James Version and the New International Version both have "wild ox" where the KJV had "unicorn." Probably more accurate, but not nearly as picturesque. The KJV's mentions of unicorns are the reason that many paintings of Noah's ark show the unicorn among the animals.

482. cockatrice

"And the sucking child shall play on the hole of the asp, and the weaned child shall put his hand on the cockatrice' den" (Isa. 11:8 KJV). In the realm of legend, a cockatrice is a kind of serpent that can kill with its glance. The cockatrice appears several times in the King James Version (particularly in Isaiah), but later versions have "viper" or "adder" or such. We have no way of knowing whether the King James translators actually believed that the fearsome cockatrice existed.

483. the monster behemoth

The Bible mentions a water monster named *behemoth* (Job 40:15). The Bible scholars aren't sure if the Hebrew name refers to some mythical water beast or to something real, such as a hippopotamus or perhaps the elephant. The word passed into the language as referring to any kind of hulking animal or monster.

484. the monster leviathan

As with the behemoth, Bible scholars aren't sure just what is being referred to. The beast is described in some detail in Job 41, but we still can't be sure if the writer is describing some mythical sea beast or referring to an actual animal, such as the crocodile or whale. Psalm 104:26, which refers to leviathan frolicking in the sea, is likely referring to the huge sperm whale, which can be sighted off Israel's coast.

485. dragons

"Praise the LORD from the earth, ye dragons, and all deeps"—so says Psalm 148:7 in the King James Version. Did the King James translators really believe in dragons, or were they simply stumped (as translators still are) by certain Hebrew words that are difficult to pin down? Probably the latter. The word *dragon* appears many times in the King James Version, while contemporary versions are (probably) more accurate with such words as "serpent" (as in Ps. 74:13) or even "jackals" (as in Job 30:29; Ps. 74:13). However, the wicked dragon in Revelation is supposed to be just that: a dragon.

486. satyrs

In Greek mythology, satyrs were strange creatures of the wild, having a manlike torso and arms, but with the hind legs, ears, and horns of a goat. In other words, they never existed. However, the prophet Isaiah mentions satyrs twice: "Wild beasts of the desert shall lie there; and their houses shall be full of doleful creatures; and owls shall dwell there, and satyrs shall dance there" (13:21); "the satyr shall cry to his fellow" (34:14). So reads the King James Version. Contemporary translations, such as the New King James, are probably more accurate in using "wild goats" instead of "satyrs."

INSECTS AND SUCH

487. fleas

These tiny bloodsuckers are a nuisance to man and can be life-threatening, since they sometimes carry diseases such as the bubonic plague. The flea is mentioned twice by David, who compared Saul's pursuit of him to pursuing a flea (1 Sam. 24:14; 26:20). Since fleas, with their amazing jumping ability, are difficult to catch, David may have been suggesting that he himself was difficult to catch.

488. worms

Earthworms are not mentioned in the Bible, and in all likelihood, "worm" always refers to the maggots of flies.

Crawly, wormlike maggots feed on the dead animals in which they hatch. Jesus spoke of hell in terms of a place where the worm (maggot) never dies but continues to feed on the corpse (Mark 9:48). Worms' presence on the human body was a reminder of life's fleetingness (Job 7:5; Isa. 14:11).

489. flies

They were and are a threat to man, not only being a nuisance, but carrying disease and even sucking man's blood. They were one of the plagues on Egypt (Ex. 8:24), and some form of fly could even ruin crops (Deut. 28:40; Hab. 3:17). (See 488.)

The pagan god Beelzebub's name means "lord of the flies" (2 Kings 1:2–6).

490. gnats

They aren't particularly dangerous, but they can be a dreadful nuisance. They were one of the plagues God sent upon Egypt (Ex. 8:16–18), though some scholars believe the Bible may be referring to sand flies, which have a nastier bite than gnats. Jesus scolded the teachers of the Law for straining out a gnat but swallowing a camel—figuratively speaking, of course, for He was referring to being fussy over the Law's details while missing the larger goal, loving God and our neighbor (Matt. 23:24).

491. locusts

One of the most feared creatures in the Bible is . . . a grasshopper. Known as locusts, in huge swarms they can strip a region of its food crops in a matter of hours. They were a serious threat in Bible times (remember the plague of them in Egypt, Ex. 10), capable of causing famines (Isa. 33:4), and even today they can do considerable damage. Curiously, the locust was listed as a creature that the Israelites could eat (Lev. 11:22)—appropriate, since more often the shoe was on the other foot, with the locusts being the eater and doing man harm instead of good.

492. ants

As in the old fable of the grasshopper and the ant, so the Bible shows admiration for the ant's industry (Prov. 6:6; 30:25). Though small in size, they work hard and use the division-of-labor principle, and their strength is all out of proportion to their size.

493. hornets

The ancient peoples respected and feared hornets as much as we do. Though hornets are basically beneficial to man (they eat flies), they can be vicious in defending their papery nests. The Bible states that God used hornets to drive away the enemies of Israel (Ex. 23:28; Deut. 7:20; Josh. 24:12).

494. bees

We know that the Israelites appreciated honey, as the frequent phrase "land of milk and honey" indicates. The book of Judges tells the famous story of bees building their honeycomb in the carcass of a lion Samson had killed with his bare hands (Judg. 14). We aren't sure if the Israelites "kept" bees for the honey or simply depended on finding wild honey whenever they could. Some of Israel's enemies were compared to swarms of bees (Deut. 1:44).

495. moths

The ancient peoples were as annoyed by the common clothes moth as we are today. The moth itself does not eat fabric: it lays its eggs at night, and its larvae hatch out and do the damage. Jesus spoke of the moth in connection with the fleeting value of clothes and other worldly goods (Matt. 6:19). Job 13:28 compares man's wasting away to the wasting of garments by moths.

496. spiders

People fear them, but most of them are quite harmless and even beneficial to man. Common as they were and are, they are rarely mentioned in the Bible. Job 8:14 refers to something being as fragile as a spider's web. (Technically, yes, they are arachnids, not insects.)

GREEN GROW THE PLANTS

497. almonds

The almond tree was prized for various reasons: the nuts are edible, and the pink blossoms are beautiful. The Israelites liked the almond blossom so much that they used the image in decorating their ritual vessels (Ex. 25:33–36). Almonds were prized so much that Jacob included almonds among the gifts he sent to Joseph's brothers in Egypt (Gen. 43:11). The most famous almond branch was Aaron's rod: placed in the Lord's tabernacle, the stick put forth buds, blossoms, and ripe almonds (Num. 17).

498. carob

In our nutrition-conscious age, carob is popular, sometimes as a substitute for chocolate. The carob tree produces pods in which seeds are embedded in a sweet pulp. Some people believe that the "locusts" John the Baptist ate were actually the pods of the carob, and thus carob has been called "St. John's bread." The "pods" eaten by the down-and-out prodigal son were probably carob (Luke 15:16).

499. bulrushes

These plants are best remembered because Moses' mother hid her baby in the river in a basket made of bulrushes (Ex.

2:3), protecting him from Pharaoh's slaughter of the Hebrew children. Most likely the "bulrushes" were the papyrus plant, the same plants whose stalks were used to make the world's first paper. Papyrus grew commonly along the Nile's shores and in wet areas throughout the world.

500. cinnamon, solid and liquid

The cinnamon tree, about twenty feet high, produces an inner bark used to make the spice we call cinnamon. The tree also yields a fragrant oil used in perfume and medicines. It was used in Israel's sacred anointing oil (Ex. 30:23).

501. citrus, but not for eating

Were there citrus fruits in the Bible? Not oranges, lemons, or grapefruits, but perhaps the citron tree, which is mentioned as a source of wood (not edible fruit) in Revelation 18:12.

502. aloes, scented and unscented

These are mentioned many times in the Bible, but probably not in reference to the small fleshy houseplant that is so popular today as a source of soothing juice for the skin. John 19:39, which mentions the materials brought to embalm Jesus, may refer to our familiar aloe plant, but elsewhere "aloe" probably refers to a tree called the eaglewood, whose inner wood gives off a fragrant resin used in perfumes (see Ps. 45:8; Prov. 7:17; Song 4:14).

503. "under his fig tree"

The first specific plant mentioned in the Bible is the fig—because its leaves were used as Adam and Eve's first (makeshift) clothing (Gen. 3:7). Figs grow well in the Middle East, and the tasty food was plentiful enough to be known as the "poor man's food." The phrase "every man under his vine and under his fig tree" occurs several times in the Old Testament, suggesting peace and prosperity (see 1 Kings 4:25; Mic. 4:4; Zech. 3:10).

504. cypress or gopherwood?

The King James Version says Noah's ark was made of gopherwood, as do several other versions. Some more recent translations say the ark was made of cypress, an extremely hard, durable wood, sometimes called "the wood eternal." It may be that gopherwood was simply an older name for cypress.

505. apples

In the first place, the Bible never says that the forbidden fruit in the Garden of Eden was an apple. In the second place, the Bible probably does not mention apples at all. They were introduced fairly recently into Palestine and have not grown well there. Where the King James Version and some other versions refer to "apples" in various verses, newer translations have "apricots" or some similar fruit. Apricots grow quite well in the region.

506. balm and balsam

Both words refer to an aromatic resin from plants, used for medicinal purposes. The most famous balm is that mentioned by Jeremiah: "Is there no balm in Gilead, is there no physician there?" (Jer. 8:22). One source of balsam is a shrub that grows abundantly near the Dead Sea.

507. hyssop

In the Old Testament, this was an herb belonging to the mint family. Its hairy stem holds fluids, and thus the plant was used for sprinkling blood during the Passover rituals (Ex. 12:22; Lev. 14; Heb. 9:19). Yet John 19:29 mentions hyssop used an entirely different way: a sponge filled with wine was placed on hyssop and raised up to Jesus on the cross. The plant experts agree: this had to be a much larger plant than the hyssop mentioned in the Old Testament. The hyssop in John 19:29 may have been a stalk of sorghum cane, which would have been tall enough for the purpose John mentions.

508. grass

Grass, as in "lawn turf," was unknown in the Bible. In fact, the word we translate as "grass" in English covers a variety of low-growing plants, mostly wild ones. More important than any botanical precision is what grass symbolizes in the Bible: the fleeting brevity of life, as in Isaiah's lament: "All flesh is grass, and all its loveliness is like the flower of the field . . . The grass withers, the flower fades, but the word of our God stands forever" (Isa. 40:6, 8). See Psalms 37:2; 90:5; 92:7; 102:11; 103:15; Matt. 6:30.

509. lentils

These were popular in Bible times as they are today, and then and now they found their way into soups and stews. Like peas and beans, they belong to the general category known as legumes. The "pottage" that the overly hungry Esau traded for his birthright was probably a stew made from red Egyptian lentils (Gen. 25:30–34).

510. lilies

This name applies to many kinds of unrelated flowers, and there is no doubt that the "lilies" of the Bible were not the familiar trumpet-shaped flowers we associate with Easter. As so often when dealing with Hebrew and Greek words, we can't be sure just what the Bible's lilies were. Jesus Himself praised the beauties of the "lilies of the field" (Luke 12:27), saying that "Solomon in all his glory" was not so beautiful to behold.

Many Bible readers remember the "lily of the valley" mentioned in Song of Solomon 2:1: "I am the rose of Sharon, and the lily of the valleys." This does not refer to the low-growing ornamental plant of today (which took its name from the Bible, actually). Somehow a Christian tradition developed that the "rose of Sharon and lily of the valley" was Jesus Himself, and several old hymns refer to Him as the "lily of the valley." The Song of Solomon, full of lush nature images, mentions lilies several times.

511. mandrakes

This plant has a large, forked root, which many people thought resembled a human body. Perhaps for this reason the plant gained a reputation as an aphrodisiac, a "love apple" that would also help barren women produce children. The root tastes terrible and is even slightly poisonous, but even so, it was highly valued by the barren. We see this in Genesis 30:14–16, where Jacob's wives, the sisters Rachel and Leah, quarrel over some mandrakes. Apparently the roots worked, for the formerly barren Leah finally conceived.

512. mustard

No, not the yellow stuff used on hamburgers, but the original plant itself, whose tiny seeds are used to make a powder or paste in cooking. From the very small seeds grows a plant about fifteen feet high, a fact that Jesus used in His famous parable of the mustard seed (Mark 4:31).

513. palms

As in the Pacific Islands today, the palm in ancient Palestine was a multipurpose plant: dates for eating, sap for making syrup and vinegar, leaves for weaving into mats, fibers for thread and rigging boats. Aside from this, the trees are just plain pretty, something the weary Israelites realized (Ex. 15:27; Num. 33:9). Palm fronds were used in the Jews' Feast of the Tabernacles (Lev. 23:40), and, most famously, were laid in front of Jesus as He entered Jerusalem (John 12:13). The book of Revelation indicates that palm branches were a symbol of victory (Rev. 7:9). The ancient city of Jericho, whose "walls come atumblin' down," was known as the "city of palms." According to Psalm 92:12, "The righteous flourish like the palm tree" (KJV).

514. oaks

Throughout human history, the sturdy, long-lived oak has symbolized strength and longevity. Several times the Old

Testament mentions the "oak of Bashan," which apparently refers to a species that especially impressed people with its durability (Isa. 2:13; Ezek. 27:6; Zech. 11:2). It was under the "oaks of Mamre" that Abraham encountered the Lord in the form of three strangers (Gen. 13:18; 18:1).

515. pistachio

Yes, the same pretty green nut in a red shell that we enjoy today was enjoyed in Palestine for thousands of years. The ancient Israelites used it not only for food but as a food coloring as well. Along with almonds, pistachios were among the gifts carried by Jacob's sons into Egypt (Gen. 43:11).

516. reed

This was a common hollow-stemmed water plant, growing in rivers and lakes. Its stalks, which grew up to twelve feet, were commonly used in animal pens. However, the reed was easily moved by the wind and water, and for the Israelites it came to be a symbol of weakness and instability (see 1 Kings 14:15).

517. rose

Several plants are referred to as "rose" in the King James Version, but none of these are the well-loved rose of gardens today. The famous "rose of Sharon" mentioned in Song of Solomon 2:1 is very likely the shrub *Hibiscus syriacus*, known today as hibiscus or as rose of Sharon.

518. saffron

Also known as the autumn crocus, this little flower's stigmas yield the deep yellow-orange matter used to flavor and color food and to dye clothing. In the Bible it is mentioned only in the Song of Solomon (4:14), which indicates that it was as valued for its fragrance as for its color.

519. nard and spikenard

The names aren't pretty, but this was a costly herb highly valued for its fragrant root. A rose-red ointment was made from it, and it was a favorite perfume in Bible times (Song of Solomon 1:12; 4:13). It was stored in an alabaster jar, which helped preserve the fragrance, and it was with this costly substance that Mary anointed Jesus' feet (Mark 14:3).

520. sycamore

This is not the same sycamore as grown in North America today, the tall, white-barked tree that grows on riversides. The sycamore of the Bible was a sycamore-fig (*Ficus sycomorus*), which bears figs, though of inferior quality.

Egyptians made their mummy cases from its wood. The prophet Amos described himself as "a sheepbreeder and a tender of sycamore fruit" (Amos 7:14). The best-known sycamore tree was the one climbed by the tax collector Zacchaeus, who was so short he climbed the tree to get a better look at Jesus (Luke 19:4).

521. thistles and thorns

In the dry, rocky soil of Palestine, plants of this type grow abundantly, and no one likes any of them. According to Genesis 3:18, the ground did not originally produce such nuisances, but they grew up as part of Adam's curse for disobeying God. Jesus spoke of such plants: "You will know them by their fruits. Do men gather grapes from thornbushes or figs from thistles?" (Matt. 7:16). The thorns used to make the "crown" for Jesus were possibly those of the *Paliurus spina-christi* (today known as the "Christ's-thorn"), which has pliable branches that would lend themselves to making a sort of crown.

522. tumbleweeds

We associate these with the American West, but they lived in ancient Palestine also. You won't find them in the King James Version, however, which speaks of a "wheel" (Ps. 83:13) or "rolling thing" (Isa. 17:13), though the New International Version has "tumbleweed."

523. vine of Sodom

This is mentioned in Deuteronomy 32:32, and scholars have had fun trying to identify it with an actual plant. Most likely the Bible authors were using "vine of Sodom" in a poetic way, reminding people of the wicked city of Sodom. Obviously any "vine of Sodom" would bear poisonous fruit.

524. walnut

Our familiar English walnuts were grown in ancient Palestine (though not known as "English walnuts" in those days, of course). It is likely that the "nut" trees referred to in Song of Solomon 6:11 were walnut trees. As today, they were highly valued for the nuts and for the excellent wood.

525. corn

This is mentioned many times in the Bible—or, at least, in the King James Version. It definitely does *not* refer to the corn we grow in America (formerly called maize or Indian corn), which is strictly an American plant, not grown in Europe when the King James translators were at work. Where the King James has "corn," modern versions have "grain." For the King James scholars—and for all Englishmen today— "corn" simply refers in a generic way to any kind of grain.

526. willows

The most familiar willow to us is the weeping willow (*Salix babylonica*), which grows well in wet sites. It may have been the willow mentioned in Psalm 137:1–2: "By the rivers of Babylon, there we sat down, yea, we wept when we remembered Zion. We hung our harps upon the willows in the midst of it." The *Salix babylonica* was given its name because scientists suspected it might be the willow of Psalm 137.

527. gourds

These are all American plants, so there is no way the "gourd vines" mentioned in the Bible are the same plants we know today. In all likelihood the "gourd vine" that grew up over the prophet Jonah was the colocynth, a trailing vine with orange-sized fruit, vaguely resembling an actual gourd plant. Most modern versions of the Bible simply have "vine" instead of "gourd vine" in Jonah.

528. flax and linen

The flax plant yields both linen and linseed oil, so it was widely grown in Bible times. Linen is fairly strong and is resistant to moisture, plus it has a cooling effect on the wearer, so it would have been a suitable material for wearing under the hot sun of ancient Palestine.

529. pomegranates

These attractive and tasty fruits were highly regarded in the Bible. The fruit was edible, the juice was drinkable, and the plant's blossoms could be made into medicine. Small images of pomegranates were sewn onto the edge of the robe of Israel's high priest (Ex. 28:33–34).

11

Daily Life in Bible Times

MAKING ONESELF PRESENTABLE

530. beards

All the great men of the Bible are usually shown in art-work with beards, and with good reason: Jewish men wore beards. It was a mark of an adult male, and having one's beard forcibly shaved was a horrible humiliation (see 2 Sam. 10:4–5; Isa. 50:6; Jer. 48:37). The Law of Moses strictly prohibited trimming the beard too closely (see Lev. 19:27).

Beards are never mentioned in the New Testament, but we know that Jewish men continued to wear them (as they have through the centuries) and that Roman men did not, looking upon beards as a mark of barbarians.

A few times in Christian history authors have written books, such as the 1860 work *Defense of the Beard*, stating biblical reasons why beards should be worn.

531. bathing

The Greeks and (even more so) the Romans made bathing into a major ritual, the more often and longer, the better. The people in Bible lands were less addicted to it, water being less plentiful. Most often, "bathing" refers to partial washing—usually just the hands and feet. The dusty roads of the region made footwashing a necessity, and servants were employed by the wealthy to wash guests' feet (Gen. 18:4; John 13:10). It appears that in Jesus' time Jews washed their hands before eating (Mark 7:3–4).

532. girdles

This didn't have the same meaning in Bible times as it does today. In the Bible, a girdle was a fairly large piece of cloth, tied around the waist like a wide sash, with its folds forming pockets for carrying small articles. A leather girdle, sometimes studded with metal, was a wide belt that men wore, suitable for securing daggers, a leather bag, etc. For poor folks, the leather girdle was usually just a rawhide strap.

533. no unisex

Despite the unisex look in so much casual clothing today, men and (especially) women have always enjoyed dressing very differently from the opposite sex. In the Old Testament, this was not just habit but law, for the Israelites were absolutely prohibited from dressing like the opposite sex (Deut. 22:5).

534. no makeup

As in our own time, people in Bible times used cosmetics to make themselves more fragrant and attractive. While the Bible never actually says, "Wear no makeup," some stricter Christians point out that the Old Testament prophets condemned people who made themselves pretty on the outside but behaved abominably (see Isa. 3:16; Jer. 4:30). In the New Testament, Peter admonished Christian women to pursue inward beauty rather than fussing over their hair, jewelry, and clothing (1 Peter 3:3).

535. scarlet

We know it as a color, but the name originally applied to the dye (scarlet, of course) produced by the kermes insect, which breeds on the kermes oak tree. The richly colored dye was used to color linen and wool thread (Gen. 38:28; Num. 4:8; Heb. 9:19). To be dressed in scarlet was a sign of wealth, even royalty (Ex. 28:5–6; Lam. 4:5; Rev. 18:12), which is obvious when the Roman soldiers mock Jesus by putting a scarlet robe on Him (Matt. 27:28). The most famous mention of scarlet is in Isaiah 1:18: "'Come now, and let us reason together,' says the LORD, 'though your sins are like scarlet, they shall be as white as snow.'"

EATING AND DRINKING

536. nonkosher catfish

The kosher laws in Leviticus 11 mention that fish are permitted as food—but only fish with fins and scales (Lev. 11:9–12). Thus any kind of seafood without scales is prohibited—which would include not only shellfish like lobsters and oysters, but also scaleless fish such as catfish.

537. three square meals a day?

Not usually. So far as we can tell, people in Bible times usually ate two meals per day. The first might be served any time from morning to noon, usually after the morning's work was completed. The evening meal was at no set time, but whenever work was ended. It was usually the main (i.e., heaviest) meal of the day. Jesus' amazing feat of feeding the five thousand people was an end-of-the-day meal (Matt. 14:15).

538. kneading troughs

These were not as big as horses' drinking troughs, but they were exceptionally large bowls, used for kneading bread dough. They were made of wood or clay and were part of every household's furnishings. Exodus 12:34 mentions that the Israelites leaving Egypt carried their kneading troughs with them. Some translations have "kneading bowls," but "troughs" gives a better idea of their size.

539. sop

There were no "place settings" at tables in Bible times, and the most common utensils were the human fingers. Since most meals included bread, people would use bread to "sop" wine, gravy, or any liquids on the plate—adding flavor to the bread, and also making good use of any liquids left on the plate. The most famous, or infamous, sop was that handed by Jesus to the traitor Judas, for Jesus identified the traitor as the one "to whom I shall give a sop, when I have dipped it. And when he had dipped the sop, he gave it to Judas Iscariot" (John 13:26–30 KJV). Judas then left to do his dirty work.

540. gleaning

The Bible existed before welfare and food stamps, and yet the Old Testament law made provision for the poor to eat. Farmers were required to leave some of their harvest in the field for the poor and for travelers to eat (Lev. 19:10). The book of Ruth speaks of the heroine rising at dawn to join other widows and orphans who collected grain along the edges and corners of fields.

ABOUT THE HOUSE

541. up on the roof

Since most people's homes were crowded (usually just one room), the home's roof was more than just something to keep out the rain and sun. The flat roofs of Israelite homes were good places for catching a cool breeze if there was one, for chatting with one's neighbors (who would likely be out on their roofs), and for surveying the passersby. On a more practical level, roofs were places to ripen fruits and vegetables, dry flax for cloth, and dry the wash.

542. parapets

Just as highways today often have galvanized steel guardrails along the shoulders, so houses in the ancient world had their own form of guardrails. They were called *parapets*, and according to the Law given to the Hebrews, every homeowner had to have a parapet on his house's upper stories so he wouldn't be to blame if someone fell from the roof (Deut. 22:8). It was the ancient world's form of consumer protection and liability insurance.

543. bottles or skins?

Though we often encounter the word *bottle* in English Bibles, in most cases the "bottles" in the ancient world were actually containers made of goatskin, with the hair on the outside. Newer goatskins were more elastic than old ones, which is what Jesus had in mind when He spoke of putting new wine into old wineskins. His hearers would have known that new wine expands as it ferments and would burst an old goatskin (Luke 5:37–38).

544. closet

Jesus told His followers not to make a big show of praying in public, but rather to go into a "closet" and pray privately to God (Matt. 6:6; Luke 12:3). The Greek word here is *tameion*, which may refer to a sort of storage room (closet, that is), perhaps used for storing the mats used as bedding. It does not imply the rather tiny areas that we call "closets" today. Some modern translations have "room" instead of "closet."

545. boundary stones

The Bible shows a deep respect for private property, as is seen in the curse for those who move their neighbor's boundary stones (Deut. 27:17). The curse is not only a curse upon stealing (trying to increase one's acreage at the expense of the neighbor) but also a curse upon disrespect for a family's lands, which might have been held for generations.

546. bricks

We read in Exodus that the Israelite slaves in Egypt were forced to make bricks without straw (Ex. 5:7–19). Good bricks used straw as a kind of "binder," so making them without straw was a severe burden.

Bricks in ancient times were square instead of oblong like bricks today. Often they were stamped, before they dried, with the name of the country's ruler. Usually they were fired in ovens to harden the clay, just like today, but in hot, sunny Egypt they could be baked in the sun.

547. cisterns

In a desert or semidesert, people take water any way they can get it. Wells were highly valued in ancient Israel, as were rivers, but Israel was not blessed with many of either. Many people relied on cisterns, which are in-ground tanks or reservoirs used for storing water, usually rainwater but sometimes springwater as well. Many cisterns were fed rainwater from the runoff from roofs. Some cisterns were a hundred feet deep, and the temple area in Jerusalem had about thirty-seven cisterns, one of them holding about three million gallons. Cisterns were sometimes used as temporary prisons: Joseph was cast into one by his jealous brothers (Gen. 37:22), and the prophet Jeremiah was lowered into one with a muddy bottom (Jer. 38:6).

548. ivory palaces

Ivory wasn't uncommon in Bible times, but it was always considered a luxury item. The rich used it for utensils, game pieces, beds and couches, and boxes. Apparently Israel was prospering (materially, anyway) under wicked King Ahab, for Ahab had an "ivory house" (1 Kings 22:39). The prophet Amos condemned the idle rich, who had no concern for the poor and who reclined on couches and beds of ivory (Amos 3:15; 6:4).

MARRIAGE AND CHILDREN

549. betrothal

"Getting engaged" doesn't carry any legal weight these days, but it did in Bible times. A betrothed couple were legally bound to each other (even though sexual relations weren't allowed until marriage). From the time of the betrothal, the bride-to-be's father would refer to the groom-to-be as his "son-in-law." So over the period of the betrothal (usually one year) a family feeling could begin to develop. The seriousness of engagement is seen clearly in the matter of Joseph and Mary: Mary was with child (though not by Joseph), so Joseph faced the choice of marrying her as planned or legally "divorcing" her, which would have had the effect that Mary could not have married anyone else. Joseph, being the righteous man that he was, married her.

550. levirate marriage

In the Old Testament, having children to carry on the family line was *very* important. For this reason the Old Testament law had an arrangement for cases of a husband who died before he had fathered any children: his surviving brother was expected to marry the widow and father children by her, children which were (figuratively speaking) the children of the man who died. This was known as levirate marriage, and refusal to comply with it brought shame on the brother's house (Deut. 25:5–9).

551. salty infants

In the days before disinfectants, parents made do with whatever was available—such as salt. After a newborn was washed clean with water, salt was rubbed over his body, presumably as a kind of purifier (see Ezek. 16:4).

552. women as heirs

The Bible has been accused of being antiwoman, but the Law in the book of Numbers shows that women could inherit property—under certain circumstances, anyway. The general rule: when a man died, his sons inherited his property, the eldest son getting a double share. But if a man had no sons, his property went to his daughters (Num. 27:8). If he had no daughters, his estate went to his brothers and, if there were no brothers, then to his father's brothers. The main idea: as far as possible, keep property in the family, and certainly within one's tribe.

553. birthright

Our view of a person's last will and testament has changed radically from Bible times. People today can divide their property equally among their children if they choose, and no law or custom requires showing favor to the firstborn. But in Bible times the firstborn, especially the first son, held pride of place. Isaac's sons Esau and Jacob were twins, but technically Esau was born first, so he had the privilege of the "birthright," which is the background for the story of his selling it to the wily Jacob in order to get some food (Gen. 25). The Bible abounds in stories of later-born sons who become preeminent over their first-born brothers—Jacob's younger son Joseph, Moses (younger than his brother Aaron), David (who had many older brothers), etc. Incidentally, the idea of birthright is still followed in countries with hereditary kings, where the throne always goes to the firstborn son.

Making a Living

554. fullers

In the Bible, "fullers" were launderers, who washed clothes by treading them or beating them with sticks.

Apparently the business (in the pre-Tide era) was quite smelly, for fullers were required to do their work outside the city walls (see 2 Kings 18:17; Isa. 7:3; Mark 9:3 KJV).

555. carpenters

Everyone has seen the bumper sticker: "My boss is a Jewish carpenter." The carpenter was, of course, Jesus Himself, practicing the same trade as His legal father, Joseph (Matt. 13:55; Mark 6:3). Carpenters built not only roofs, doors, and window shutters for homes, but also plows and yokes for farm use. Some carpenters were skilled in working with stone and metal as well as wood. From the earliest days of Christianity, believers noted the irony of Jesus, a worker in wood, being executed on two pieces of wood.

556. cupbearer

This doesn't sound like such a great job: the one in charge of the king's cup. But in fact it was quite prestigious, and it involved some danger as well, for the cupbearer ("butler" in some translations) had to taste foods and beverages, testing them for poison before the king could touch them. If they served well, they were highly esteemed by their masters (1 Kings 10:5; 2 Chron. 9:4). One book of the Bible is named for a cupbearer: Nehemiah, the faithful Jew who used his clout as cupbearer to the king of Persia to get aid in the rebuilding of Jerusalem.

557. fishermen

This occupation is mentioned three times in the Old Testament, but only in passing. Most of what the Bible says about fishing is found in the Gospels, and appropriately so, since four of Jesus' disciples (Peter, Andrew, James, and John) were fishermen. Most of the fishing on the Sea of Galilee was done by casting out nets, and also by the use of dragnets. As John's gospel shows, someone standing on the shore can sometimes see schools of fish that the fisherman in the boat cannot see (John 21:4–6).

558. hunting

Throughout history, and even today, many people have survived by hunting, killing, and eating wild game. But where people do not have to find their food by hunting, it turns into recreation rather than necessity, and for centuries it has been a favorite pastime of royalty (see Gen. 10:9; 27:3; 1 Sam. 26:20; Job 38:39). In the days before firearms, large game was shot with bow and arrow, or trapped in pits covered over with brushwood. Small game like quail and ducks were snared by nets and cages. The hunter *par excellence* was the famous Nimrod (Gen. 10:9).

559. perfumers

Travelers in Third World countries today will testify to the pronounced *smell* of primitive life. This was certainly true in Bible times, which explains why perfumers performed such a valuable function. All towns had makers and sellers of all kinds of sweet-smelling substances, including pressed cakes, powders, oils, leaves, and barks—anything to make life more bearable in a time when sanitation was hardly what it is today. With bathing facilities at a minimum, people would (if they could afford it) perfume their skin and hair as much as possible. Some versions of the Bible, notably the King James Version, have "apothecaries" instead of "perfumers."

560. potters

Clay was the most plentiful substance for making everyday containers, and so potters served a valuable function in Bible times. The familiar potter's wheel, still used today, is not so different from the one the ancient Hebrews would have used. Broken pottery cannot be repaired, so the broken pieces—sherds, or shards—were thrown into the "potter's field" (see Matt. 27:7, 10).

561. watchmen

The closest thing an ancient city had to municipal police were its watchmen, who stood guard on the city's walls or at its gates, watching for any danger approaching. They might also patrol the city streets and try to break up any violence that erupted. Like the town crier of medieval times, they also called out the passing hours of the night. God's prophets were referred to, figuratively, as His "watchmen," warning of moral and spiritual dangers (see Isa. 21:6).

562. centurions

The Latin word *centum*, meaning "a hundred," is the root of our "cent" (there are one hundred in a dollar). Naturally a centurion was a military man in charge of one hundred soldiers. As despised as the conquering Romans were (and the military in particular), a few centurions were of noble character. A centurion of Capernaum was noted for his aid to the Jews, and for his faith that Jesus would heal his servant (Luke 7:2–10). One centurion present at Jesus' crucifixion uttered the famous words, "Truly this was the Son of God!" (Matt. 27:54). The God-fearing centurion Cornelius was converted to Christianity by the apostle Peter (Acts 10). The centurion Julius had the duty of taking the prisoner Paul to Rome, and he saved Paul's life when the soldiers wished to kill all the prisoners (Acts 27); Paul, in turn, acted to save the centurion and the entire ship's company.

563. money changers

Anyone who has tried to exchange money in another country knows that it can't be done for free. The bank or whoever swaps one currency for another always makes a profit on the transaction. This was true in the temple at Jerusalem, where coins of all types had to be swapped for the Jewish shekel, in order to pay the temple tax. Jesus may have frowned on the trade (as many visitors to Jerusalem did), but His anger at the money changers was not so much their trade as their doing it in His Father's house, which they had turned into an exchange bureau. This led to the one act of violence we connect with Jesus, His driving the money changers out of the temple court with a whip (Matt. 21:12).

DEALING WITH DEATH

564. no mourning for priests

Christians cannot imagine a funeral without enlisting the services of their minister, but in ancient Israel the priests were specifically *not* to have anything to do with mourning or funeral rituals (Lev. 21:1–4, 10–11). The Old Testament Law was very strict about keeping the priests "clean," and that included having them avoid contact with any dead thing, including a corpse.

565. professional mourners

The Old Testament speaks of "skillful wailing women" (Jer. 9:17–22), referring to women hired to wail and grieve at funerals. This strikes most readers as rather tacky, actually *hiring* people to pretend to be in mourning. Obviously the richer a person was, the more mourners his family would hire to lament his passing. While this was, strictly speaking, fakery, the hiring itself was the family's sign of sincere grief over the departed.

566. mourning hair

Jewish men in Bible times took their facial hair very seriously. For them to cut their beards in any way involved some dramatic change in life—such as a death in the family or some national disaster. In such extreme cases they would either cut off their beards or pull out the hairs with their hands (Ezra 9:3).

567. coffins

Coffins, or caskets, were not used among the Israelites. When an Israelite died, he was carried to his grave on a bier, a flat board. Joseph, Jacob's son who became a high official in Egypt, is mentioned as being buried in a coffin, as was customary among the Egyptians (Gen. 50:26).

568. snow

Snow is rare in Bible lands, most often seen only on mountaintops. Snow symbolized, then and now, the highest purity, such as the purity of the redeemed soul (Ps. 51:7; Isa. 1:18; Matt. 28:3; Rev. 1:14). "White as snow" was as common a phrase in Bible times as it is today.

569. rain

Israel is not quite as dry as the almost rainless Egypt, but Israel's rain is very unevenly distributed through the year. From the first of May to mid-October, almost no rain falls, so the Bible speaks of the "latter rains" (in spring) and the "former rains" (in fall). In the heat of the rainless summer, many people slept on their roofs to be as cool as possible.

An extended drought was a great threat to crops and to life in general. Pagans would engage in ritual orgies to induce their gods to send rain, but the Israelites were prohibited from such activities.

570. hailstones

Hail still frightens people today, particularly farmers, for large hail can do major damage to crops. The worst hailstorm on record was the plague of it sent by God upon the Egyptians, killing their livestock and crops all over the land (Ex. 9:18–26). Another momentous hailstorm occurred when the Israelite armies faced the armies of Gibeon, in a battle where "the LORD cast down large hailstones from heaven on them . . . and they died. There were more who died from the hailstones than the children of Israel killed with the sword" (Josh. 10:11).

Hail is mentioned several times in the visions of Revelation, most notably in 16:21, which speaks of a storm in which every hailstone weighed about a hundred pounds.

571. earthquakes

These are pretty intimidating, and probably were even more so in the ancient world. Several significant ones are mentioned in the Bible: the one that occurred at Horeb for the prophet Elijah (1 Kings 19:11), one referred to by Amos (1:1) and Zechariah (14:5) that occurred in the reign of King Uzziah, one that occurred at Christ's resurrection (Matt. 28:2), and the very helpful one at Philippi that freed Paul and Silas from their chains (Acts 16:26).

572. east wind

For the people of Israel, the east wind was a hot, dry wind, since it blew in from the desert regions. Almost always in the Bible the east wind is connected with bad news: the plague of locusts on Egypt (Ex. 10:13), withered heads of grain (Gen. 41:6), withered plants (Ezek. 17:10), dried-up fountains (Hos. 13:15), and Jonah's faint (Jonah 4:8). Sometimes the east wind could signify God's judgment (Isa. 27:8; Jer. 18:17). On the other hand, on one occasion—the parting of the Red Sea for the Israelites to cross—the east wind did some good (Ex. 14:21).

And Things Left Over

573. fathom

The measurement known as a fathom was supposed to be the distance between one's fingertips when the arms are outstretched. It is, as most people know, a nautical term, and thus the only mention of fathoms in the Bible is in the account of Paul and the storm at sea (Acts 27:28).

574. bath, homer, ephah

The ancient Hebrews used weights and measurements different from ours, and scholars have to guess at just what these were. Bath, homer, and ephah appear to have been standard measurements. Apparently for solid goods ten ephahs were equal to one homer. For liquids, ten baths equaled one homer. A homer was, we think, about five bushels (see Ezek. 45:11).

575. bells, but not many

Bells are often connected with churches, but bells are rarely mentioned in the Bible. The only ones of note are the bells around the hem of the high priest's robe (see Ex. 28; 39). The prophet Zechariah mentions horses' bells, presumably worn on the bridles (14:20). Bells are never mentioned in the New Testament.

576. taxes

Griping about taxes—but paying them anyway—is as old as history. In the days before it had a king, Israel had minimal taxation. When the people asked for a king, the leader Samuel warned them about the coming burden of taxation (1 Sam. 8:11–18). His prediction came true under Saul and David, and more so under Solomon, whose immense building projects (his palace, the temple, etc.) required oppressive taxation. By the time he died, the people had grown so tired of heavy taxes that the ten northern tribes broke away to form a separate kingdom (1 Kings 12). (See 577.)

In the New Testament period, the Roman government followed the system of "farming out" taxes—that is, having local people collect the taxes, extorting whatever extra money they could, which explains why tax collectors were so hated in Jesus' day.

577. tribute

Tribute is "bully" money (or goods) paid by a small power to a bigger power that threatens it. Israel, being a fairly small and relatively powerless nation, was often faced with this threat from the great powers around it: pay us or we conquer you. The large empires—Assyria, Babylonia, etc.—could often force heavy tribute from Israel (see 1 Kings 15:19–20; 2 Kings 23:33; 2 Chron. 10:18; Ezra 7:23–24). When a king of Israel found himself forced to pay tribute, he often passed the tribute along to the people in the form of higher taxes. Not paying tribute often resulted in conquest (as under the Romans), and the conquered power had to pay taxes to the conquerors. Tribute, taxes, or both were the price paid for being a small nation.

578. cleanness of teeth

Beggars were, and still are, a part of the culture in the Middle East. Sometimes beggars asked for food, or for money to buy food, but they also used the gesture of bringing the index finger across the teeth and holding it up to show that it was "clean"—that is, no trace of food in their mouths. For this reason, prophets such as Amos used the phrase "cleanness of teeth" to mean hunger (Amos 4:6).

579. charity

In the King James Version, the Greek word *agape* was often translated "charity," while today we almost always translate it as "love." Neither is an ideal translation, since our "love" has so many meanings attached, most of them having nothing to do with the unselfish love Paul describes in 1 Corinthians 13. When the King James was published in 1611, "charity" had a meaning pretty close to *agape*, but in time "charity" came to mean "giving to the poor," which is why translators no longer use it.

580. borrowing

One of the Ten Commandments forbids stealing, but the Ten say nothing about borrowing. But other commandments in the Old Testament make it clear that God frowns on borrowers who are careless about what they borrow (Ex. 22:1–15). In general, the Israelites preferred not to borrow unless absolutely necessary, which makes sense, since too often the borrower is the servant of the lender (Prov. 22:7). However, the compassionate Jesus instructed His followers not to turn their backs on those who need to borrow (Matt. 5:42).

581. *ptuo* and *ptui*

Sometimes words make such perfect sense: the Greek word for spit is *ptuo*, not far from our modern "ptui." In ancient times as today, spitting in the face was a great insult (see Num. 12:14; Deut. 25:9; Isa. 50:6; Luke 18:32). Among the many insults heaped upon Jesus at His trial was having His face spit in (Matt. 26:67; 27:30).

582. slander

The Bible has stern warnings about that very abusive part of the human body, the tongue. One of the Ten Commandments forbids bearing false witness against another person (Ex. 20:16). Leviticus 19:16 has a similar command: "You shall not go about as a tale-bearer among your people." Paul told the early Christians to "let all bitterness, wrath, anger, clamor, and evil speaking be put away from you, with all malice" (Eph. 4:31).

583. slavery

As American slave owners knew quite well in the years before the Civil War, the Bible does not actually condemn slavery. It was common practice in the ancient world, and the Jews and some of the early Christians owned slaves. Even so, the Old Testament Law did govern the treatment of slaves, and in general, the Hebrews treated their slaves better than other nations did. (The Hebrews had to be reminded sometimes that they themselves had been slaves in Egypt.) Slaves could be acquired as prisoners of war, by purchase, by being born to slaves already owned, and even as a way of paying off a debt. Jesus said nothing directly against slavery, nor did the apostles, but in the Christian community, where being slave or free-born did not matter, inevitably antislavery feelings began to surface.

584. Sabbath day's walk

Since the Sabbath was to be a day of rest, no long journeying was to be done on that day. Thus a "Sabbath day's walk" was a very short trip. It is mentioned in Acts 1:12 as being the distance from Mount Olivet to Jerusalem. The rabbis taught that it was limited to 2,000 cubits—roughly 3,000 feet.

585. prison

Jesus commended people who visited those in prison (Matt. 25:36–44) and foretold that His disciples would themselves be thrown into prison (Luke 21:12). This certainly came to pass, for Peter and John were imprisoned for preaching the faith (Acts 4:3; 5:18–25), and Paul was in prison several times (2 Cor. 11:23): in Philippi (Acts 16:23–40) with Silas, in Jerusalem (Acts 23:18), in Caesarea (Acts 25:27), and on a ship (Acts 27:1, 42).

Righteous people were imprisoned even before the time of Jesus. Joseph was thrown into an Egyptian prison (Gen. 39–40), Samson was imprisoned by the Philistines (Judg. 16:21), the righteous prophet Micaiah was imprisoned (1 Kings 22:27), as was Jeremiah (Jer. 29:26; 37:14–21). It appears from the Bible that there will be many former prisoners in heaven.

586. land of iron and copper

The Bible many times refers to the promised land as a "land of milk and honey," an image of agricultural abundance. But man does not live by food and drink alone, for minerals are a necessary part of human existence. On one occasion Moses spoke of the promised land as "a land whose stones are iron and out of whose hills you can dig copper" (Deut. 8:9).

587. STDs

Were there sexually transmitted diseases in Bible times? Most definitely. Proverbs 7:22–23 speaks of the physical ailments that follow consorting with harlots. The disease known as the "botch of Egypt" in Deuteronomy 27:28 (KJV) was probably syphilis, and the "bodily discharge" described in some parts of the Law may have been a symptom of gonorrhea. In the days before antibiotics, such diseases were not just a nuisance; they could be fatal in the long run.

588. bubonic plague

The "Black Death" that killed so many people in Europe in the Middle Ages was bubonic plague, a horrible disease transmitted by rats (or, more precisely, by the fleas that live on rats). In all likelihood, the plague that struck the Philistines when they captured the ark of the covenant was bubonic plague, as evidenced by the rodents mentioned in connection with the story (1 Sam. 6:5). The ancient Hebrews knew nothing of the microorganisms that actually caused plague, but they were certainly aware that rats had something to do with it.

589. dwarfs

We know that giants are mentioned in the Bible (Goliath being the most famous), but what about dwarfs? The one time they are mentioned is in Leviticus 21:20, in a long list of defects that would have disqualified a man from the priesthood of Israel. The defects included blindness, lameness, being hunchbacked, being a eunuch, etc. These strict regulations do not mean that God doesn't love the handicapped, only that Israel's law would not let them serve as priests.

590. Roman citizenship

We take "citizens" to mean "everybody," but that wasn't its meaning in the Roman Empire. To be a Roman citizen meant having equal rights with the inhabitants of Rome itself. Citizenship could be earned, usually by pleasing the emperor in some way (including bribing him with money). A Roman citizen was exempt from some of the empire's crueler punishments, such as crucifixion and flogging. Citizens could also appeal to Caesar for trial before him, as Paul did in Acts 25:11. Paul had been born a citizen, which means his father or some ancestor had been granted citizenship. He was rather proud of his citizenship and on occasion could use it to his advantage. However, Paul let Christians know that they are citizens of heaven, something of far more value than citizenship in the empire (Phil. 1:27; 3:20).

591. brooks and wadis

In a country that is largely desert, with hardly any major rivers, brooks were deeply appreciated, as witnessed by the many that are named in the Bible (see 1 Sam. 30:9; 2 Sam. 15:23; 1 Kings 17:3–7). But some of the brooks were actually what today are called "wadis"—not permanently flowing streams, but actually ditches that filled with water in the rainy seasons but were dry most of the time.

592. avenger

In the Old Testament, the Hebrew word *goel* refers to the "next of kin," the relative who takes our side when we need aid. But often the *goel* had to play the violent role of avenger, taking the vengeance that the law demands (Num. 35:11–34). So *goel* is sometimes translated "redeemer" (which has a positive sound) or "avenger" (which has a negative sound). In the case of murder, the avenger had to do the required thing and kill the murderer. In Job's famous statement, "I know that my Redeemer lives" (Job 19:25), he actually used the Hebrew *goel*, which is why some translations have "I know that my Avenger lives."

12

Digging Up the Bible

593. finding the lost ark

No, not the ark of the covenant in the Harrison Ford movie. Rather, people have long wondered if Noah's ark, or parts of it, might still exist. In 1887, a bishop from India scaled lofty Mount Ararat in Turkey. (Ararat, according to Genesis, is where the ark came to rest when the Flood subsided.) The bishop claimed he came upon a ship 900 feet long and 100 feet high—but the Turkish authorities blocked his efforts to explore further. In 1955 a Frenchman, Fernand Navarra, brought back pieces of timber from the mountain, found in a glacier at an elevation of 13,000 feet. He persuaded some experts that the wood was old enough to be the wood of Noah's ark. Scientists who tested the wood said it was indeed old— maybe a thousand years old, but certainly not old enough to date back to Noah.

594. tear bottles

Mourning in the ancient world was *real* mourning, with no holding back of tears or wailing (and, psychologically speaking, this was much healthier than holding in the grief). In some Egyptians tombs archaeologists have found beautifully designed "tear bottles," small containers used for holding the tears of those who mourned the deceased person. This practice is mentioned in Psalm 56:8: "Put my tears into Your bottle."

595. Luke on a roll

As mentioned in 967, the earliest Christian writings were more often in codices (books) than on the traditional scrolls. The archaeologists have found that this is less true of Luke's gospel and the other book by Luke, Acts. Why so? It seems likely that Luke's two books (which may have originally been one) were intended for "public consumption"—reaching out to pagans who wanted to know more about the new religion. For this reason, Luke and Acts may have been copied more often on scrolls because copyists knew that pagans preferred scrolls to the newfangled codex form.

596. digging up David

In the 1800s, many skeptics liked to claim that the great names of the Bible did not even exist—that people like

Moses, David, and Solomon were pure fiction. Most historians now are not so skeptical. They are fairly certain that David, Solomon, and the other kings mentioned in the Old Testament were real people. But it wasn't until 1993 that anyone had unearthed any inscription referring to David— that is, any "scientific" proof outside the Bible that a man named David was king of Israel. In 1993 archaeologists at Tel Dan in northern Israel found a stone inscription referring to the "house of David" and naming David as "king of Israel."

597. neck charms, with Scripture

The oldest biblical inscriptions ever found were discovered in 1979, in a cave near the site of the Jerusalem temple. They were thin pieces of pure silver, rolled up in the form of tiny scrolls, apparently designed to be charms worn around the neck. The tiny charms contained the famous "priestly blessing" from Numbers 6:24–26: "The LORD bless thee, and keep thee: The LORD make his face shine upon thee, and be gracious unto thee: The LORD lift up his countenance upon thee, and give thee peace" (KJV). Some Hebrew craftsman inscribed this text more than 2,600 years ago.

598. foundation sacrifices

Sacrificing infants was common in the ancient world, though the Israelites abhorred the practice. When a city was being built, it was common practice to encase the dead infants in the city's foundations. This explains why when archaeologists dig around the walls and foundations of ancient cities in the Middle East, they often stumble upon the skeletons of babies. (For an example of this horrid practice, see 1 Kings 16:34.)

599. Jehu, king but servile

As mentioned elsewhere in this book, skeptics used to insist that the people of the Bible, particularly the Old Testament, were pure fiction, including the men named as kings of Israel. Hardly anyone believes this anymore. As early as 1846, an explorer discovered the famous Black Obelisk in the region that is now Iraq (and, in the past, Babylon and Assyria). The six-foot-tall four-sided obelisk is a monument inscribed with the conquests of the Assyrian king Shalmaneser II. The obelisk shows King Jehu of Israel (see 2 Kings 9–10), bowing down in obedience to Shalmaneser. The obelisk calls Jehu the "son of Omri," referring to an earlier king of Israel (the father of Ahab, 1 Kings 16). Technically, Jehu was not Omri's son, but the obelisk probably is referring in general terms to what the Assyrians believed was Israel's ruling dynasty.

600. Tacitus and Christus

The historian Tacitus is famed as author of the *Annals of Imperial Rome*, which gives the glorious (but mostly sordid) history of Rome and its often depraved emperors. His history records that the immoral Emperor Nero, who may himself have ordered the burning of Rome, decided to place the blame on the people known as Christians, since he knew that the population at large was suspicious of them. Tacitus wrote that "Christus, the founder of the name of the group, was put to death by Pontius Pilate, procurator of Judea in the reign of Tiberius, but the pernicious superstition, repressed for a time, broke out again, not only through Judea, where the mischief originated, but through the city of Rome also." Tacitus confirms several of the historical details found in the Gospels and in Acts.

601. politarchs

In Acts 17:6 we find a mention of "politarchs," meaning "city rulers." For years scholars believed that Luke, author of Acts, invented the word *politarchs*, which proved (so they said) that Acts was unreliable as history. No one had ever seen "politarch" in any literature or inscription from that era, so it seemed the skeptics were right. But not so. Several years ago archaeologists did find an inscription in Greece that speaks of "the days of the politarchs." Luke was correct, and the skeptics were wrong.

602. the Moabite Stone

For many years it was commonly agreed that the stories of the Old Testament kings were pure legend. However, beginning in the 1800s, archaeologists began to find items confirming that many of the Bible characters were genuine. In 1868 a Germany missionary traveling in Israel found the Moabite Stone, a basalt plaque about two feet by four feet, with an inscription referring to Omri, king of Israel, and Mesha, king of Moab, both mentioned in the Old Testament (see 1 Kings 16:23–28; 2 Kings 3:4). Part of the inscription reads as follow: "I, Mesha, king of Moab, made this monument to Chemosh [a Moabite god] to commemorate deliverance from Israel . . . Omri, king of Israel, oppressed Moab many days and his son after him."

603. "To the Unknown God"

The ancient Greeks had many gods, a fact the apostle Paul noticed when he visited Athens, full of statues and other images of the many gods. Paul even found an altar that was inscribed "To the Unknown God" (Acts 17:23). Paul told the Athenians that this "Unknown God" was actually the one true God of the universe. Archaeologists tell us that such altars to "unknown gods" were common in ancient Athens.

604. theater

The Jews themselves had no tradition of theater, and the only theaters in the Holy Land were those built by the Romans. The only theater mentioned in the Bible is the one in

Ephesus, the scene of a riot of the people who worshiped the pagan goddess Artemis (Acts 19:21–41). Apparently most of the town had gathered in the theater, where Paul and his companions came very near to being lynched. Archaeologists have located the ruins of the Ephesus theater, finding that it seated about 25,000 people.

605. the middle wall of division

Paul wrote that Christ is "our peace," the One who has "broken down the middle wall of separation" (Eph. 2:14). He was speaking figuratively of the "walls" that separate people of different classes and ethnic backgrounds, saying that as Christians those divisions no longer matter. But he had in mind a literal wall, the wall in the temple complex in Jerusalem that no non-Jew could pass beyond. A notice on the wall in Greek and Latin warned that death might await any non-Jew who ventured farther. In 1871, archaeologists actually found this inscription, carved on a pillar. Paul himself was in danger of his life because he escorted a non-Jew, Trophimus the Ephesian, past the wall of division (Acts 21:29).

606. images of God

One of the Ten Commandments forbids the making of "graven images," that is, idols. This included making images of God Himself. Israel was unique among ancient cultures in that it did not allow any visual representations of its God. While the Israelites frequently broke God's commandments, they were very strict about this one, for the archaeologists tell us that in all the digging around Israelite sites, no one has ever found an image of the God of Israel.

13

Reform and Revolution: The 1500s

THE GREAT MARTIN LUTHER

607. *sola Scriptura*

This Latin phrase means "Scripture only" or "the Bible alone." The phrase was spoken often in the 1500s, after a monk named Martin Luther ignited the religious movement we call the Protestant Reformation. One aim of Luther and other Protestant leaders was to "get back to the Bible," doing away with meaningless rituals and church traditions that had no basis in the Bible. *Sola Scriptura* meant that Christian beliefs and practices had to have a clear basis in the Bible, not in man-made traditions.

608. "do penance" or "be penitent"?

The Roman Catholic Church has seven sacraments, one of which is *penance*. This involves repenting of a sin, then doing something to show one is truly sorry. One basis of the practice of penance is Matthew 4:17, which in the Latin Bible read *penitentiam agite*—usually translated as "do penance." But in the 1500s Martin Luther and other church Reformers went back to the Greek original and noticed that the Greek wording actually means "repent" or "be penitent" or, literally, "change your mind." This discovery is the main reason the Protestant churches did away with the sacrament of penance.

609. "my Patmos"

German Reformer Martin Luther found himself on the lam several times in his life, which is not surprising, since the Protestant Reformation that he launched upset the Catholic authorities and the secular rulers. Labeled as a heretic, Luther was hidden in Wartburg castle, a safe but extremely gloomy place that he labeled "my Patmos." He was referring to the Greek island of Patmos, where the exiled apostle John wrote the book of Revelation (see Rev. 1:9). Using his time in Wartburg wisely, as John did, Luther penned his famous German translation of the New Testament.

610. "the true pilgrimage"

Christians have always liked to visit sites associated with Jesus and the early Christians. German Reformer Martin Luther realized that, while there is nothing wrong with these trips—known as pilgrimages—we would do better to follow the Bible than to walk where its people walked: "The true Christian pilgrimage is not to Rome or to Jerusalem, but to the Prophets, the Psalms, and the Gospels."

611. Luther's mug

Martin Luther, the great German Reformer, saw nothing wrong with a glass of wine or beer. He had his own mug, on which were three rings. He claimed the three rings represented the Ten Commandments, the Lord's Prayer, and the Apostles' Creed. Even when drinking, Luther was reminded that he was a Bible-believing Christian.

612. Moses the German

Martin Luther's translation of the Bible into German is considered a classic of German prose. Luther, who continued revising his Bible until his death in 1546, claimed that he wanted to make it so accessible to German readers that "Moses will seem so German that no one would suspect he was a Jew."

613. the Peasants' Revolt

Bible reading can be revolutionary. In 1524, the peasants of Germany felt so oppressed by high taxes and other abuses of their lords that they took up arms, probably 300,000 peasants in all. One of the prime factors was the Protestant faith of Martin Luther, who encouraged reading the Bible. The peasants' leaders noted, "We do find in the Scriptures that we are free, and we will be free." They overlooked the fact that the Bible promises *spiritual* freedom, not necessarily freedom from political oppression. Martin Luther was severely criticized then and later for urging the government authorities to use force to put down the revolt.

614. the "apocryphal" New Testament

When Martin Luther translated the New Testament into German, he put four of its books in a sort of "appendix" at the end: Hebrews, James, Jude, and Revelation. Luther did not deny that these were inspired Scripture, but felt they were somehow less valuable than the other books of the New Testament. He wrote prefaces to the four books, explaining why he thought they were less important than the others. When William Tyndale published his English New Testament in 1526, he followed Luther's arrangement, putting Hebrews, James, Jude, and Revelation last, though he did not in fact agree with Luther's opinion about them.

615. Philip of Hesse

Can Christians divorce? For centuries the Catholic Church has said no, but . . . *annulments* are sometimes possible. When Protestantism arose in the 1500s, Protestant leaders said no divorce at all, period. Martin Luther and other Protestant leaders believed that in this they were following the Bible. An odd situation arose: Philip (1504–1567), ruler of the German state of Hesse, was a devout Protestant but unhappy with the wife that his parents had forced on him as a political match. He wanted a wife he could truly love and be faithful to, but since he could not divorce, he was offered by Luther and others a way out of the dilemma: do as Old Testament men did and have more than one wife. Philip's bigamy was one of the great scandals of the early Protestants.

616. Thomas Munzer

In the 1500s the Protestant Reformation was a "back to the Bible" movement, an attempt to get Christian beliefs and practice in line with the New Testament. In some cases, though, a few extreme Protestants decided the Bible itself wasn't essential—in fact, Christians could be led by inspired prophets. After all, they said, the people in the Bible were led by the direct inspiration of God, not by the Bible (since it was still being written, obviously). One of these extremists was the German leader Thomas Munzer, at one time an associate of the great Reformer

293

Martin Luther. Like Luther, Munzer wanted to throw out the Catholic Church and its meaningless rituals. But Munzer went well beyond Luther, going so far as to organize his followers into an armed band, ready to use the sword on behalf of the gospel, hoping to create the kingdom of God on earth. Luther and the other Protestants were as alarmed by this as the Catholic authorities were. Luther said the Bible had no place for using force to defend the faith. Munzer helped incite the Peasants' War, but, appropriately, in 1525 he was captured, tortured, and beheaded, a classic case of a good man being led to foolish extremes.

ENGLAND UNDER KING HENRY VIII

617. Thomas Cromwell

Cromwell (1485–1540), an able English statesman, is an easy person to dislike. He was incredibly ambitious, greedy, and unscrupulous. As it happens, he was also the most active force in helping turn England from a Catholic nation to a Protestant one, and that included getting English Bibles into the people's hands. Cromwell had some nonspiritual reasons for making England more Protestant: decreasing the power of the Catholic Church meant increasing the power of his master, King Henry VIII. Cromwell made many enemies, and they were pleased to watch his fall and execution—mostly because he arranged Henry's disastrous fourth marriage.

618. reading aloud, but only when proper

In the 1500s the English people enjoyed their new freedom: the ability to read from an English Bible. Since most people could not afford their own copies, they would go to churches, where the large pulpit Bible was available for public reading. Sometimes people got carried away, however—they would read the Bible aloud while worship service was in progress! In 1539 King Henry VIII had to issue a proclamation forbidding laymen to read the Bible aloud during worship. Perhaps the people found the Bible more interesting than whatever the pastor was saying.

619. Henry in his glory

The Great Bible, published in 1539 and given the stamp of approval by King Henry VIII, has an interesting illustration on its title page: Henry on his throne delivers the Word of God with his right hand to Thomas Cranmer (the archbishop of Canterbury) and with his left hand to Thomas Cromwell (Henry's chief political aide at that time). Cranmer and Cromwell in turn deliver the Word to the clergy and laity, who form a motley group calling out "God save the king." God looks approvingly on the whole scene, using these words from Acts 13:22: "I have found a man after My own heart, who shall perform all My desire." Presumably this man was Henry VIII.

620. the pope and Caiaphas

The Gospels tell us that the Jewish high priest at the time of Jesus' trial and crucifixion was named Caiaphas. According to John 18:14, Caiaphas uttered a truth that was bigger than he realized: "Now it was Caiaphas who advised the Jews that it was expedient that one man should die for the people." Christians understood the larger meaning of Caiaphas's advice: Christ did indeed die for the whole people, to save them from their sins.

Miles Coverdale's Bible, the first complete printed English Bible, contains a preface in which it compares the pope to Caiaphas. What was the connection? The pope had, years earlier, bestowed the title "Defender of the Faith" on King Henry VIII. The reason: Henry, at that time a faithful Catholic, had written a book about the "heretic" Martin Luther. Things changed, Henry moved England from Catholicism to Protestantism, and now he was giving his approval to a Bible in English—something he had outlawed back in his Catholic days. So Protestants believed that now the title "Defender of the Faith" was more appropriate than when the pope first bestowed it.

621. the new Josiah

Fat, diseased, many-times-married King Henry VIII of England died in 1547, and his successor was his nine-year-old son, Edward VI. While Henry VIII had broken the Church of England away from Catholicism, Henry was anything but a gung ho Protestant. However, young Edward had been brought up with Protestant tutors, and on Henry's death many Protestants proclaimed Edward "the new Josiah," harking back to the religious king of Israel (2 Kings 21–23), a welcome change from Josiah's ungodly father, Amon. As has often happened in history, deeply religious people see events of the day as "recaps" of events in the Bible. England did in fact become more Protestant under Edward, although, since he was only a boy, it was due more to his guardians than to Edward himself. He died after less than six years on the throne and thus accomplished much less than Josiah of Israel.

622. Bloody (and Bible-less) Mary

Henry VIII's daughter Mary became queen of England in 1553, and as a staunch Catholic she tried to turn England from a Protestant country back to Catholicism. Because she ordered so many Protestant leaders executed, she has gone down in history as "Bloody Mary." She also put a stop to the practice of printing the Bible in English, so during her five-year reign all English Bibles were printed elsewhere and smuggled into the country.

623. Stephen's martyrdom, again

Under Catholic queen Mary, England witnessed the burning of many Protestants. One of the more notable was the archbishop of Canterbury, Thomas Cranmer. While being burned at the stake in 1556, Cranmer several times repeated the last words of the first Christian martyr, Stephen: "Lord Jesus, receive my spirit" (Acts 7:59). Over the centuries, many martyrs have repeated Stephen's words.

624. "that Jezebel"

Scottish Reformer John Knox wrote a famous book, *Against the Monstrous Regiment of Women*, in which he railed against the various women rulers in Europe at that time. He combed through the Bible and found no justification for woman as monarchs, and, indeed, the Bible presents us with some nasty queens such as Jezebel and Athaliah. Knox directed much of his fire at England's Catholic queen Mary—"Bloody Mary"—who was turning many Protestants into martyrs. Knox often referred to Mary as "that Jezebel."

ENGLAND'S ELIZABETH

625. "marvelous in our eyes"

During the reign of the Catholic queen Mary Tudor ("Bloody Mary"), her Protestant half sister Elizabeth sometimes feared for her life. Mary tried (and failed) to turn England from Protestantism back to Catholicism. She suspected Elizabeth of being in cahoots with

Protestant traitors, and it was no doubt a relief to Elizabeth (and all Protestants) when Mary died after a five-year reign. Elizabeth greeted the news of her half sister's death with a verse from the Psalms: "This is the LORD's doing; it is marvelous in our eyes" (118:23 KJV). Mary's death ended Catholic rule and, incidentally, made Elizabeth the new queen. When Elizabeth took the throne, she had the words from Psalm 118:23 stamped on England's coins.

626. "the jewel"

England grew tired very quickly of the Catholic queen Mary Tudor, so there was rejoicing at her death and at the new queen, Mary's half sister Elizabeth I. When Elizabeth entered London to be crowned, she made a public show of kissing the English Bible and speaking of it as "the jewel that she still loved best." She promised to "diligently read therein," a promise she kept.

627. Elizabeth I (1533–1603)

The woman known to history as "Good Queen Bess" and "Gloriana" was the daughter of much-married King Henry VIII, who broke England away from Catholicism. His daughter Elizabeth, who herself seems to have been a skeptic about religion, had to handle England's religious situation carefully: she had to keep it Protestant (which sometimes meant dealing with rebellious Catholics) without it becoming *too* Protestant (which meant controlling the more zealous Protestants known as Puritans). In an age when people were often punished or martyred for their faith, both Catholics and Puritans suffered under Elizabeth's laws. There were stiff censorship laws in those days, but, take note: neither Elizabeth nor the dreaded Court of Star Chamber took any steps to suppress the popular Puritan version of the Bible, the famous Geneva Bible. In fact, most of the editions of this popular Bible (first published in 1560) were issued by the queen's own printer, Christopher Barker. The Puritans saw God's hand at work in this.

628. Elizabeth I and Zerubbabel

In the past people liked to make comparisons between their contemporaries and people in the Bible. Consider Queen Elizabeth I, who came to the throne following the rule of her Catholic half sister Mary ("Bloody Mary," because she had many leading Protestants executed). Some of Elizabeth's contemporaries referred to her as Zerubbabel, for she reminded them of the Old Testament figure who rebuilt the Jerusalem temple after a long exile in Babylon. Protestant Englishmen observed that the "Babylonian captivity" (Catholic rule under Mary) was over, and the Protestant queen Elizabeth would rebuild "the ruins of God's house."

629. Elizabeth's morning exercises

In the past, people were less body-conscious and more brain-conscious. "Morning exercises" would more likely refer to stimulating the mind, not the muscles. Thus England's Queen Elizabeth I, a highly intelligent woman, started the day by reading the New Testament in Greek, then would read some of the classic Greek dramas.

630. the bishops' dining rooms

The Bishops' Bible of 1568 was published with the approval of Queen Elizabeth I. Three years later the English Church's ruling council ordered that every English bishop should have in his home a large copy of the Bible, placed "in the hall or the large dining room, that it might be useful to their servants or to strangers."

VOICES OF CHANGE

631. Erasmus's *Enchiridion*

Desiderius Erasmus, a noted Dutch scholar of the 1500s, was a powerful force in making scholars familiar with the original Greek New Testament. Erasmus also wrote a book with the forbidding Latin title *Enchiridion Militis Christiani*—"The Christian Soldier's Handbook," with "soldier" referring to any serious Christian, not just military men. Written in 1502, the book stresses the duty of studying the New Testament and making it the sole basis of one's beliefs and morals. It was translated into English by William Tyndale, who is today remembered for his translation of the Bible.

632. Hebrew, the Holy Tongue

Since the Reformation was a "back to the Bible" movement, there was an increased interest in learning Hebrew, so as to read the Old Testament in the original language. The Swiss Reformer Ulrich Zwingli was enthusiastic about Hebrew studies. He called Hebrew the "Holy Tongue," and claimed that "no other language so delights and quickens the human heart." The flip side: some Christians found it tiresome when preachers insisted on quoting Hebrew and Greek in their sermons.

633. Obbe Philips

The Mennonites, named after Dutch pastor Menno Simons, were originally called the Obbites after Obbe Philips (1500–1568). Philips was an early leader of the Anabaptists, Protestants who believed that infant baptism had no basis in the Bible, which taught only believers' baptism. It was Philips who baptized and ordained Menno Simons.

634. Olivetan

The Frenchman born Pierre Robert was a powerful influence on his younger cousin, the great theologian John Calvin. As a student, Pierre Robert (1506–1538) earned the name "Olivetan" because he burned the midnight oil (the oil used in lamps in those days being *olive* oil). Olivetan was not only an early Protestant leader but also a translator of the Bible into French.

635. praying through saints

According to the apostle Paul, "There is one God and one Mediator between God and men, the Man Christ Jesus" (1 Tim. 2:5). In other words, we need no one but Christ as the "middleman" between us and God. Nonetheless, Catholic and Orthodox Christians pray to (or through) saints, particularly to Jesus' mother, Mary. The practice was severely criticized in the Protestant Reformation of the 1500s, and today most Protestants pray only to God or Christ, not through the saints.

636. how often Communion?

How often should Christians celebrate the Lord's Supper? The New Testament suggests that it should be at every Christian gathering. Note how Paul reported Jesus' own words on the subject: "This cup is the new covenant in

My blood. This do, as often as you drink it, in remembrance of Me" (1 Cor. 11:25). Apparently the earliest Christians did celebrate the Lord's Supper every time they gathered together. But as time passed, an elaborate ritual grew up around the Lord's Supper, making it a long (and some would say boring) affair. With the coming of the Protestant Reformation in the 1500s, the Lord's Supper was often simplified—and also done less frequently. Many churches today take it only three or four times per year.

637. disapproving suicide

The Geneva Bible of 1560 included the Apocrypha, but also included a preface indicating that the Apocryphal books were not to be used as a foundation for Christian belief and practice. Specifically, some deeds recorded in the Apocrypha were not to be imitated, such as the suicidal heroics recorded in 1 Maccabees 6:43 and 2 Maccabees 14:41.

638. the Geneva Bible and the pope

There were no "interdenominational Bibles" in the 1500s. Catholics and Protestants strongly detested each other, and Bibles would include footnotes interpreting the Scriptures in a way that condemned the other side. Thus most Protestant Bibles had strongly anti-Catholic footnotes. The Geneva Bible of 1560 was typical in this, particularly in the notes on the book of Revelation. For most Protestants of that time, the pope was the AntiChrist, the beast from the bottomless pit (Rev. 11:7). For this verse, the Geneva Bible includes in a note the statement that the beast is "the Pope, which hath his power out of hell and cometh thence."

639. "every man's humor"

As far as Bibles in English were concerned, England had gone from famine to feast: several centuries with no Bible in English, then, in the 1500s, a dozen different translations. In 1603, Richard Bancroft, bishop of London, complained about this situation: "If every man's humor were followed, there would be no end of translating." Bancroft uttered those words just before work began on a new translation, the one we today call the King James Version.

640. from Switzerland to Scotland

In the 1500s, Switzerland and Scotland had something in common: they both went Protestant, and they both adhered to the version of Protestantism known as Calvinism (after John Calvin) or the Reformed faith. John Knox, Scotland's leading Reformer, had spent time in Geneva, Switzerland, learning from John Calvin. Knox returned to his native Scotland determined to make it another Geneva. He largely succeeded, and in 1560 when the English version known as the Geneva Bible was published, the Church of Scotland almost immediately accepted it as its official Bible.

641. Ben's ancestors

Benjamin Franklin was hardly a traditional Christian, but in his famous *Autobiography* he told a pious tale from his family's history: during the reign of "Bloody Mary," who had outlawed Protestantism and the Bible in English, Franklin's great-great-grandfather kept his family's Bible hidden underneath a stool. While he read from it during the family's devotional time together, one of his children would stand at the door to watch for any of Mary's government officials. Had one of these appeared, the family would have quickly hidden the Bible away.

642. prayers for the dead

Here is a Christian practice based on a single passage from the Apocrypha: 2 Maccabees 12:39–45 speaks of offering prayers and sacrifices for the sins of Jews who were slain on the battlefield. Nothing in the New Testament supports praying for the dead, yet it was fairly common practice by the second century. Prayers for the dead were common in the Catholic Church, but from the time of the Reformation, Protestants rejected the practice.

643. old, but not senile

Theodore Beza (1519–1605) was John Calvin's friend and successor as head of the Protestant Reformation in Geneva, Switzerland. Like all the Protestant leaders, Beza emphasized getting "back to the Bible," studying the Hebrew and Greek originals closely and translating them into the languages people actually spoke. Beza led a long, full life, and even in his eighties he could recite, in Greek, all the Epistles of the New Testament.

644. Old Testament, New Testament, and "other"

The books that Protestants call the "Apocrypha" are included by Catholics in the Old Testament. Not so for Protestant Bibles. Beginning with Miles Coverdale's Bible in 1535, the books of the Apocrypha were included in a separate section between the Old and New Testaments. Protestants generally did (and do) place the Apocrypha on a lower spiritual plane than the other books. As time passed, many Protestant Bibles simply discarded the Apocrypha altogether.

645. "wholesome doctrine and comfort"

The Protestant Reformation was pro-Bible—not just the Bible, but specifically the Bible in language the people could read. Most English church officials began to encourage the people to read the Bible for themselves. In 1538, Nicholas Shaxton, bishop of Salisbury, required his clergy to ensure that an English Bible should be chained to the desk in every parish church, so that literate laymen might read, and illiterate ones might hear, "wholesome doctrine and comfort to their souls."

14

The Amazing
King James Version

646. a Bible not fit for a king

Before the King James Version of 1611, the most popular
Bible among the English laity was definitely the Geneva
Bible, published in 1560. Like all Bibles of that time, it
had notes explaining the text. Some of these notes bothered people—specifically, they bothered King James I.
James objected to the annotation on Exodus 1:17, which
approved the Hebrew midwives who disobeyed the
Egyptian king's orders. (Most kings would object to a
footnote approving of people disobeying their ruler.)
James also disapproved of the note on 2 Chronicles
15:16, which stated that King Asa's idol-worshiping
mother should have been not deposed but executed.
Perhaps for James this reflected some hatred for his own
executed mother, Mary Queen of Scots.

647. "ratified by royal authority"

King James I, shortly after he took the throne of England, declared that he had never seen a Bible well translated into English. He specifically detested the very popular Geneva Bible (ironic, since it was well loved in his native Scotland). James pressed the Church of England to produce a new uniform translation, one "ratified by royal authority" (for James had a high opinion of himself as king). The new version would be, he insisted, "read in the whole church, and none other." In the course of time (but not his own lifetime) he got his wish: the 1611 version named for him was for many centuries *the* English Bible, "read in the whole church, and none other."

648. Shakespeare in the Psalms?

William Shakespeare was alive (though retired from the stage) when the King James Version of the Bible was being prepared. Some people have fancied that he may have had a hand in the KJV himself. Some say that he helped with the wording of Psalm 46—and note that in Psalm 46, the forty-sixth word from the beginning of the Psalm is "shake," while the forty-sixth word from the end is "spear." And note: in 1610, the year in which the KJV was being completed, Shakespeare was forty-six years old. Coincidence? Almost assuredly, yes.

649. "authorized" by whom?

The beloved 1611 Bible that Americans call the King James Version (or KJV, for brevity's sake) has always been called the "Authorized Version" in its native England. The funny thing is, though the KJV's title page says that it is "appointed to be read in churches," it was never in any real sense "authorized" by any authority. It was definitely undertaken with the encouragement of King James I (hence its common name), but, legally speaking, neither the king nor Parliament nor any official church body ever "authorized" it. Perhaps this was a blessing, for as well loved as the KJV—or Authorized Version—has been, the Church of England never forced it upon anyone, nor discouraged anyone from revising or modernizing it. It gained popularity not because it was "authorized," but because it was great.

650. noteless Bible

One novel feature of the King James Bible: it has no footnotes. All other Bibles of the time did, particularly the popular Geneva Bible of 1560, with its anti-Catholic and strongly pro-Protestant annotations. King James I detested the Geneva Bible (perhaps because its notes hinted that it was legitimate to get rid of an unworthy king) and agreed that the new version under his sponsorship would be a noteless Bible.

651. the Trinity verse

The word *Trinity* does not appear in the Bible, but in Matthew 28:19 Jesus tells His disciples to baptize people in the name of the Father, Son, and Holy Spirit. This is the one verse that supports the idea of God as Trinity. But in the King James Version, there is another, 1 John 5:7: "For there are three that bear record in heaven, the Father, the Word, and the Holy Ghost: and these three are one." The Word here is, of course, the same as the Son. One problem, though: this verse does not appear in any of the really old Greek manuscripts of the New Testament. In fact, it appears to have been added some- time in the 300s by a Spanish Christian named Priscillian. Yet it made its way into the King James Version of 1611, and there was loud complaining when the English Revised Version of 1881 dropped the verse. (After all, it had been in the King James Bible for centuries, and was one of only two verses mentioning the Trinity.) Most contemporary Bibles either leave out the verse entirely or include it as a footnote.

652. the Christian Song of Solomon

In most old versions of the Bible, such as the King James Version, it is clear that the translators saw Christian mean- ings in the Old Testament. Christ is never mentioned by name in the Old, yet the King James Version of Psalm 93 bears the subtitle "The majesty, power, and holiness of

Christ's kingdom." That is, the translators believed that this pre-Christian psalm was actually a prophecy of Christ's kingdom. They applied the same logic to the Song of Solomon: though on the surface it appears to be a collection of fairly erotic love poems, the King James translators indicated that it was actually an exchange of love songs between Christ and His church.

653. dating the Creation

Beginning in 1701, most King James Bibles included in the margins a note on the date of creation. It was (according to Irish bishop James Ussher, who died in 1656) the year 4004 B.C., and well into the twentieth century many Bibles included this bit of data.

654. Wesley's edited KJV

John Wesley, founder of the Methodist movement in Britain, issued his own revision of the King James Version in 1768. The Methodists had a knack for reaching out to poor and working-class people, and Wesley claimed his revised Bible was for "plain, unlettered men who understand only their mother tongue." Wesley made about twelve thousand alterations, mostly minor matters of updating archaic words.

655. one devil, many demons

Some Greek words are fairly easy to translate: *diabolos* easily translates into "devil," and *daimon* easily becomes "demon." (It so happens that these two Greek words are, obviously, the root words of our English equivalents.) One thing worth noting as you read different translations: some versions speak of plural "devils," but in fact there is only one *diabolos* (Satan, obviously), but more than one *daimon*. People in the New Testament suffered from "demons" but not (in the Greek, anyway) from "devils." Most contemporary versions are accurate in this, but the King James Version has many instances of "devils"—probably because they chose never to use "demon" in singular or plural.

Oh, How Words Have Changed . . .

656. quick changes in languages

The King James Version was published in 1611, and after almost four centuries, English has changed so much that most people no longer read the KJV. But, oddly, as early as 1653 someone decided that the KJV was hard to read and needed a helpful paraphrase. Henry Hammond in that year published *A Paraphrase and Annotations upon All the Books of the New Testament*, which contained the KJV New Testament and Hammond's paraphrase side by side. Similar paraphrases were published in 1675 and 1685.

657. jot and tittle

According to Jesus, not "one jot or one tittle" of the Old
Testament Law shall pass away until all has been fulfilled
(Matt. 5:18). So the King James Version reads. The "jot"
was the *yodh*, the smallest letter in the Hebrew alphabet.
A "tittle" was a small horn-shaped mark, used in Hebrew
to indicate an accent. Jesus was saying that the tiniest par-
ticle of the Law was still valid. Since most people now
have no idea what jots and tittles were, contemporary versions have readings like this one from the New
International Version: "not the smallest letter, not the
least stroke of a pen, will by any means disappear from the
Law."

658. candles

Putting it bluntly, wax candles didn't exist in the biblical
world. Yet "candle" and "candlestick" appear in many
Bibles. The item called "candlestick" in the King James
Version, the Hebrew *menorah*, was in fact a lamp stand,
with the light coming from burning oil. Ditto for "light
a candle" and "candlestick" in Jesus' Sermon on the
Mount (Matt. 5:15): Jesus was referring to the typical oil
lamp of His time, not to candles and candlesticks as we
know them.

659. sodding pottage

Consider the King James Version's reading of Genesis 25:29: "And Jacob sod pottage: and Esau came from the field, and he was faint." Crystal clear? Perhaps it is more so in the New King James Version: "Now Jacob cooked a stew; and Esau came in from the field, and he was weary."

660. outlandish

We use "outlandish" to mean weird, odd, off-the-wall. In the King James era it meant just what it says: something from an out-land—that is, something foreign. Thus the King James Version of Nehemiah 13:26 records that Solomon was caused to sin by "outlandish women"—that is, the many foreign wives he had married. Likewise, 1 Kings 11:1 notes that "Solomon loved many strange women"—"strange," meaning "foreign."

661. a change of bowels

In the 1600s, the word *bowels* didn't just mean "intestines" but could generically mean "inward parts," which could include a person's emotions. Knowing that, the King James Version of 2 Corinthians 6:12 might make some sense: "Ye are not straitened in us, but ye are straitened in your own bowels." The New King James Version might be clearer still: "You are not restricted by us, but you are restricted by your own affections."

662. meat or food?

An old proverb has it that "one man's meat is another man's poison." In that proverb—and in older versions of the Bible—*meat* meant "food," not necessarily the flesh of animals. In the King James Version, an offering of grain is referred to as a "meat offering" (Lev. 14:10).

663. cherishing David

In 1 Kings 1:1–2, we read that old King David needed warmth, so a young virgin was sought to "cherish the king." So the King James Version reads. Curiously, *cherish* in the 1600s meant "to keep warm" and had no emotional meaning. Later versions have changed "cherish" appropriately.

664. glass

When the Bible uses the word *glass*, it usually means "mirror," as in Paul's famous statement on seeing "through a glass, darkly" (1 Cor. 13:12 KJV), which in most modern versions reads "mirror" (NKJV). Mirrors in Bible times were not actually glass but were highly polished metals.

When the word *glass* occurs in Job 37:18 and James 1:23, it may actually mean a bright, transparent mineral such as quartz. We know that the ancient Egyptians made actual glass, but this glass, the material we are familiar with today, is not mentioned in the Bible.

665. helpmeet or helpmate?

"And the LORD God said, It is not good that the man should be alone; I will make him an help meet for him." So reads Genesis 2:18 in the King James Version. What is "an help meet"? The KJV was using "meet" in the old sense—"suitable" or "appropriate." God intended that Adam would have a suitable helper. Over the centuries, "help meet" evolved into "helpmate," which is not accurate, though the idea is a pleasant one. The New King James Version reads "a helper comparable to him," and the New International Version has "a helper suitable for him."

666. Parbar westward

For 1 Chronicles 26:18, the King James Version has this: "At Parbar westward, four at the causeway, and two at Parbar." This may qualify as the most bizarre verse in the KJV. Happily, our knowledge of Hebrew has advanced since the KJV debuted in 1611. A more contemporary translation makes slightly more sense: "As for the court to the west, there were four at the road and two at the court itself" (NIV).

667. "appearance of evil"

The apostle told Christians to "abstain from all appearance of evil" (1 Thess. 5:22 KJV)—a perfectly valid Christian idea, but not really a good translation of the Greek. People who read it in the King James Version assume it means "Don't do anything that appears evil," which is fine, but the Paul's Greek originally meant something more like "avoid every form of evil."

668. "debts" or "trespasses"?

One verse from the Lord's Prayer has proved difficult to translate. Consider Matthew 6:12 in the King James Version: "And forgive us our debts, as we forgive our debtors." Some later versions have "trespasses" instead of "debts," and some contemporary versions have "sins" or "wrongs." Strictly speaking, "debts" is a literal translation of the Greek. But some translators point out that beyond the Greek lie the Aramaic words (and ideas) Jesus Himself would have used, and while the Gospel uses the Greek words for "debts" and "debtors," the idea is really closer to "sins" and "those who sin against us."

669. another man's wealth

"Let no man seek his own, but every man another's wealth" (1 Cor. 10:24 KJV). Doesn't sound very

Christian, does it? When the King James translators were writing, *wealth* actually meant "welfare" or "well-being"—and with that idea, the verse sounds very Christian. Worth noting: in that period, *wealthy* did not mean "rich" but rather "contented" (see the KJV: Ps. 66:12; Jer. 49:31).

670. virtue and virtuous

We use the word *virtue* to mean "moral" or "righteous." In 1611, the year the KJV was published, it *could* mean that, but it normally meant something more like "powerful" or "competent." In Proverbs 31, the praise of the "virtuous" woman might be more correctly praise of the "competent" woman. And consider the KJV reading of Jesus' encounter with the woman who touched the hem of His garment: "And Jesus, immediately knowing in himself that virtue had gone out of him, turned him about in the press, and said, Who touched my clothes?" (Mark 5:30).

671. feebleminded and fainthearted

We use "feebleminded" to mean "stupid" or "mentally slow." It meant something else to the King James translators, something like what is found in the New King James Version at 1 Thessalonians 5:14: "comfort the fainthearted."

672. quick, and also alive

The Apostles' Creed states that Jesus will "come to judge the quick and the dead." The word *quick* is used in the old sense, the same as in the King James Version of the Bible: it meant "alive." Not once does that version use its current meaning of "rapid." (See Num. 16:30; Ps. 119:25; John 5:21; Heb. 4:12; 1 Peter 3:18.)

673. Bethlehem's coast

Literature buffs like to snicker at Shakespeare's mention of the "coast of Bohemia," for the country of Bohemia has no coast. Some similar readings are found in the King James Bible—for example, the "coasts" of Bethlehem (Matt. 2:16), even though Bethlehem is nowhere near a sea. A simple explanation: for the King James translators, *coast* could mean "district" or "the adjoining region."

674. champaign, campaign, etc.

Certain words all have the same root: *campaign, camp, champaign, campus*, etc. All come from the Latin *campus*, meaning "plain" or "field." Knowing this, the King James reading of Deuteronomy 11:30 makes some sense: "in the land of the Canaanites, which dwell in the champaign over against Gilgal." Most modern versions show "plain" instead of "champaign."

675. cousin John

It has long been assumed that Jesus and John the Baptist were cousins. This is based on the King James Version's translation of Luke 1:36, which speaks of Mary, Jesus' mother, and Elizabeth, John the Baptist's mother, as cousins. In fact, as newer translations indicate, "cousin" in the King James is probably more accurately translated as "relative" or "kinswoman," which could mean distant cousins. So Jesus and John were, in some way, related by blood, although they were second cousins at best, and probably more distant than that.

676. the Galatians contradiction

Many readers look for contradictions in the Bible, and certainly Galatians 6 seems to have one: in the King James Version, verse 2 has "bear ye one another's burdens," while verse 5 reads, "every man shall bear his own burden." Hmmm. The problem (in the King James Version, anyway) is that two different Greek words are both translated with the English "burden." Verse 2 uses *baryos*, meaning "heavy or burdensome weight," while verse 5 uses *phortion*, meaning simply "something carried," not necessarily heavy or burdensome. So the two verses don't contradict at all: we should each try to carry our own normal loads (v. 5), but we should help one another with the heavier ones (v. 2).

677. fetching the compass

Acts 28:13 relates that Paul and his companions "fetched a compass"—yet we know for a fact that navigational compasses did not exist in those days. This is the fault of the King James Version. The actual meaning of Acts 28:13 is, as the New King James states it, "We circled round."

678. the coat of many colors

Generations of Bible readers have smiled at the familiar story of Jacob giving his favorite son, Joseph, a "coat of many colors." It has served as the subject of numerous paintings, as well as the popular musical *Joseph and the Amazing Technicolor Dreamcoat*. But, frankly, "coat of many colors" in the King James Version is probably not accurate. Most likely (though the scholars aren't absolutely certain) the item given to Joseph was a fine robe with long sleeves—something that would be worn by a man's designated heir. Thus Joseph's jealous brothers weren't envying the robe's beauty but, rather, that it symbolized that Joseph, the next-to-the-youngest brother, was being elevated above his older brothers.

Still, it does seem a shame to part with "coat of many colors," doesn't it?

679. "Drink ye all of it"

At the Last Supper, Jesus spoke of the cup of wine He was holding and told His disciples, "Drink ye all of it" (Matt. 26:27). So reads the King James Version. Some people have taken this to mean that when churches have Communion service, all the wine (or juice) must be consumed, with none left over. But in fact, the word *all* in the verse is connected with "ye," not with "it" (the wine). The New King James more accurately reflects the Greek: "Drink from it, all of you."

680. condemning lawyers

The world abounds with lawyer jokes, and they are of one profession that people feel free to mock and despise. Jesus Himself had harsh words to say about "the lawyers and the Pharisees," as the King James Version has it. But the "lawyers" He preached against were not lawyers in our modern sense. They were (as newer versions have it) "teachers of the law," people knowledgeable about the Old Testament law and how to apply it to daily life. Jesus condemned them, along with the Pharisees, for focusing too much on the law's details and missing the "big picture"—loving God and our fellow man. What Jesus would have thought of lawyers today is anybody's guess.

681. "all glorious within"

Sermons have been preached on Psalm 45:13: "The king's daughter is all glorious within." So the King James Version has it. And what a wonderful and very Christian idea: a woman that is beautiful inwardly, spiritually. But this is not what Psalm 45 actually meant. The New King James is more accurate: "The royal daughter is all glorious within the palace."

682. "where there is no vision"

In the King James Version, Proverbs 29:18 reads, "Where there is no vision, the people perish." That verse has been quoted, and preached on, countless times, and most people would accept it as true: where a culture lacks a vision for itself, the people perish, spiritually speaking. However, the way we use "vision" is not quite what the author of Proverbs had in mind. He meant something more like "oracle from a prophet," or "revelation" (which is what the New King James Version has, and is correct).

683. biblical organ

The Bible, at least the King James Version, mentions the organ as a musical instrument (Gen. 4:21; Job 21:12; Ps. 150:4). This is most definitely *not* the large instrument with several keyboards that we know today. Newer translations have "flute" or "pipes," which is probably more accurate. (Technically, these are all *wind* instruments, since modern organs do have pipes through which air is passed.)

684. denarius

The common coin in New Testament days was the Roman denarius, called "penny" in the King James Version, but usually "denarius" in newer translations. It was silver and resembled the U.S. dime. A denarius was, in those days, about a day's wages. Just as our modern coins have the heads of famous statesmen, so the Roman denarius had a man's head, always the head of the reigning emperor, as seen in the story of Jesus and the question of paying taxes (Matt. 22:19); the coin mentioned there would have had the image of either Tiberius or Augustus.

685. worshiping scarecrows

The prophet Jeremiah mocked people who worshiped idols: "Like a scarecrow in a melon patch, their idols cannot speak; they must be carried because they cannot walk. Do not fear them; they can do no harm nor can they do any good" (Jer. 10:5 NIV). Put another way: the false gods aren't real gods at all, having no power to act any more than a scarecrow does. Incidentally, while most Bible versions now read "scarecrow," the King James Version reads "palm tree," which is most likely wrong.

686. "desire" or "caper-berry"?

The King James Version was not perfect—but then, neither were the various attempts to update and improve it. Consider the KJV wording of Ecclesiastes 12:5: "desire shall fail." The English Revised Version of 1881 "improved" it with this wording: "the caper-berry shall fail." Better? Wisely, the New International Version states "desire no longer is stirred," and the New King James Version "desire fails." Sometimes "new and improved" isn't.

15

Some Choice Tidbits: Old Testament

687. light from first to last

The first recorded words of God are "Let there be light," right at the beginning of the Bible (Gen. 1:3). Likewise the book of Revelation, at the very end of the Bible, closes with a vision of heaven, the New Jerusalem, in which there will be no more night, no need for lamp or the sun, "for the Lord God gives them light" (Rev. 22:5).

688. lesser light, greater light

Ancient peoples almost all worshiped the sun and the moon. The Hebrews would not, since God alone was to be worshiped. Not surprisingly, in the account of the world's creation, God creates light before He creates the sun and moon—that is, light has its origin in God Himself, not in the heavenly spheres He created. When

Genesis does speak of the sun and moon (which are created *after* the land and the plants), they are not even called by their names but are referred to as "the greater light" (the sun, that is) and "the lesser light" (the moon). Genesis was reminding people that as amazing as the sun and the moon are, they are not divine and are not to be worshiped.

689. tired God?

Most Bible versions tell us that God "rested" on the seventh day, after His six days of creating. While no one has ever suggested that the Lord Almighty was truly *tired*, that is what "rested" suggests. In fact, the Hebrew word there simply means "ceased His activity." Humans need rest, but God does not.

690. the original sprinkler system

Man did not invent lawn sprinkler systems—not the first one, anyway. According to Genesis 2:5–6, before there was any plant growing on the earth there had been no rain (which makes sense), "but a mist went up from the earth and watered the whole face of the ground."

691. the lost rivers of Eden

The Bible is pretty specific about where the Garden of Eden is. In fact, Genesis mentions four rivers in connection with Eden: Hiddekel (Tigris), Euphrates, Pishon, and Gihon (Gen. 2:10–14). Well, the Tigris and Euphrates are there in Iraq for all to see. But scholars have puzzled over the Pishon and Gihon—were these just mythical names? Dr. Juris Zarins, a scholar at Southwest Missouri State University, came up with an interesting possibility: the two "lost rivers" are today two gulleys, Wadi Rimah and Wadi Batin—dry today, but originally the courses of the rivers Pishon and Gihon. Zarins has another interesting theory: the site of the Garden of Eden is now under the waters of the Persian Gulf, into which the four rivers flowed.

692. vegetarian world

According to Genesis 1, in the world as originally created there was no eating of meat. God gave mankind all seed-bearing plants and all fruits to use as food. Likewise all the beasts, birds, and reptiles were to subsist on plant food, not on each other.

After the Flood, things changed: God gave man every living thing, including animals, as food (Gen. 9:3).

693. gold first and last

Appropriately, since gold is the "king" among metals, it is the first to be mentioned in the Bible: "the whole land of Havilah, where there is gold. And the gold of that land is good" (Gen. 2:11–12). Appropriately, it is also the last metal mentioned, for gold is widely used in the heavenly Jerusalem. In fact, the city was measured with a rod of gold (Rev. 21:15, 18, 21).

694. Josephus and Cain

Why did God prefer Abel's sacrifice over Cain's? The Bible itself provides no answer. It only reports that Cain's jealousy led to his murder of his brother. The Jewish historian Josephus had a theory, one popular among many Jews in the ancient world: God preferred Abel's offering (sheep) over Cain's (crops) because He preferred what grew according to nature over what man forced from nature.

695. the first polygamist

For centuries Christians and Jews have felt some embarrassment over the polygamy of some of the great men of the Old Testament—notably David, and also Solomon, with his enormous stable of wives and concubines. Interestingly, the Bible attributes the origins of polygamy to descendants of the first bad guy, Cain. Cain was the first murderer, the slayer of his brother Abel, and his grandson Lamech (also a killer) was also the first man to take more than one wife (Gen. 4:19). Even while the people of Israel tolerated polygamy, they apparently felt uncomfortable with it, connecting it with rogues such as Lamech.

696. Jubal at the organ?

According to Genesis 4:21, Jubal was "the father of all such as handle the harp and organ" (KJV). Did they really have organs in Bible times? Hardly. More recent versions of the Bible have "harp and flute," which is more accurate.

697. the original blacksmith

Iron, one of man's most durable and widely used metals, is mentioned very early in the Bible. The first "blacksmith" is Cain's descendant Tubal-Cain, "an instructor of every craftsman in bronze and iron" (Gen. 4:22). By the way, many older translations use "brass" but the correct translation is "bronze."

698. daughters of Cain

Readers are puzzled by Genesis 6:1–4, which tells of the "sons of God" who mated with the "daughters of men" and fathered children by them. An old Jewish tradition, adopted by many Christians, states that the "sons of God" were fallen angels. But there is another interesting Christian interpretation of the passage, also very old: the "sons of God" were the descendants of Adam's good son Seth, while the "daughters of men" were descendants of Adam's evil son Cain.

699. from 969 to 70

At the time of David and Solomon in the Old Testament, seventy years was about the average life span for a human being (see Ps. 90:10). But it is obvious in the book of Genesis that people lived a long, *long* time in the old days. Take the longest-lived, Methuselah, who lived to be 969. Much later, the patriarch Abraham lived to be 175. How do we explain such life spans? Was this just a wild legend, a fond but foolish belief that in the past life was much better—or at least longer? Hard to say. We know nothing of what life on earth was like in those days, but certainly it may have been healthier in some ways—and certainly moved at a slower pace than today.

700. Kircher's ark

In the 1600s, a Catholic priest named Athanasius Kircher drew a floor plan of Noah's ark. In Kircher's design, the ark has three decks, Deck One being the Bird Deck, with various types of birds being in different stalls. Deck Two is the Food Deck, with stalls not only for fruits, vegetables, and grains, but also for animals used as meat. Deck Three was the Beast Deck, with stalls for the various animals—keeping the predators separated from the beasts they preyed on, of course.

701. the table of nations

This is the name scholars give to Genesis 10, a long list of genealogies of Noah's three sons. A key idea here: all the peoples on the earth are, in fact, one family, all being descended from Noah. The sons of Noah's son Ham are said to populate Egypt, Mesopotamia, Ethiopia, Babylon, and Canaan. The sons of Japheth are identified with the people of Greece, Asia Minor, and the Mediterranean islands. And the sons of Shem include the Hebrews, the chosen people, later known as Israel.

702. the Tower of Babel

What was the original language of man? Hebrew, according to Jewish tradition? The Bible is clear that there was definitely *one* language at the beginning. This changed when mankind decided to overreach itself, building a tower whose top would reach into the heavens. On the plain of Shinar (near what later became Babylon) builders constructed a huge brick tower. Seeing this display of pride, God went down and confused their speech, so the workmen could not understand one another. They ceased building and scattered over the earth. "Therefore its name is called Babel, because there the LORD confused the language of all the earth" (Gen. 11:9). Our word *babble* has its origin in Babel, of course.

703. life changes, name changes

The Bible mentions several characters whose names were changed, often at God's command. Abram and his wife Sarai were renamed Abraham and Sarah (Gen. 17). The name of Abraham's grandson Jacob, father of the twelve tribes, was changed to Israel, which means "struggled with God" (Gen. 32:22–30; 35:9–10). Ruth's mother-in-law Naomi (which means "pleasant") suffered such calamities that she told Ruth to call her Mara (meaning "bitter," Ruth 1:20).

704. Egypt as refuge

Even though the Israelites' fleeing slavery in Egypt is one of the key stories of the Bible, the Bible is also filled with stories of people deliberately choosing Egypt as a place of refuge. First was Abraham, who went to Egypt because of a famine in Canaan. The same situation drove Jacob and his sons to Egypt. Centuries later, Solomon's aide Jeroboam fled his master's wrath and went to Egypt, returning when he heard of Solomon's death. When the

Babylonians deported many Israelites to Babylon, some Israelites fled to Egypt, taking the prophet Jeremiah with them. But of course, the most famous refugees to Egypt were Joseph, Mary, and the newborn Jesus, who fled to Egypt to escape Herod's slaughter of the infants of Bethlehem. They did not return to Israel until after Herod's death.

705. the cave of Machpelah

This cave became the burial place of some Old Testament notables. Abraham purchased it to be the tomb of his beloved wife, Sarah (Gen. 23:4–9), and in time it also held the remains of Abraham himself, and also Isaac, Rebecca, Leah, and Jacob.

706. *teraphim*

In the ancient world, many families and individuals kept their "household gods" or small idols in the home. The Hebrew word for these is *teraphim*, which some Bibles don't bother to translate at all. The New King James Version reads "household idols," as in Genesis 31:19, where Rachel, fleeing with her husband, Jacob, steals her father's idols. (See 31:34 for the clever way she keeps her father from finding them!) In 1 Samuel 19:13 we find that David's wife, Michal, hid one of these idols in her husband's bed to deceive the men who were searching for him.

707. wrestling in prayer

Genesis 32:23–32 tells the curious story of the patriarch Jacob wrestling all night with a mysterious visitor (the angel of the Lord). Jacob will not give up until the visitor blesses him. Many early Christian authors saw the story in symbolic terms: the Christian must struggle in prayer, and if he perseveres (painful as it may be), God will bless him.

708. the rape of Dinah

Sex and violence are definitely there in the Bible, particularly in the Old Testament. One of the most sordid stories of all concerns Dinah, daughter of Jacob (Gen. 34). She attracts the attention of Shechem the Hivite, who rapes her, then (a surprising element in any rape story) decides he loves her and wants to marry her. Her father and her twelve brothers aren't pleased at the rape, needless to say, but they pretend to consent to a wedding—on the condition that Shechem and all his tribesmen consent to be circumcised (which, for an adult male in the days before anesthesia, was quite serious). On the third day after the surgery, "when they were in pain," the men had two bloodthirsty visitors: Dinah's brothers Levi and Simeon. Finding the Hivite men incapacitated, they murder them all and plunder their goods (and took Dinah with them as well). Jacob laments this, saying it will lead to further bloodshed. The brothers' reply: "Should he treat our sister like a harlot?" (Gen. 34:31).

709. the eunuch Potiphar

Genesis 39 tells the story of Joseph, sold as a slave by his brothers, in the service of the Egyptian official Potiphar. In the famous story, Potiphar's randy wife tries to seduce Joseph, and when he resists, she tells her husband that Joseph tried to rape her—resulting in Joseph being thrown in prison. Interestingly, the Hebrew text says that Potiphar was a *saris*—technically, a eunuch. If this was literally true, it might explain why Potiphar's wife was so lascivious. But the Bible scholars believe that *saris* in Genesis 39 does not refer to an actual castrated male but to a royal official.

710. civil disobedience, Hebrew style

Some scholars see the first recorded example of civil disobedience in Exodus 1. The two women who served as midwives to the Hebrew slaves in Egypt were called on the carpet by Pharaoh, who had instructed the women to kill the sons born to Hebrew women. The two spunky women resisted this horrible order by telling a lie: the Hebrew women, they told Pharaoh, were so physically fit that they delivered their sons before the midwives could arrive to help! So, through the hand of God, the number of Hebrews grew, in spite of Pharaoh's plan that they would decrease in number.

711. slow of speech

Moses, called by God to lead the Israelites from Egypt, stated that he was not eloquent, for "I am slow of speech and slow of tongue" (Ex. 4:10). Some readers have taken this to mean that he had some speech impediment, such as stuttering. Most likely he meant that he was not someone to whom words came readily.

712. Moses and the magicians

In the ancient world, the Egyptians had a reputation for dabbling in magic and sorcery. This is evident in the book of Exodus, where the pharaoh had court magicians who could duplicate some of the miraculous feats done by Moses. The miracles of Moses came through the power of God, of course, but because the magicians could seemingly do some of the same stunts, Pharaoh was not convinced that God was on Moses' side.

Did pharaoh's magicians really work magic—or were they like "magicians" today, clever illusionists? Hard to say. Exodus makes it clear that the magicians could not duplicate all of Moses' miracles, and eventually the stubborn Pharaoh realized he was dealing with a power mightier than magic.

By the way, though the Old Testament does not tell us the names of the court magicians, Jewish tradition names them Jannes and Jambres (whose names are mentioned in 2 Timothy 3:8).

713. fire and cloud as guide

When the liberated Israelite slaves left Egypt, they had no road map to the promised land. They did however, have a miraculous guide that God provided: a pillar of cloud by day and a pillar of fire by night (Ex. 13:17–22). The pillar moved ahead of the mass of people, showing the way.

714. the water sweetener

After the famous crossing of the Red Sea, the Israelites faced another problem: they were in the wilderness three days without water. They came to a place called Mara, which had water, but water too bitter to drink. (The name Mara means "bitter.") Moses cried out to the Lord for aid, and the Lord showed him a tree, which Moses cut down and cast into the waters, taking out the bitterness (Ex. 15:22–26).

715. the first cheerleader

Perhaps the world's first cheerleader—or the first in the Bible—was Moses. While the Israelites were fighting the Amalekites, Moses stood where the Israelites could see him, holding his rod up high. This amazing morale booster was so effective that when Moses' arms got tired, Hur and Moses' brother Aaron came to hold Moses' arms up (Ex. 17:11–13).

716. the ephod

Sometimes Bible translators make their work easier by simply not translating a word. A good example is the Hebrew word *ephod*, which refers to a garment worn by Israel's high priest. It is described in detail in Exodus 28:6–14. It was made of gold and of blue, purple, and scarlet linen, with two onyx stones on which were engraved the names of the twelve tribes of Israel.

At times other people could wear ephods. Samuel wore one (1 Sam. 2:18), and David wore one while he danced before the ark of the covenant (2 Sam. 6:14).

Apparently the item could be used in some way to determine the Lord's will (1 Sam. 23:6; 30:7–8). The judge Gideon made an ephod from gold he had captured from the Midianites, and the Israelites made it into an idol (Judg. 8:27).

717. lying

Does the Bible actually say "Thou shalt not lie"? No, although honesty is consistently held up as a great virtue and deception is frowned upon. In the Ten Commandments, the ninth is, in a sense, a prohibition against lying: "bearing false witness" against one's neighbor not only refers to lying in court, but also to making any false (and potentially harmful) statements against another person. So the ninth commandment is a prohibition against perjury, lying, and slander.

718. why a calf?

People are familiar with the Israelites' golden calf idol, if only because it figures so prominently in the movie *The Ten Commandments*. While Moses was receiving the commandments from the Lord, Aaron his brother fashioned a golden calf for the Israelites, who turned the occasion into a sort of religious orgy (Ex. 32). Ironically, one of the commandments that Moses was receiving at that time specifically prohibited making any kind of idol.

Why a calf? We think of calves as sweet, innocent creatures, not the sort of thing one would worship. One possibility: the "calf" may have been a young bull—in short, a bull full of vigor, an obvious symbol of fertility. One other possibility: the idol may indeed have been a bull, and the Egyptians (the people the Israelites had just fled from) worshiped their god Hapi in the form of a bull. Calling it a "calf" may have been the way the author of Exodus was pouring scorn on the idol.

719. fasting to the max

According to Exodus 34:28, Moses abstained from all food and water for a period of forty days. *Forty days?* Scientifically speaking, a person can go without food for twenty-eight days, but even less time without water— seven days, in fact. Other than God's miraculous sustaining, there is no explanation for Moses' lengthy fast.

720. the Holiness Code

How are God's people supposed to behave? Obviously they are, like God Himself, to be *holy*. Chapters 17 through 26 of the book of Leviticus are sometimes called the Holiness Code, for this section is a long set of regulations, not only for correct ritual in the worship of God, but also for sexual ethics and general morality. Appropriately, the section contains the most-quoted verse, Leviticus 19:18: "You shall love your neighbor as yourself."

721. unequally yoked

The laws governing the Israelites were strict about mixing unlike things—such as two different kinds of fabric in one garment (Lev. 19:19). Likewise it was illegal to yoke two different kinds of beasts—such as a donkey and an ox—to a plow (Deut. 22:10). These laws sound silly to us today, but they were everyday reminders to the Israelites that they themselves were distinct from the pagan cultures around them.

722. the quail—miracle or coincidence?

Skeptics enjoy explaining away the miracles of the Bible, but sometimes an obvious question remains: If something "just happened" or is just "natural," how do we account for it happening at a particular time? Couldn't that be part of God's miracle as well? Take, for example, the miraculous provision of quail for the Israelites to eat in the wilderness after they left Egypt (see Num. 11:31–32). Many people in the past have witnessed the same amazing event described in the Old Testament: huge flocks of quail, fatigued from their migrations over open water, land in certain areas, and are so tired they can be taken with nets or even by hand. A "natural" event? Yes. But who arranged it that the Israelites would encounter these fatigued—and edible—birds at just the right time?

723. Egyptian cuisine

Once the Israelites had been delivered out of their slavery in Egypt, they never ceased to gripe. Wandering for forty years in the wilderness before they reached the promised land, they had various reasons to complain. One thing they certainly missed: the food they had had in Egypt. Even though they had been slaves, there apparently had been food in abundance: "We remember the fish, which we did eat in Egypt freely; the cucumbers, and the melons, and the leeks, and the onions, and the garlick" (Num. 11:5 KJV). Their wilderness fare did not, it appears, compare favorably with their former foods.

724. "like grasshoppers in their sight"

Numbers 13 tells the curious story of the Israelite spies—reconnaissance men, actually—who ventured into Canaan to see what the land was like. They were impressed: the land bore wonderful fruit, including a huge cluster of grapes so large that two men carried it between them on a pole. The spies reported this to Moses, but also gave him the bad news: the inhabitants of the land were strong and large—giants, in fact. Compared to them, "we were like grasshoppers." The report produced such fear that many of the Israelites wanted to oust Moses and select a new leader to guide them back to Egypt. God pronounced a death sentence on these rebels.

Incidentally, the two men carrying the large cluster of grapes is today the official symbol of Israel's tourism board.

725. Israel's first draft

Military drafts are nothing new, and neither are censuses. In Numbers 26:1–2 we read of God telling Moses to take a census of all Israel, partly to take account of how many men there were above the age of twenty, men who would be required to go to war. (The book of Numbers, by the way, takes its name from the censuses, which take up most of chapters 1–3 and 26.)

726. "strange fire"

"And Nadab and Abihu died, when they offered strange fire before the LORD" (Num. 26:61 KJV). What exactly was the "strange fire" that Nadab and Abihu, the sons of Aaron the priest, offered to the Lord? The story is told in Leviticus 10:1–3, which speaks of the two sons being devoured by fire for their sin. To be honest, we don't know just what the "strange fire" was. Apparently the two had performed the incense ritual wrong in some way. Leviticus 10:9, which closely follows the story of the "strange fire," is prohibition against priests being drunk on the job, and some scholars think that might have been the sin of the two men. As a result of their untimely death, Israel's priesthood was passed on not through Nadab and Abihu but through Aaron's younger son, Eleazar.

727. the iron bed man

Beds as pieces of furniture were rare in the ancient world. Most ordinary folks slept on mats on the floor, and only the privileged had actual beds. King Og of Bashan had a famous iron bed, more than thirteen feet long and six feet wide (king-size, obviously, Deut. 3:11). Og was supposed to be the only one remaining "of the remnant of the giants."

728. the mutilation law

Israel's law in the Old Testament made no provision for mutilation of offenders—except in one notable case.

Deuteronomy 25:11–12 states that if two men are fighting, and the wife of one of them intervenes by grabbing the privates of the other man, she shall be punished by having her hand cut off.

729. everlasting clothing

Most people would say that clothing that lasts for forty years is mighty sturdy. Such were the clothes—even the shoes—of the Israelites who left slavery in Egypt and wandered in the wilderness for forty years. Nothing wore out, a sign that God was with His people through their long days of wandering (Deut. 29:5).

730. -ites

The Bible, particularly the Old Testament, often uses the -*ite* suffix or ending to designate a particular tribe. Thus the people of Israel are Israelites, people of Moab are Moabites, people of Edom are Edomites, and so on. (But people of Egypt are Egyptians, not Egyptites.)

731. beer and *shekhar*

Was there beer in Bible times? We know the Egyptians brewed beer from grain, but we aren't sure if the drink indicated by the Hebrew word *shekhar* was beer or something else. The New International Version reads "beer" in several verses (1 Sam. 1:15; Prov. 31:4; Isa. 24:9; Mic. 2:11). The New King James Version reads "intoxicating drink" or "strong drink," and "strong drink" was the preferred translation for the KJV and RSV. Today's English Version sometimes uses the most neutral word of all: "alcohol."

732. Jericho's curse

Jericho may be the world's oldest city. The book of Joshua tells the familiar story of the Israelites marching around it, blowing their trumpets, "and the walls come a-tumblin' down" (Josh. 6). What is often forgotten is that Joshua, Israel's military leader, put a curse on the city—or, rather, a curse on anyone who dared to try rebuilding it (6:7). Inevitably, someone did. In the days of King Ahab, a man named Hiel rebuilt Jericho. But when the foundations were laid, his firstborn son died. When the city gates were set up, another son died. The curse had worked (1 Kings 16:34).

733. Ai the ruin

The most appropriately named city in the Bible has to be Ai, a name that means "ruin." Joshua 8 tells of how the heathen city was totally destroyed by the Israelites and made "a heap forever."

734. sun standing still

In Joshua 10 we read of one of the Bible's most amazing miracles: while Joshua and the armies of Israel fought against their enemies, the sun stood still and did not go down for a whole day. Joshua uttered his famous words: "Sun, stand still over Gibeon" (10:12). How to explain this? To some people it is simply legend, nothing more. To some, it did literally happen through the hand of God. Author Immanuel Velikovsky, in his book *Worlds in Collision*, had an interesting theory: the sun stood still because of a near collision between earth and a comet, which caused a temporary halt in the earth's rotation.

735. "devoted" and destroyed

In ancient times, part of the pleasure in defeating any enemy was taking his property. The Israelites, like the nations around them, took booty from their defeated enemies. (This included making slaves of the survivors, of course.) However, some cities or nations were so extremely wicked that the Israelites were instructed to keep nothing that was captured. In such cases the enemy's goods were to be "devoted" to the Lord—which meant totally destroying them so they would be of use to no one. This included killing the survivors instead of enslaving them. The idea seemed to be that pagans, allowed to live, might influence God's people with their wicked beliefs and practices (see Josh. 6:18–21; Deut. 20:14–18; 1 Sam. 15).

736. death by cattle prod

Electric-charged cattle prods are a fairly recent invention, but in Bible times there was the ox goad, a long-handled stick used to poke and prod the animals along. One of Israel's judges (military leaders, that is) named Shamgar once killed six hundred Philistines with an ox goad (Judg. 3:31).

737. no glorious actions

No news is good news. Consider the judge Abdon, who led Israel for eight years (Judg. 12:13–15). The Bible says nothing about his leadership, which means there were probably no major wars during the time. The Jewish historian Josephus wrote that Abdon's time was peaceful, which indicates that Abdon "had no occasion to perform glorious actions."

738. Samson the gatekeeper

The Philistines thought they had finally captured their mighty enemy, the Hebrew strongman Samson. In those days cities had walls and gates, and could literally be locked up at night. Samson was trapped—so they thought—in the city of Gaza. But not so: in the middle of the night Samson lifted Gaza's gates and gateposts right out of the ground and left the city (Judg. 16:1–3).

739. muscleman and child

Judges 16 tells the tale of the strongman Samson's end: blinded and imprisoned by the Philistines, Samson's strength gradually returned, unknown to his captors. They brought him to their temple to make sport of him. Samson asked a little boy to guide him to the temple's pillars, which he then pushed down, literally bringing the house down on the Philistines. More than three thousand people died.

740. lap child

The book of Ruth mentions an ancient custom that is very touching: Ruth, who stuck by her mother-in-law Naomi after Naomi's husband and two sons had all died, had her own son, the boy Obed. After his birth, Naomi took the child into her lap—a symbol that she wanted to adopt Obed and treat him as her own son. Thus the child became Naomi's heir, in place of the sons she had lost (Ruth 4:14–17).

741. Eli's greedy sons

Sometimes good people have vile children. A case in point: the priest-judge Eli, spiritual mentor to the boy Samuel, whose sons were notoriously greedy. Serving as priests at Shiloh, Hophni and Phinehas made a point of getting for themselves the choicest cuts of meat from the sacrificed animals (1 Sam. 2:12–25). A prophet warned Eli that both his worthless sons would die on the same day (2:27–36). It happened that the two sons were killed at the same time that the ark of the covenant was captured by the Philistines. All the bad news at once caused poor Eli—old, nearly blind, and very fat—to fall off his seat, break his neck, and die (1 Sam. 4:12–18).

742. the future king's pursuits

Sometimes the Bible is so painfully straightforward that we know no one could have invented it. Take God's man Samuel, told to anoint Israel's first king, Saul. What was Saul doing when Samuel found him? Nothing even remotely "royal." He was out hunting donkeys that belonged to his father (1 Sam. 9:1–20). On the other hand, though it wasn't exactly a "kingly" activity, it did prove that he was a dutiful son with no pretense about him.

743. why five smooth stones?

One of the most beloved stories of the Bible is that of the spunky shepherd boy David, who brings down the giant warrior Goliath with only a rock and a sling. But the Bible tells us that David took "five smooth stones," not just one. Why five? Were the other four his "backup"? No indeed. Goliath had four brothers (who, we must assume, were probably as large and fierce as he was), so the other stones David carried were just in case the other four brothers showed up. As it turned out, the four brothers of Goliath did later die in battle with David and his soldiers (see 2 Sam. 21:22).

744. Rizpah the faithful

One of the forgotten women of the Bible was a truly faithful woman—so faithful that she stood watch over the dead bodies of two of her sons and five of her grandsons. She was Rizpah, mother of two of the sons of the ill-fated King Saul. When the Gibeonites demanded that King David revenge Saul's slaughter of some of their men, David reluctantly complied by handing over Saul's two sons and five grandsons, who were hanged (2 Sam. 21:9). No one was allowed to bury the bodies of the executed men. But day and night, from spring to late autumn, the faithful Rizpah guarded the hanging bodies, keeping away birds of prey and scavenging animals. David heard of her vigil and consented for the men's bones to be buried with Saul's.

745. mutant giants

Goliath was not the only giant David faced. There were several among the Philistine warriors, but David and his men defeated all of them. One of them was not only a giant in size but a mutant in another respect as well: he had six fingers on each hand and six toes on each foot (2 Sam. 21:20–21).

746. David the inventor

David, king of Israel, was credited with being an excellent musician and writer of song. According to the prophet Amos, David was even more: he invented new musical instruments to play (Amos 6:5).

747. Absalom's ego

King David of Israel's favorite son was the handsome, popular, and extremely egotistical Absalom. Part of Absalom's plot to make himself king in his father's place involved always having a crowd around him: specifically, he enlisted fifty men to run ahead of him when he went out in his chariot (2 Sam. 15:1).

748. father and son songwriters

David—king of Israel, shepherd, warrior, husband of many wives, "man after God's own heart"—was also a fine musician and poet. Of our 150 psalms in the Bible, 73 are attributed to him. Apparently his wise son Solomon was even more prolific: 1 Kings 4:32 says that Solomon wrote in excess of a thousand songs.

749. peace temple

King David, the "man after God's own heart," wanted to build a temple for his Lord—a plan that God frustrated. Why? David was, God told him, a man of war, who had shed much blood, thus he was not the man to build the temple. That task would fall to his son Solomon, a man of peace (1 Chron. 22:2–10).

750. Solomon's daily bread

The wealthy need a lot of supplies to maintain their households. Take wise and wealthy King Solomon of Israel: on a daily basis his household required 195 bushels of flour, 30 cows, and 100 sheep (see 1 Kings 4:22–23). Since he had 700 wives and 300 concubines, obviously the needs were substantial.

751. quiet construction

Most construction sites are pretty noisy places, especially with modern power tools. They were noisy in Bible times as well, but not when the Jerusalem temple was being built. The temple "was built with stone finished at the quarry, so that no hammer or chisel or any iron tool was heard in the temple while it was being built" (1 Kings 6:7). This little detail added by the author of 1 Kings suggests that even before the temple was finished there was a feeling of holiness about it.

752. Solomon's giant finger bowl

One of the most impressive items in Solomon's temple was called "the Sea." Described in detail in 1 Kings 7:23–26, it was a giant wash bowl in the temple courtyard. Made of cast bronze, it was decorated with ornamental flower buds and rested on the backs of twelve bronze oxen. The Sea held about twelve thousand gallons of water and was used by the priests to wash their hands and feet when they were ministering in the temple.

753. the land of Good for Nothing

When Solomon built his magnificent temple in Jerusalem, one of his chief benefactors was Hiram, king of Tyre. Hiram supplied Solomon with cedar, cypress, and gold for his project. For this, Solomon gave Hiram twenty cities in northern Israel. Hiram went to visit them, "but they did not please him." He was so peevish that he named the cities "Cabul," which means "good for nothing" (1 Kings 9:10–13).

754. Solomon's throne

Wise and wealthy King Solomon made a deep impression on history, as seen by the detail used to describe his household in 1 Kings. As just one example, his throne: it was made of ivory overlaid with gold, situated at the top of six steps. At the ends of each step were figures of lions—twelve in all, a reminder of the twelve tribes of Israel. "Nothing like this had been made for any other kingdom" (1 Kings 10:18–20).

755. no silver, thank you

Silver and gold are both beautiful, but silver tarnishes while gold is . . . well, gold is the best. This fact was not overlooked by the writer of 1 Kings, who mentions that gold was a prominent feature in the household of King Solomon of Israel. Even Solomon's cups were of gold: "not one was of silver, for this was accounted as nothing in the days of Solomon" (1 Kings 10:21).

756. the land of Omri

Omri, king of Israel and father of wicked King Ahab, was himself a wicked king, heartily condemned in the Old Testament (see 1 Kings 16). Still, though Omri was a spiritual failure, he must have had some political success, for other nations referred to Israel as the "land of Omri" for several generations after his death.

757. halting between two opinions

The mighty prophet Elijah's victory over the false prophets of Baal is related vividly in 1 Kings 18. Elijah asks the people this question: "How long halt ye between two opinions? if the LORD be God, follow him: but if Baal, then follow him. And the people answered him not a word" (18:21 KJV). "Halt" is rendered "limp" in some versions, "falter" in others. The key idea: the people dally with both Baal and the Lord, so they are "limping" along, unsteady in their devotion.

758. "as small as a man's hand"

The most famous cloud in the Bible is the one seen by Elijah's servant. The cloud, "as small as a man's hand," symbolized the end of the three-year drought declared by the prophet Elijah. After Elijah's victory over the heathen prophets of Baal, he declared that the drought could end. It was from that site, Mount Carmel, that Elijah's servant saw the small cloud that, as Elijah predicted, brought the much-needed rain (1 Kings 18:41–45).

759. the running prophet

One of the most famous showdowns in the Bible is the confrontation between the heathen prophets of Baal and Elijah, the sole prophet of the true God. In the confrontation on Israel's Mount Carmel, Elijah and God won the contest—but the day wasn't over yet. Wicked King Ahab, who had been led into Baal worship by his wife, Jezebel, ran away from the scene, pointing his chariot

toward Jezreel, seventeen miles away. Elijah had no chariot at all, but relied on his own feet—and, we may assume,
on the power of God—to speed him to Jezreel ahead of
Ahab's chariot (1 Kings 18:45–46).

760. "a still small voice"

Sometimes the Lord's people go from a "high" to a major
"low." Elijah the prophet, after the amazing victory over
the pagan prophets of Baal, found himself on the lam
from wicked Queen Jezebel. Hiding out on Mount
Horeb, the distraught Elijah encountered the power of
God, manifesting Himself in a powerful wind, then an
earthquake, then a fire. "And after the earthquake a fire;
but the LORD was not in the fire: and after the fire a still
small voice" (1 Kings 19:12 KJV). Apparently the mighty
Ruler of all nature can also speak in a whisper at times. In
this "still small voice," God encouraged His prophet.

761. iron horns

The Bible includes the words of God's prophets—and
the words of false prophets also. In 1 Kings 22 we read
of the true prophet Micaiah, who told wicked Ahab
(king of Israel) and Jehoshaphat (king of Judah) that
disaster would result if they went to war against Syria.
Quite the opposite was the false prophet Zedekiah.
Telling Ahab exactly what he wished to hear, Zedekiah

told Ahab that his army would win against the Syrians. And to make his point clear, Zedekiah wore a set of iron horns on his head, telling the kings, "With these you shall gore the Syrians until they are destroyed" (v. 11). The false prophets chimed in. Micaiah was put in prison, but his words came to pass: Ahab died in battle with the Syrians.

762. the prophet's mantle

The prophet Elijah's mantle was more than an article of clothing—it was a symbol of his power and charisma. When he was taken into heaven in a fiery chariot, he left his mantle to his successor, Elisha, who had acquired Elijah's gifts as prophet and wonder-worker. In fact, Elisha used the mantle in performing one of the same miracles Elijah had done: parting the waters of the Jordan River (2 Kings 2:8, 14).

763. acoustic trickery

Sometimes you don't need an army to defeat another army—you simply need the *enemy* to think there is an army. When the Syrian army had surrounded Israel's capital, God caused the Syrians to hear the sounds of chariots and galloping horses. The Syrians feared that the Israelites had joined forces with larger armies, and they fled in fright (2 Kings 7:6–7).

764. temple repair fund

Even the best buildings need repair from time to time. In the days of King Jehoash, this was true of the temple in Jerusalem. To promote a building fund, the priest Jehoiada took a chest, bored a hole in its lid and placed it beside the altar so that people could contribute money as they saw fit. In effect, it was the world's first piggy bank. The money was used to pay the masons, carpenters, and other workmen for temple repairs (2 Kings 12:8–12).

765. nehushtan

Idolatry is a horrible sin in the Bible, and yet God's people constantly fell into it. In 2 Kings 18:4, we learn that the people preserved the bronze snake that Moses had set up on a pole to heal snakebite. Later generations had turned this relic—which they called *nehushtan*—into an object of worship. Godly king Hezekiah destroyed the relic to keep the people from their idolatry of it.

766. Hezekiah's sundial

The book of Isaiah tells us that King Hezekiah of Judah had a sort of sundial, which served as a kind of clock. In fact, the Hebrew word that was translated "dial" or "sundial" in old versions is more accurately "steps" or "stairs." The likely meaning: Hezekiah marked time by observing how a shadow—perhaps one cast by a building or monument—moved along a flight of steps (Isa. 38:1–8).

767. the Book of the Law

Josiah, one of the few really good kings in the Old Testament, instituted a great religious reform in Judah, and what prompted him to do so was the finding of the Book of the Law in the temple (2 Kings 22). Scholars generally agree that the Book of the Law was a scroll containing what we today call the book of Deuteronomy.

768. Nebuzaradan

The Babylonian god Nebo's name crops up as part of a lot of Babylonian names, such as the king Nebuchadnezzar, and also the king's general, Nebuzaradan. This formidable military man was responsible for the siege and sacking of Jerusalem (2 Kings 25). Among Nebuzaradan's various atrocities, "He burned the house of the LORD and the king's house; all the houses of Jerusalem, that is, all the houses of the great, he burned with fire" (v. 9). He also forced into exile all the well-to-do people, leaving only the poorest. One who chose to stay was the prophet Jeremiah (Jer. 40:1–6).

769. Chronicles and "the annals of the kings"

Our 1 and 2 Chronicles were originally one long book, divided into two for convenience' sake. They weren't called "Chronicles" until around 400, when the Bible scholar Jerome gave them that name. Some people mistakenly believe they are mentioned elsewhere in the Bible, because several times the Old Testament mentions "the book of the chronicles of the kings of Israel" (1 Kings 14:19; 15:31; 16:5) and "the chronicles of the kings of Judah" (1 Kings 14:29; 15:7). It appears that the author of 1 Kings was drawing on some old court histories, but Bible scholars are quite sure that he was not referring to the Chronicles in our Bible. To avoid this confusion, some modern translations use "annals" instead of "chronicles."

770. king in the bedroom

Nasty Queen Athaliah is one of the Bible's most unpleasant characters. To hold her throne, she had most of the royal heirs put to death—most, but not quite all. Young Joash was hidden, along with his nurse, in a bedroom for six years, until a coup would rid the land of Athaliah (2 Chron. 22:11–12).

Curiously, "bedroom" doesn't mean what it does today, a sleeping room in a house. It probably refers to a storage room where the mats for bedding were kept—in effect, a large closet for sleeping bags.

771. Cyrus of Persia

Generally speaking, foreign rulers get a bad rap in the Bible, and for the obvious reason that most of them were tyrants, and pagans to boot. One ruler who is mildly approved by Scripture is Cyrus of Persia. After Persia overran the Babylonian Empire (which had sacked Jerusalem and taken its leading citizens into exile in Babylon), Cyrus took a lenient stance toward the conquered people and allowed any Jews who wished, to return to their homeland. Cyrus even encouraged the rebuilding of the temple in Jerusalem. Cyrus is favorably reported in 2 Chronicles 36:22–23 and Ezra 1:1–6, and is called "the anointed" in Isaiah 45:1.

772. clergy exemption

Churches and other religious institutions are tax-exempt in the United States. A similar situation existed in Bible times: the Persian emperor Artaxerxes gave a tax exemption to all the workers in the Jerusalem temple—priests, Levites, choir members, gatekeepers, and attendants (Ezra 7:24).

773. shutting down Jerusalem

Keeping the Sabbath day holy was never easy, for human greed made people want to treat the day as any other, a day to make money and transact business. In the days after the Jews returned to Israel from their exile in Babylonia, the spiritual leaders were determined to have the people obey all God's commandments—including keeping the Sabbath strictly for worship and rest. The leader Nehemiah found an effective way to make the Sabbath a "no-business" day: he ordered the gates of Jerusalem shut on the Sabbath, ensuring there would be no commerce on that day (Neh. 13:17–22).

774. Rahab the monster

The most famous Rahab was the prostitute who aided Joshua's spies (Josh. 2), but another Rahab was a sort of mythical monster, something like a dragon. Mentioned in Job 9:13, Psalm 89:10, and Isaiah 51:9, the monster Rahab symbolizes evil and disorder, but is conquered by the Lord.

775. "laws of the Medes and the Persians"

"If it please the king, let there go a royal commandment from him, and let it be written among the laws of the Persians and the Medes, that it be not altered" (Est. 1:19 KJV). When people were more Bible-literate, a writer or speaker could refer to "the laws of the Medes and the Persians," and his audience would know he meant "something set in concrete, subject to no change at all."

776. speechless friends

Much of the book of Job is filled with the speeches of Job and his three friends—and mostly the three friends were telling Job that because he had suffered so many calamities, he must have sinned to deserve them. But to give the friends credit, when they first came to visit poor Job, they were so grieved that they were speechless—in fact, for an entire week they sat on the ground and said nothing, so deeply were they moved at what had befallen their friend Job (2:11–13).

777. can you say "imprecatory"?

Some of the Old Testament's psalms are lovely hymns of praise to God—some, but not all. A few of the psalms call for God's swift vengeance upon an enemy. These are called the *imprecatory* psalms (the word means "calling down a curse"), and they are Psalms 2, 37, 69, 79, 109, 137, and 143. In today's lingo, they would be considered "mean-spirited"—the rantings of a man who believes he is righteous, calling for God's brutal smashing of the enemies. Consider one of the most famous imprecatory rants, Psalm 137, written as a lament for being conquered by the cruel Babylonians: "O daughter of Babylon, who are to be destroyed, happy the one who repays you as you have served us! Happy the one who takes and dashes your little ones against the rock" (137:8–9).

Christians have for centuries been bothered by these

psalms. They seem cruel and vindictive—not exactly "Christian." But stop and consider: the author of these psalms was not taking vengeance into his own hands (which the Bible forbids). He was asking God, the Righteous One, to reward the good and punish the wicked—something that Christians can agree with. While we may not like the stark tone of these psalms, they remind us of something: God will ultimately destroy evil.

778. the most common name

The most popular name for a man in the Bible is Shemaiah: twenty-seven men bore that name. Another name curiosity: Israel's king David is one of the best-loved men in the Bible, yet he is the only man with that name.

779. a year, but not quite

We have known for a couple of centuries that, scientifically speaking, a year consists of 365.25 days—the reason we add an extra day to February every fourth year. Curiously, in the ancient world, including Israel, a year was presumed to have precisely 360 days—twelve months of thirty days each. A neat and easy-to-remember system, but (according to the sun and earth's path around it, anyway) not quite precise.

780. the real Lemuel

Proverbs 31 claims to be the "words of King Lemuel." There was no king of Israel by this name, and if it refers to some foreign king, we have no idea where he hailed from. Some Bible scholars have suggested that Lemuel—the name means "devoted to God"—might be another nickname for King Solomon, the author of Proverbs 1–29. Considering how many hundreds of wives Solomon had, the glowing description of the perfect wife in Proverbs 31 makes one ask, "Which of his wives was he describing here?" Or did this amazing woman exist only in his imagination?

781. Qoheleth

The Old Testament book known as Ecclesiastes has the title *Qoheleth* in Hebrew. The word is hard to translate, but it has the general meaning of "speaker in the assembly," and when the word appears in the book, translators have used "Preacher" or sometimes "Teacher."

782. astrology

The Old Testament includes severe warnings against any kind of magic or occult dealing, including trying to "read the stars" (see Isa. 47:13; Jer. 10:2). The Babylonians and Egyptians were notorious for trying to read the future of nations or individuals through the movements of the stars and planets. The "Magi" or "wise men" who came to see the infant Jesus were astrologers (Matt. 2), a fact that does not change the Bible's very negative view of astrology.

783. a long, long name

Names in Bible times meant something—for example, the name Jeremiah means "exalted by the Lord." The longest name on record also had a meaning: the prophet Isaiah was told by God to name his son Maher-shalal-hash-baz, meaning "your enemies will soon be destroyed."

784. the queen of heaven

Who was this? The Old Testament mentions the name several times as a pagan goddess that the Israelites were prohibited from worshiping. While many pagan religions had an "earth mother," a kind of fertility goddess, some religions also had a "sky mother," called by different names in different nations. In some ways she was like the earth mother—the divinity that people prayed to for fertile crops, for children, for general well-being. Israel's prophets reminded the people that if they worshiped her, or any other pagan deity, they would inevitably be conquered by the pagan nations around them (see Jer. 7:18; 44:17–19).

785. circumcised but not really

The Hebrews were the only people in the ancient world who attached any religious meaning to the ritual. Many of the neighbor nations of Israel also practiced circumcision, either on infants or on boys coming of age. But the prophet Jeremiah reflected the Israelite view when he spoke of people who were "uncircumcised in heart"—that is, the physical operation had been the same, but only the people of Israel saw circumcision as a sign of God's covenant (see Jer. 9:25).

786. "the hammer of the whole earth"

The Bible is clear on one thing: the proud and the mighty will inevitably fall. The prophet Jeremiah looked at the mighty empire of Babylon, which had ravaged Israel and carried away its people into exile. Yet he predicted—correctly—that "the hammer of the whole earth," Babylon, would be broken and made desolate (Jer. 50:22–25).

787. book eaters

Two men in the Bible were ordered to eat books—or, more accurately, *scrolls.* The prophet Ezekiel was told to eat a scroll, then deliver its message to the people. Ezekiel ate the scroll and found it tasted like honey (Ezek. 3:1–4). In Revelation, John had a slightly different experience: an angel told him to eat a scroll, which would taste like honey—then sour in his stomach (Rev. 10:9–10).

788. the Ancient of Days

This curious phrase occurs only in the book of Daniel, and obviously it refers to the Eternal One, God. In a vision, Daniel sees the Ancient of Days: "His garment was white as snow, and the hair of His head was like pure wool. His throne was a fiery flame" (Dan. 7:9). Obviously "Ancient of Days" is another way of saying "the One who has existed for all eternity."

789. a wife of harlotry

The prophet Hosea was ordered by God to take for himself "a wife of harlotry." Most readers assume the obvious: he married a prostitute. But this may not be correct. More likely it means that the woman (whose name was Gomer) participated in the fertility cults common at the time, cults condemned by righteous prophets such as Hosea. Gomer probably engaged in the ritual intercourse common in fertility rituals—then the rest of the time pursued a normal life. In other words, she wasn't a prostitute, but just an average worldly woman of her time. Even so, her acts are heartily condemned, for God demands total fidelity to Himself. Hosea's love for her symbolized God's love for "whoring" Israel, always chasing after other gods.

790. burden

Literally, a burden is something that must be carried. Figuratively, it refers to a responsibility or a sorrow. Several of the Old Testament prophets referred to their messages to their people as "burdens"—usually as "the burden of the Lord" (see Isa. 13:1; Jer. 23:34 (KJV); Ezek. 12:10; Nah. 1:1; Hab. 1:1; Zech. 12:1; Mal. 1:1).

791. moon turned to blood

Joel 2:31 contains this ominous prophecy: "The sun shall be turned into darkness, and the moon into blood." Some translations have "the moon will turn blood red," which is likely the real meaning. Does this ever happen? Indeed. When the earth comes between the sun and the moon, there is an eclipse of the moon. Because the earth's atmosphere bends the rays of light, the sun's light is reflected by the moon and returned to earth, causing the eclipsed moon to appear red (just as the sun often appears when it is setting).

792. Old in New: the most quoted

The New Testament many, many times quotes the Old, particularly the books of Isaiah, Psalms, and Deuteronomy. The most quoted verse is Psalm 110:1: "The LORD said to my Lord, 'Sit at My right hand, till I make

Your enemies Your footstool.'" The verse, which is interpreted as God speaking to Christ, is quoted or alluded to 16 times in the New Testament. The second most quoted verse is Leviticus 19:18: "You shall love your neighbor as yourself," quoted ten times.

16

Some Choice Tidbits: New Testament

JESUS' LIFE AND WORK

793. gospel singular, not plural

We speak of the "four Gospels" and of the "gospels of Matthew, Mark, Luke, and John." But in the vocabulary of the early Christians, there was only one gospel, *the* gospel—in Greek, *euangelion*, "good news," singular. Thus in the early manuscripts of the New Testament the scribes appended the titles that are sometimes used today: "The Gospel According to Matthew," "The Gospel According to Luke," etc. The first Christians were certain that though there were four authors, there was only one Jesus and one gospel to communicate to the world.

794. Incarnation

This is from Latin, meaning "being in the flesh," and it refers to Jesus, the Son of God, taking on human flesh. The word itself is not found in the Bible, but the idea is certainly there, as in John 1:14: "And the Word became flesh and dwelt among us, and we beheld His glory." The idea is also found in Philippians 2:5–11, where Paul speaks of Christ "taking the form of a bondservant, and coming in the likeness of men. And being found in appearance as a man, He humbled Himself and became obedient to the point of death, even the death of the cross." The New Testament authors are clear on this point: Jesus Christ was fully divine, yet also fully human.

795. Zechariah the doubter

What is the punishment for doubting the word of an angel? Sometimes it is muteness. The aged Zechariah was told by the angel Gabriel that he and his wife, Elizabeth, so long childless, would have a son. Zechariah doubted, and until the birth of the son (who turned out to be John the Baptist) he was unable to speak (Luke 1).

796. the hidden years

The New Testament has a huge gap in it: it tells us nothing about Jesus' life between age twelve (when He was at the Jerusalem temple with Mary and Joseph) and age thirty, probably the age when He began His ministry. Scholars speak of Jesus' "hidden years." Various false gospels were written to fill this gap, most of them silly tales about the boy Jesus performing miracles, and so forth. Luke's gospel does tell us something important about the hidden years: "Jesus increased in wisdom and stature, and in favor with God and men" (Luke 2:52).

797. dating Jesus' baptism

Can we assign specific dates to Jesus' life? In some cases, yes. Luke's gospel tells us that Jesus was baptized in the fifteenth year of the reign of the Roman emperor Tiberius (Luke 3:1). Historians are almost 100 percent certain that this would have been the year 27 or 28.

798. twelve disciples

Twelve is a very biblical number, especially because the nation of Israel was composed of twelve tribes, the descendants of Jacob's twelve sons. Jesus chose twelve men to be His disciples, His closest companions, and we can assume He did so as a symbol that a new Israel was taking shape, based not on descent from Jacob's sons, but on a spiritual connection with Christ.

799. Boanerges

Jesus bestowed this nickname on His two disciples James and John, brothers and fishermen (Mark 3:17). It means "sons of thunder" and may have been used because of their sometimes violent tempers (Luke 9:54–56).

800. Jesus' brothers

At least four men are referred to as Jesus' brothers: James, Joseph, Simon, and Jude (Matt. 13:55; Mark 6:3). Since the Bible refers to Jesus as Mary's firstborn, most readers assume the obvious: these four were younger brothers of Jesus, all of them sons of Joseph and Mary. However, many Catholics, because of their belief that Mary remained a virgin throughout her life, believe that these were actually stepbrothers, the sons of Joseph from a previous marriage. One thing is clear: His brothers did not, during His earthly ministry, accept Him as the Messiah (John 7:5).

Of the New Testament writings, two (the Letters of James and Jude) may have been written by brothers of Jesus, which indicates that at least two of His brothers did become believers at some time.

801. adultery

As the Ten Commandments make clear, adultery was serious business. Put another way, marriage was taken very seriously, a covenant that should never be violated. It was punishable by death in Israel, and even the morally lax pagan nations frowned on adultery. Jesus took the commandment against adultery further: not only should we refrain from the actual deed, but we should avoid thinking adulterous thoughts (Matt. 5:27–30). Like the Old Testament prophets, Jesus could use "adulterous" in a spiritual sense: God's people being unfaithful to Him. Paul claimed that adulterers could not inherit the kingdom of God (1 Cor. 6:9).

802. "abomination of desolation"

This phrase occurs three times in the book of Daniel and was later referred to by Jesus (see Dan. 11:31; 12:11; Matt. 24:15). Just what is the "abomination of desolation"? Probably it refers to some sort of spiritual defiling of the Jerusalem temple at the end of time. Various foreign enemies have defiled (or, in the case of the Roman Empire, destroyed) the temple over the centuries. The phrase may be a symbolic way of referring to an evil power that tries to blaspheme God in some way.

803. how many "Jesuses"?

The name Jesus appears 700 times in the four Gospels and in Acts, but fewer than 70 times in the Epistles. On the other hand, the name Christ appears 60 times in the Gospels and Acts, but 240 times in the Epistles and in Revelation.

804. fire from heaven

In a Samaritan village, Jesus was rejected by villagers. Two of His disciples, the brothers James and John, asked Him, "Lord, do You want us to command fire to come down from heaven and consume them?" (Luke 9:54). The disciples had in mind the great prophet Elijah, who had indeed called down fire upon his enemies (2 Kings 1:12). But Jesus declined. Though He was, like Elijah, the Lord's prophet and a worker of miracles, He was teaching His disciples a new view of loving one's enemies.

805. Simon Bar-Jona

Was the apostle Peter a zealot, one of the anti-Roman revolutionaries who were willing to take up arms to drive out the Romans? Probably not, but more than once in John's gospel, Jesus refers to Simon Peter as "Simon, son of John" (1:42; 21:15–17), but scholars think that when Jesus first spoke in his native tongue of Aramaic, He called Peter "Simon Bar-Jona"—which can mean "Simon, son of John [or Jonah]" but can also be connected with the Semitic word *baryona*, meaning "outlaw," a name that sometimes applied to the Zealots. Matthew 16:17 actually uses *baryona*. Consider that it was Peter who, when Jesus was arrested, wielded a sword (John 18:10).

806. Yeshua the Savior

Did Jesus' contemporaries actually call Him Jesus? Generally, no. Jesus—*Iesous*, in the Greek New Testament—is the Greek form of the Aramaic name *Yeshua*, the name as Jesus would have known it in His own language. Yeshua is the Aramaic form of the older Hebrew name Joshua, one of the great men of the Old Testament. All three names mean "Savior" or "Deliverer."

807. bloods, plural

The word *blood* is hardly ever used in the plural, but that is just what occurs in John 1:13, which speaks of the children of God, who are born not of "bloods." The plural form may mean "genealogies" or "bloodlines," but it may also be referring to Israel's old system of blood sacrifices. According to John, neither human bloodlines nor the old system of blood sacrifices suffices to make a person a child of God.

808. the Old Testament Gospel

Of the four Gospels, Matthew's is unique in citing the Old Testament forty-one times. This is twice as many times as Mark and Luke cite the Old Testament. A distinctive feature of Matthew: he sees these Old Testament passages as being "fulfilled" in the life and work of Jesus. Matthew is concerned to show that Jesus was, in fact, the fulfillment of all that the Jews had hoped for over the centuries. Most scholars believe that Matthew's original readers were Jews who had been converted to Christianity.

809. the "Roman" Gospel

We don't know for certain where the Gospel of Mark was written, nor who made up its original audience. But a very old tradition connects Mark's gospel with Rome. It's fairly clear from reading the gospel that (unlike Matthew) Mark wrote it for non-Jews, for he makes little attempt (as Matthew does) to connect Jesus' deeds with the Old Testament. Like Luke's gospel, Mark's was probably written for pagans who had become Christians.

810. the Gentile Gospel

Luke, author of the Gospel that bears his name, was probably a Gentile, not a Jew. Thus he may be the only Gentile author of a book of the Bible. Luke's gospel is believed to have been written for a Gentile audience. If this is so, and it probably is, there is one curiosity: nowhere in the gospel does Jesus preach to the Gentiles.

811. the Gospel of the Poor

The poor are, all throughout the Bible, the particular concern of God, and God's people are to be judged by the compassion they show the poor. Of the four Gospels, all four show Jesus' love for the poor, but it is especially Luke's that is sometimes called the "Gospel of the Poor." Luke's account is brimming over with attention to the poor, such as the story of the shepherds in Bethlehem (which the other Gospels leave out), Mary's song of praise for the God who lifts up the poor and scorns the proud, the parable of the rich man and the beggar, and many other "pro-poor" touches.

812. "father" minister?

Jesus told His disciples, "Do not call anyone on earth your father; for One is your Father, He who is in heaven" (Matt. 23:9). The Catholic Church has neglected this verse, for most Catholic priests are called "Father" by the people of their parishes. Most Protestant churches do not refer to their pastors as "Father," although the whole message of Matthew 23—being humble, not trying to make oneself seem important—would seem to rule out "Reverend" and "Doctor" also.

813. "Savior," but sparingly

We so often speak of Jesus Christ as Savior that it surprises people to learn that the New Testament hardly ever refers to Him with that word. He is called Savior only twice in the Gospels (Luke 2:11; John 4:42), and a handful of times in Paul's letters, but, curiously, the brief letter known as 2 Peter calls Him Savior five times. The Bible scholars suspect that one reason the New Testament authors used the title sparingly is that many pagan cults used the name Savior to refer to heathen gods. The name was also connected with worship of the Roman emperors, something the early Christians shunned.

814. the no-exorcism gospel

Jesus had power to deliver people from demons, and often used it—but not in the gospel of John. Matthew, Mark, and Luke give a prominent place to Jesus' exorcism, but for some odd reason this activity is never mentioned in John's gospel.

815. shaking the dust off one's feet

"Whoever will not receive you nor hear you, when you depart from there, shake off the dust under your feet as a testimony against them" (Mark 6:11). So Jesus told His disciples. His meaning was this: when you preach the gospel in a place and they reject you, then leave that place to the judgment of God. "Shaking the dust off" was, spiritually, a way of saying, "We are no longer responsible for what happens to you." Apparently some of His apostles followed this advice, for Acts 13:51 tells us that the apostles Paul and Barnabas "shook off the dust from their feet against them."

816. washing one's hands of the matter

Matthew's gospel records an interesting detail that the other three Gospels omit: at Jesus' trial, the Roman governor Pilate seemed to think Jesus innocent of any serious crime, yet the crowd of Jews pressed for Jesus' execution. Weary of the whole matter, Pilate "took water and washed his hands before the multitude, saying, 'I am innocent of the blood of this just Person. You see to it'" (Matt. 27:24).

817. omnipotence

This refers to being "all-powerful," which God is. The word itself does not occur in the Bible, but the idea is everywhere. Unlike the gods of Greek and Roman mythology, who were powerful but bound by fate (or by the interference of some other god), the God of Jews and Christians is all-powerful, with no other god to thwart His will (see Job 42:2; Jer. 32:17; Luke 1:37). Jesus' words "With God all things are possible" (Matt. 19:26) sum up the Bible's view.

818. abomination

This English word translates several Hebrew and Greek words, all connected with idol worship and detestable pagan practices. The basic idea is of something repugnant to the true God and His faithful ones. In the Old Testament the prophets often railed against such pagan horrors as ritual orgies and child sacrifice. The book of Daniel speaks of some horrible abomination in the future (Dan. 9:27; 11:31; 12:11). Some scholars believe this was fulfilled when the Syrian ruler Antiochus Epiphanes set up a pagan altar in the Lord's temple and sacrificed a pig on it. Jesus also predicted a horrible abomination in Jerusalem (Matt. 24:15; Mark 13:14), which may refer to something in the end times or to some events perpetrated by the Romans years after Jesus' ascension.

819. raising the roof

Jesus' reputation as a miraculous healer spread far and wide. A paralyzed man had four friends who took him to Jesus, but because of the crowd they could not get to Him. They were so desperate that they literally tore through the house's roof, lowering the paralyzed man on his mat. This must have made quite an impression—as did Jesus, who told the man to rise, take up his bed, and walk home (Mark 2:1–12).

820. simplicity

In the Beatitudes, Jesus said, "Blessed are the pure in heart" (Matt. 5:8). The New Testament frequently commends the person who is honest, guileless, lacking an ulterior motive. Several Greek words are translated "simple," as, by contrast, are Greek words like *dipsychos* in James 1:8, which is also translated "double-minded" but literally means "double-souled."

Simple does not mean "stupid." It means simple in a moral sense—the simple person is just as he appears to be, with no hidden agenda. Such a person finds favor with God: "The LORD preserves the simple" (Ps. 116:6). On the other hand: "Cleanse your hands, you sinners; and purify your hearts, you double-minded" (James 4:8).

821. "the poor always with you"

Jesus said, "The poor always ye have with you; but me ye have not always" (John 12:8 KJV). Some people find this verse shocking, considering how much Jesus said about showing love and compassion to the poor. Some callous Christians have taken the words to mean "Why bother with social assistance at all?" Clearly that was not Jesus' meaning. He spoke the words when Judas, His disciple, scolded a woman for "wasting" some expensive ointment to anoint Jesus' feet. Jesus took her act for what it was: a spontaneous act of sweetness. He probably also knew that Judas didn't really care for the poor (as the Gospels make clear) but was merely looking for a chance to criticize the woman.

Christians who tour Third World countries—or even the U.S.—and see poor people in the streets in the shadow of a grand cathedral often remember Jesus' words.

822. wheat and tares

Jesus' parable of the wheat and tares is straightforward enough: we cannot always tell righteous people from unrighteous, but God can, and at the Last Judgment, the two will be finally separated (Matt. 13:24–30). Just what are "tares"? Jesus was probably referring to a plant called "darnel," a noxious weed that does resemble wheat. Most readers won't know what "tares" or "darnel" are, so some versions, such as the New International, made a wise choice by using "weed."

823. *raca*

This Aramaic word from the Sermon on the Mount means something like "stupid" or "emptyheaded" or even "loser." Speaking of the commandment not to murder, Jesus extended it a bit further: not only should we not murder, but we also should not nurse anger against someone else, nor call him contemptible names. So we should not call someone "raca," or "fool," or we may be in danger of hell (Matt. 5:21–22). Did Jesus mean that one angry slip of the tongue can send us to hell? Hard to say. Obviously His point was that we can do a lot of harm with our words and that God is listening.

824. the naked detail

All the Gospels give us details about Jesus' arrest, trial, and crucifixion. One curious detail is recorded only in Mark's gospel: a young man was following Jesus the night of the arrest, clad only in a linen sheet (which may mean a sort of nightshirt). The soldier who arrested Jesus grabbed the young man, who slipped out of his only garment and fled away naked. (For the record, "naked" here may not mean "stark naked" but "underdressed," meaning he still had on a sort of loincloth.) Why was this apparently useless detail included? Bible scholars think that the young man may have been Mark himself, including this peculiar detail as a way of saying, "I was there as an eyewitness to these events."

825. Simon of Cyrene

In most crucifixions, the condemned man had to carry on his own shoulders the horizontal beam on which he was to die. Jesus was so exhausted by the horrid chain of events—his trial, the scourging, the crown of thorns— that He fell under the beam's weight. The Roman soldiers forced a bystander, Simon of Cyrene, to carry the beam to the place of execution. We aren't sure why the Gospels even mention this unimportant detail, unless, perhaps, Simon or some of his kin were well known among the early Christians.

826. vinegar as beverage

While in agony on the cross, Jesus was offered a sponge soaked in vinegar—or wine, in some translations. The liquid was in fact a wine vinegar used not just for seasoning but for drinking as well. It was popular among the poor (not being of the best quality as wines go) and among Roman soldiers, who enjoyed it as a sort of "camp drink." When offered to crucified persons, the wine vinegar was mixed with gall or myrrh, the idea being to intensify the numbing effect of the wine. It was a small way of showing some mercy to the crucified person, quenching an excruciating thirst and also helping numb the tortured body (see Matt. 27:34).

827. blood and water

John's gospel account of Jesus' crucifixion includes an interesting detail: one of the Roman soldiers pierced Jesus' side with a spear, and blood and water flowed out (John 19:34). What likely happened was that the spear pierced the heart (which still contains blood even after death) and also pierced the sac around the heart (the hydropericardium), which contains plasma (which, being clear, looks like water). Later Christian commentators, who often had vivid imaginations, said the blood and water were symbols of Communion and baptism.

828. describing the Resurrection

One thing is clear in the New Testament: Jesus was raised from the dead, and His tomb was found empty by His disciples, who later saw the risen Christ. But the Gospels do not tell us exactly how the Resurrection took place, and for a simple reason: there were no human witnesses to it. Over the centuries artists have let their imaginations run riot as they picture Jesus coming from the tomb, but the Bible itself provides no information of how the Resurrection occurred, only that it did.

THE FIRST CHRISTIANS

829. villain Caiaphas

Notorious as the extremely unspiritual high priest of Israel, Caiaphas is one of the nastier characters in the Gospels. High priest from A.D. 18 to 36, Caiaphas was one of many high-ranking Jews who believed that Jesus' activity might result in the Jewish aristocrats losing the privileges they had under the Romans. Caiaphas is credited with stating that it was better for one man (Jesus) to die than to have the whole people perish—a statement that, without his knowing it, turned into a prophecy of Jesus' work as Savior (John 11:41–53). A mockery of a trial for Jesus took place in the house of Caiaphas, who then gladly turned Jesus over to the Roman governor, Pilate (John 18:24–27). Even after Jesus' ascension, Caiaphas took part in the persecution of the apostles (Acts 4:6). Caiaphas is a classic example of the spiritual emptiness of the Jewish priesthood in the New Testament period.

830. "great lamentation"

Acts 7 tells the sad but inspiring story of the stoning of Stephen, the first Christian martyr. Acts 8 relates that some of the Christian brothers buried Stephen "and made great lamentation over him" (8:2). Worth noting: in Jewish custom, stoning was a way of punishing a criminal blasphemer, so there was to be no mourning over such a person. Acts 8:2 is telling the reader that even though the Jews of Jerusalem had "officially" stoned Stephen to death, the Christians mourned for him anyway, not accepting this execution as valid.

831. Herod and the owl

Pride, in the Bible's view, is one of the chief sins of mankind. A textbook case of it was the vain Herod, who appeared before the people of Caesar wearing a silvery robe. It so impressed the people that they began to hail him as a god. But his "divinity" didn't last long: Herod was suddenly struck down and shortly thereafter died—a divine punishment for his acting godlike (Acts 12:21–23). The Jewish historian Josephus records the same incident, but adds an interesting detail: at the moment before Herod was struck down, he saw an owl. At that moment he may have recalled a prophecy he had heard a decade earlier when he served a spell in prison: a fellow prisoner told Herod that if he ever saw an owl again, it would be an omen of his death.

832. *Christianos*

This Greek term from the New Testament is where we get "Christian," of course. The word's ending, *-ianos*, was widely used in the Roman Empire to refer to a slave of the person whose name occurred before *-ianos*. Thus a *Christianos* was a slave of Christ, belonging to Him. (See Acts 11:26; 1 Peter 4:16.)

833. Simeon Niger

Were there any Africans among the first generation of Christians? Possibly. Acts 13:1–3 speaks of a "Simeon who was called Niger" (which means "black"), who was one of the five prophets and teachers in the church at Antioch. It is possible Simeon may have simply been a very dark-skinned resident of that area, and also possible he was one of the dark-skinned Jews from North Africa.

834. the Areopagus

Ares was the Greek god of war, and the city of Athens had a rocky hill called the Areopagus, "hill of Ares." The name Areopagus also applied to the city court that assembled there, sometimes to decide questions of public morals, or to determine if a public speaker was worthy to be heard. Paul, on his missionary travels, appeared before the Areopagus. Most of the council was not impressed with his preaching, though it is worth noting that Paul's words (recorded in Acts 17) have been remembered long after people have forgotten the philosophies believed by the snobbish members of the Areopagus. One member of the Areopagus, Dionysius, did become a convert.

835. "almost persuaded"

"Then Agrippa said unto Paul, Almost thou persuadest me to be a Christian"—so reads the King James Version of Acts 26:28, Paul witnessing to his faith before the cynical official Agrippa. That verse lent the words "Almost Persuaded" to a much-used gospel song, often played at altar calls as an encouragement to people who were "almost persuaded" to give their lives to Christ.

836. Castor and Pollux

These twin brothers of Greek mythology were demigods, that is, the offspring of a god and a mortal. Zeus, the Greeks' chief god, fathered the twins by Leda, one of his many mistresses. The two were honored as heroes, Castor as a horseman, Pollux as a boxer, and after death the two were immortalized as the constellation Gemini (the Twins). The two were popular with sailors, which explains why the ship on which Paul sailed (Acts 28:11) was named for the two.

837. Phoebe

The New Testament church was full of dedicated and faithful women. Among them was Phoebe, whom Paul praised for her assistance to him and many others (Rom. 16:1–2). She was an important figure in the congregation at Cenchrea, the port of Corinth. There is an old tradition that it was she who carried Paul's Letter to the Romans to the congregation in Rome.

838. Paul's coauthors

"I, Tertius, who wrote this epistle, greet you in the Lord"—so reads Romans 16:22, indicating to us that there was Paul's coauthor of the letter—or, more likely, a scribe taking down dictation. However, 1 Corinthians opens with a greeting from Paul and from "Sosthenes our brother." Likewise, 2 Corinthians is from Paul and "Timothy, our brother." Philippians and Colossians are also from both Paul and Timothy, while 1 and 2 Thessalonians are from Paul, Silvanus (also known as Silas), and Timothy. Thus Timothy has the distinction of being not only the recipient of two letters from Paul, but also a cosender of four of Paul's letters.

How much input did these coauthors have? We have no idea. Most likely Paul did the chief composition of the letters (using a scribe, probably) and affixed these Christian friends' names as a courtesy to them. While the New Testament gives some information about Timothy and Silvanus (Silas), we know nothing whatsoever about Tertius, except that Paul obviously trusted him as a scribe. Sosthenes is another matter: he may be the Sosthenes of Acts 18:17, a synagogue ruler of Corinth who was beaten by the crowd in the presence of Gallio, a Roman official.

839. ambassador

An ambassador is one who officially represents a ruler or other eminent person. Paul spoke twice of being an ambassador, not for an earthly ruler, but for the King of kings, Christ. In 2 Corinthians 5:20 is his famous statement that all Christians are "ambassadors for Christ." In Ephesians 6:20 Paul spoke of himself as an "ambassador in chains"—the King's representative, but one who was being persecuted.

840. quadrilingual Paul

The common language of the Jews in the Near East in New Testament times was Aramaic, the everyday language that Jesus and His apostles would have spoken. Paul, with much training in the Jewish law, would have also known Hebrew quite well and, given his missionary travels around the Roman Empire, definitely knew the common Greek used across the empire. (His letters are in Greek, with an occasional word or two in Aramaic.) We can feel fairly certain that Paul knew a fourth language, Latin, Rome's official language.

841. the Mediterranean

The Romans called it *Mare Nostrum*—"our sea," since they controlled the land all around it. The ancient Hebrews really had no name for it at all. Since it was the only really huge body of water they knew, they referred to it simply as "the Sea." Because of his missionary journeys around the Roman Empire, the apostle Paul probably knew the Mediterranean better than any other Bible character.

842. barbarians

We use it to refer to people who are crude, uncivilized, even violent. In the New Testament period it meant something more specific: people who did not speak Greek. (The

Greeks, having a high opinion of themselves, said that non-Greek-speakers were merely babbling—"bar bar" referring to their babbling speech.) The New Testament uses "barbarians" in the sense of "non-Greeks." See Acts 28:2–4 (KJV), where the inhabitants of the island of Malta are called barbarians. Paul's letters make it clear that in God's sight, all are equally sinful and all can be saved— even Greeks, even "barbarians" (Col. 3:11).

843. Crete

"Cretans are always liars, evil beasts, lazy gluttons" (Titus 1:12). So said Paul, who followed this with "This testimony is true." Sounds highly prejudiced, doesn't it? He was writing to his protégé Titus, head of the Christian community on the Greek isle of Crete. Paul was actually quoting the Greek poet Callimachus, but he apparently believed the poet's words. If so, Titus had his work on the island cut out for him. Paul may have had in mind that Mount Ida on Crete was, so the myths said, the birthplace of the chief god Zeus—obviously a lie, since there was no Zeus.

844. *athlesis*

Our word *athlete* comes from the Greek *athlesis*, meaning "fight" or "strive" or "contest." Paul used the work several times, referring to the good fight of faith (1 Tim. 6:12), praying fervently (Col. 4:12), and competing for the "prize," the "imperishable crown" given to Christians who endure (1 Cor. 9:24–27). Paul made it clear that disciplining one's body to lead a moral life was just as strenuous, or more so, than being an athlete in training.

845. "abide in the same calling"

"Let every man abide in the same calling wherein he was called" (1 Cor. 7:20 KJV). So said the apostle Paul to the Christians in Corinth. And so did many Southerners in the pre–Civil War years, who took Paul's words as applying to slavery. The pro-slavery people had a point: nowhere in the Old or New Testament is slavery prohibited.

846. triumph

We use it to mean simply "victory," but in New Testament days it meant much more: a triumph was a magnificent parade in honor of a victorious general. He would enter the city of Rome in a chariot, along with high-ranking officials and, most important, the spoils of his victory— treasures he had captured from his enemies, and his captive enemies themselves, in chains. Paul referred twice to triumphs, but both times the "general" was God Himself, leading His redeemed people, while the conquered captives are the evil powers that man has been saved from (see 2 Cor. 2:14; Col. 2:15).

847. revelings

The Greek word *komos* literally means "orgy," which is how English Bibles sometimes translate it. It can also be translated "revelings," and either way it refers to lustful indulgence of the type usually associated with pagan religions. Paul includes revelings in his lists of sins that will exclude people from the kingdom of God (Gal. 5:21), and Peter likewise condemned revelings (1 Peter 4:3).

848. the love of silver

Paul's famous statement on money was that "the love of money is the root of all evil" (1 Tim. 6:10 KJV)—*not* money itself, but the love of it. The actual text in the Greek speaks of *philarguria*—"love of silver." Almost all coins in those days were silver, so someone who loved silver was a "lover of coins." In the days before paper money, "coins" was the same as "money."

849. Narcissus

In Greek myth, he was the beautiful youth who fell in love with his own reflection in a pool, and from his name we get *narcissist*, a person in love with himself. (Yes, the flower narcissus is named after him also.) There was actually a Narcissus mentioned in the Bible: Paul greeted the household of Narcissus in Rome, which doesn't necessarily include Narcissus himself (see Rom. 16:11).

850. growing a Christian

Most of the New Testament is concerned with the first generation of Christians, so most of the people who convert to the faith are adults. But a new generation of Christians was being raised by Christian parents, the best example being the young pastor Timothy, the protégé of the apostle Paul. In one of his two letters to Timothy giving pastoral advice, Paul mentions that Timothy had received his spiritual training from his grandmother Lois and his mother Eunice (2 Tim. 1:5).

851. no-Sabbath Paul

Here is a curiosity: Paul, the faithful Jew who would have grown up observing the Sabbath rest on the seventh day, never told Christians to do so. While we know the earliest Christians, all Jews, still kept the Sabbath as a day of worship, non-Jews had no particular regard for the Sabbath. Apparently Paul, the "apostle to the Gentiles," felt no obligation to impose the old Jewish Sabbath customs on non-Jews. As the faith spread among the Gentiles, they adopted the custom (which we still follow) of observing the first day (the day of Jesus' resurrection) as the day of rest and worship.

852. the lost epistle to Laodicea

The apostle Paul's letters are highly valued, but, alas, one of them has been lost: the Epistle to the Laodiceans, which Paul refers to in Colossians 4:16. What became of it? No one knows. We do know that sometime in the fourth century some devout Christian composed "St. Paul's Epistle to the Laodiceans." It circulated for many years but was never accepted as inspired Scripture.

853. what author?

Of the many epistles in the New Testament, only two do not name their author at the beginning: Hebrews and 1 John. No one is certain who exactly wrote Hebrews, but an old tradition connects 1 John with the disciple who also wrote the Gospel of John, and the epistles known as 2 John and 3 John.

854. the Catholic Epistles

This has nothing to do with the Roman Catholic Church. The word *catholic* originally meant "universal." Several of the New Testament letters—James, 1 and 2 Peter, 1–3 John, and Jude—are not addressed to specific individuals or churches but to all Christians everywhere. That is, their audience is "universal," so these have traditionally been called the "Catholic Epistles," or sometimes the "General Epistles." (Since all the New Testament letters are now read by Christians everywhere, *all* of them are, strictly speaking, General Epistles.)

855. Peter on rocks and stones

Simon the fisherman was given the name Peter (the Greek word *Petros*, meaning "rock") by Jesus (Matt. 16:18). Perhaps this image stuck in Peter's mind, for years later as a leader among the Christians he wrote a letter speaking of all Christians as "living stones," which are being built by God into a "spiritual house." Of course, Peter also noted that the chief stone was Christ Himself (1 Peter 2:4–5).

856. Peter in Babylon

Was the apostle Peter ever in Babylon? The ancient city, mostly a ruin at the time Peter lived, was way off the apostles' path. Yet 1 Peter 5:13 contains a greeting from those in "Babylon." Commentators are pretty sure that this was Peter's sly way of referring to Rome—chief city of the empire, and as notorious for its materialism and immorality as Babylon had been centuries before. Tradition says that both Peter and Paul were martyred in Rome.

857. "the elect lady"

The tiny letter known as 2 John is addressed to "the elect
lady and her children." Scholars have puzzled over this:
Was John writing to a Christian woman and her family?
If so, then 2 John has the distinction of being the only
book of the Bible addressed specifically to a woman. But
most likely John was using "lady" in a figurative sense: a
church, that is, a community of Christians (the "children"). The epistle ends this way: "The children of your
elect sister greet you." Most likely John was passing
along a greeting from another Christian congregation.

858. "the beloved Gaius"

Gaius was a fairly common name in the Roman Empire
(being the first name of the famous Julius Caesar, in fact).
There are three of them mentioned in the New
Testament, all three connected with the life and ministry
of Paul. It is possible that one of these three may be the
"beloved Gaius" to whom the brief letter known as
3 John was sent. As with other New Testament letters sent
to individuals, it is obvious that John intended the letter
to be read aloud to his Christian fellowship.

859. Diotrephes

Many pastors, particularly those of small churches, are aware that certain laymen want a "one-man church"—that is, want themselves to be the center of attention. This began early in Christian history, as the tiny letter known as 3 John indicates. John wrote the elder Gaius about a certain Diotrephes, who was attempting to dominate the Christian community. John was aware that pride and love or preeminence is what motivates such people, and it is stark contrast to the Christian ideals of humility and self-lessness.

860. apocalyptic

The Bible's last book, Revelation, is also known as Apocalypse, from a Greek word meaning "unveiling" (or even "revelation"). The term "apocalyptic" applies to the type of literature like Revelation, dealing with the end of the world, often delivering its message in dramatic and often violent symbolism. Apocalyptic literature always has an appeal to believers, particularly during times of persecution, when its message that God triumphs over evil gives hope and comfort.

861. seven stars

In the first vision of the book of Revelation, John sees Christ, who "had in His right hand seven stars" (1:16). Scholars have argued over what the stars symbolize, but one possibility is this: the Roman emperors were sometimes depicted with seven stars in their right hand, which symbolized their power over the whole world. By depicting Jesus this way, John was saying that Christ, not the Roman emperor, was the true Ruler of the world.

862. the sword of Faithful and True

Revelation 19 describes a rider on a white horse, a rider called Faithful and True, and from His mouth issues a sharp sword for striking the nations. Needless to say, the images from Revelation have been interpreted a thousand ways, but most scholars agree that the rider represents Christ (who is faithful and true) and, most likely, the sharp sword represents the Word of God, which "strikes" the nation not literally but spiritually.

863. weeding out the false books

Twenty-seven books made it into our New Testament, and a lot of very weird material didn't. The early Christians chose the four Gospels over many other false Gospels, some of them geared toward teaching Gnosticism or other religions. It appears that when

Christians were deciding which writings were and were not truly inspired by God, they used these criteria: (1) emphasis on the historical reality of Jesus' life, death, and resurrection, (2) accepting the Old Testament as God's revelation pointing toward Jesus, and (3) the firm belief that God's revelation was accessible to all, not just to a spiritual elite (which was a noted feature of the various Gnostic cults).

864. Christian cannibals

In Christianity's early days, pagans were highly suspicious of the church. There was a rumor that Christians gathered together for some kind of ritual meal where they ate the body and drank the blood of Christ. This was, of course, the Lord's Supper, where the Christians were actually eating bread and drinking wine, symbols of Jesus' sacrifice of His life. More than a few pagans accused Christians of cannibalism, eating the man (or god) they claimed to worship.

17

Songs and Music and Such

865. hymns

Were there hymns in the New Testament church? Definitely. Jesus and His disciples sang a hymn (possibly one of the Psalms) following the Last Supper (Matt. 26:30). The missionaries Paul and Silas sang hymns even while in prison (Acts 16:25), and Paul several times reminded Christians to sing hymns (1 Cor. 14:26; Eph. 5:19; Col. 3:16). Most likely the early Christian hymns were *a capella*, with no musical accompanist.

866. women in choirs

Prior to the twentieth century, women were prohibited from singing in most church choirs, particularly in Catholic churches. The church authorities based this practice on the words of Paul: "Let your women keep silent in the churches, for they are not permitted to speak" (1 Cor. 14:34). Thus Catholic churches had choirs of men and boys, but not women. (Nuns in convents could sing, since only women were present.) After the Vatican II council in the 1960s, the Catholic Church's position on this officially changed, allowing women in choirs.

867. "human composures"

Most people can't imagine a church service without hymns, but for a long time there was strong resistance to hymn-singing. In England in the 1500s, Puritans objected to hymns as being things of "human composure"—that is, not "divine composure," like the Psalms in the Bible. It took many years before this resistance to "human composure" broke down.

868. the benefits of Psalm singing

In the 1300s, noted cleric and author Richard Rolle translated some of the Psalms from Latin into English. He wrote that psalm singing had numerous benefits for Christians: "psalm singing chases fiends, excites angels to our helps, removes sin, pleases God. It shapes perfection, removes and destroys annoyance and anguish of soul."

869. More Psalms

Sir Thomas More (1478–1535), the English statesman executed because he defied King Henry VIII, was a deeply religious man who began every morning by reciting seven psalms (in Latin). While being conveyed to the Tower of London, where execution awaited him, he sang psalms, later telling his son-in-law that this singing "gave the devil a foul fall indeed."

870. Geneva jigs

In the 1500s, during the reign of Mary Tudor ("Bloody Mary," because she executed many Protestants), numerous Protestants fled to Switzerland, where they were impressed by the progress of Protestantism there. They liked the new Protestant habit of singing Psalms in worship, notably in the city of Geneva. After Mary's death, when her Protestant sister Elizabeth I came to reign, the Protestants returned to England, bringing the psalm singing with them. Elizabeth herself didn't think highly of the habit—she called the musical psalms "Geneva jigs." Yet she encouraged the people in the practice, and she herself made some attempts at setting some psalms in a rhyming, singable form.

871. two kinds of cymbals

The last psalm, 150, tells us to "praise him upon the loud cymbals; praise him upon the high sounding cymbals!"

(KJV). It isn't just repeating itself: the Israelites had two kinds of cymbals. The "loud" ones were like our modern cymbals, very large, with one held in each hand. The "high sounding" cymbals were much smaller, played by one hand, with one cymbal attached to the thumb, one to the middle finger (what we today call, appropriately, "finger cymbals").

872. symbolic psaltery

A musical instrument called the King James Version book of *psaltery* was widely used in ancient times and is mentioned in the Psalms (33:2; 92:3; 144:9). Most likely it was a ten-stringed instrument with four sides, flat like a zither (resembling what today would be called an autoharp). Early Christians liked the psaltery and saw some symbolism in its design: its ten strings symbolized the Ten Commandments, and its four sides symbolized the Gospels.

873. jingle-less tambourines

A tambourine-like instrument for beating out rhythms was the Hebrew *toph*, which is translated "tambourine" in many Bibles. It was, we think, a wooden ring with a skin stretched over it, but without the jingles that modern tambourines have. For some reason it was mostly played by women (see Ex. 15:20; Judg. 11:34; 1 Sam. 18:6).

874. trumpets

They have long been connected with the military, and this was certainly true in Bible days. The Lord instructed Moses to construct trumpets of hammered silver for calling the community together and for heading into battle (Num. 10:1–2, 9–10). But trumpets were also a call to the community to prepare for religious festivals. These were fairly simple instruments, with no valves for changing notes—more like bugles than trumpets today. There were 120 trumpets sounded by priests in the temple (2 Chron. 5:12).

875. *selah*

Sometimes Bible translators just throw up their hands and say, "We don't know what this word means!" This is true of a Hebrew word that occurs many times in the Psalms, *selah*. (Curiously, it also occurs three times in the book of Habakkuk.) Since the Psalms were often sung or recited to music, the scholars think that *selah* was some kind of musical direction, maybe an indication of a pause for a musical interlude. Some Bible translations simply omit the word because no one understands it.

A FEW SELECT SONGS

876. "Jerusalem"

Many people saw and enjoyed the movie *Chariots of Fire* without being aware that the movie's title is from the poem "Jerusalem" by William Blake (1757–1827). The song is sung by a boys' choir in the movie, though most people don't remember it. The message of Blake's poem is this: England can be spiritually transformed, with the New Jerusalem taking shape, as long as its people make spiritual war with their "arrows of gold" and their "chariots of fire." Blake claimed he based his poem on Numbers 11:29: "Would God that all the LORD's people were prophets" (KJV).

877. "Break Thou the Bread of Life"

This hymn is often used in Communion, though in fact the "bread" referred to is the Bible. Mary Lathbury's words, written in 1877, are concerned with the Scriptures being opened to the believer: "Show me the truth concealed within Thy Word, / And in Thy Book revealed I see the Lord."

878. "Father of Mercies, in Thy Word"

Anne Steele (1716–1778), a Baptist minister's daughter, faced a major setback: her fiancé died on the day of their wedding. Poor Anne, using the pen name "Theodosia," devoted herself to writing poems and hymns, notably this one about the Bible. The fourth stanza is particularly moving: "Divine Instructor, gracious Lord, / Be thou forever near; / Teach me to love thy sacred Word / And find my Savior there."

879. "Wonderful Words of Life"

Philip P. Bliss (1838–1876) was a noted writer of the rousing "gospel songs" used in evangelistic meetings, and he was an associate of noted evangelist D. L. Moody. One of his many hymns is this tribute to the Bible, with its chorus of "Beautiful words, wonderful words, wonderful words of life."

880. "The Heavens Declare Thy Glory, Lord"

Isaac Watts (1674–1748), English pastor and one of the great hymn writers of all time, based this hymn on Psalm 19, which says the "heavens declare the glory of God." But Watts put a new spin on the psalm: he turned the hymn into praise of the Bible, which declares God's glory even more clearly than the heavens do: "The rolling sun, the changing light, / And nights and days Thy power confess; / But the blest volume Thou hast writ, / Reveals Thy justice and Thy grace."

881. Ebenezer

Charles Dickens chose it as the name of the miser Scrooge in his *Christmas Carol*. The name is from the Bible, 1 Samuel 7:12: God gave Israel a victory over the Philistines, and Samuel took a stone, setting it up as a kind of monument to the victory. The stone was called *Ebenezer*—"stone of help." The word crops up in the wonderful old hymn "Come, Thou Fount of Every Blessing," which has the line "Here I raise my Ebenezer."

882. "the Bible tells me so"

A favorite hymn for children is this 1859 classic by Anna Bartlett Warner, "Jesus Loves Me," with its affirmation "Yes, Jesus loves me, / the Bible tells me so." Curiously, the twentieth-century Swiss theologian Karl Barth, who wrote massive volumes of Christian theology, once said that he could sum up his faith with the hymn's words "Jesus loves me, this I know, for the Bible tells me so."

18

The Bible and the Jews

883. did God condone polygamy?

The story of Adam and Eve suggests that God's original plan for mankind was for marriage to consist of one man with one woman. Jesus Himself certainly approved this idea (Mark 10:6–9). So why did so many notable men of the Old Testament have multiple wives as well as concubines? Think of Jacob, David, Solomon, and other notables. Just as with the pagan nations, high-ranking men of Israel had many wives, usually as a sign of wealth and status. Did God approve of this? Hard to say. Bible scholars like to say that God tolerated the practice in the old days, though by the New Testament period there is no allowance at all for polygamy. Certainly the soap opera antics of David's wives and children are a stern warning to anyone: "Don't try this—it leads to nothing but trouble!"

884. honey on the page

Here's an interesting tradition in Jewish schools, still observed in some areas: new students would touch a page of the Torah with a drop of honey on it to their lips. Perhaps the teachers had in mind Proverbs 24:13–14, which speaks of wisdom being as sweet as honey.

885. the day of the Jews

Under the rule of Rome, Jews had certain legal privileges. But on the whole, the Romans detested the Jews and their religion. They especially detested and mocked the Jews' observance of the Sabbath. To the practical-minded and materialistic Romans, Sabbath observance meant that one day out of seven was wasted, with no work being done, even among Jewish slaves. The Romans referred to the Sabbath as the "day of the Jews." After the Roman emperor Constantine became a Christian in the 300s, he mandated that one day out of seven be observed as a day of rest and worship.

886. Rome is Edom is Rome

In the New Testament period, Israel was unhappy under the Roman occupation. Knowing that the Roman Empire did not like to be criticized, the people of Israel often spoke of Rome as "Edom," the name of a heathen nation to the south and west of Israel. Edom had, centuries before, been conquered by King David of Israel, but in later times Edom was a thorn in Israel's side, often plundering Israel when larger nations (such as Assyria and Babylon) were doing the same. The people of Israel kept alive a hope that when the Messiah came He would, like David of old, again subdue "Edom"—that is, they hoped for a Deliverer who would drive out the hated Romans. It was safer to murmur against "Edom" than to speak openly about their hatred for Rome.

887. why twenty-two books?

There are twenty-two letters in the Hebrew alphabet, and, centuries ago, some Jewish scholars decided that twenty-two was also the appropriate number for the inspired books of the Old Testament. Attentive readers today know there are thirty-nine books in our Old Testament, but wait: in the old days, the twelve Minor Prophets composed one book altogether, while Samuel, Kings, and Chronicles were not divided (as now) into 1 and 2. Also, Ezra and Nehemiah composed one book. So, counted that way, there are twenty-two books in the Old Testament.

888. star of David

In Hebrew it is *magen David*, meaning "shield of David." It is the familiar six-pointed star formed by two triangles.

We don't know for certain if it originated with King David, but we do know it was later used in Israel as a kind of decorative symbol. By the time of Jesus it was a familiar symbol in Palestine. In modern times Jews have chosen it as their special symbol in the same way that Christians use the cross. It appears, naturally—on the flag of the nation of Israel (see 427).

889. boxing the Bible

In Deuteronomy 6:8, God commands the Israelites to adhere to His words: "You shall bind them as a sign on your hand, and they shall be as frontlets between your eyes." Devout Jews have taken this commandment literally, and that is why, in morning worship, some Jewish men wear the *tefillin*, small black boxes attached by straps to the head and to the left arm. The boxes contain (as the commandment requires) verses from the Bible. The boxes are also known as phylacteries.

890. tallit

The tallit is the rectangular prayer shawl worn by adult male Jews during morning service. The tallit, made of wool or silk, is white, with stripes at the ends. The wearing of it is prescribed in Numbers 15:38–39, which mandates that it have *tzitzit* (fringes or tassels) at its corners.

891. God at the door

God, speaking through Moses, told the Israelites that His commandments to them were so important that "you shall write them on the doorposts of your house and on your gates" (Deut. 6:9). Pious Jews have taken this command literally, affixing at their homes' doorposts small cases containing verses from the Old Testament. Each case is known as a *mezuzah*, and it contains Bible verses written (naturally) in Hebrew. The case has a small slit so that the Hebrew word *Shaddai* (meaning "Almighty") is visible.

892. Elijah in Jewish ritual

God's faithful prophet Elijah is one of the most appealing characters in the Bible, particularly his famous "exit" (taken to heaven in a chariot of fire, 2 Kings 2:11). At the seder meal, the ceremonial meal that marks the beginning of the Jews' Festival of Passover, one cup of wine is poured but not drunk—the cup for the prophet Elijah. According to Jewish tradition, the prophet will arrive on Passover eve to usher in the new age. After Elijah's cup is filled, the home's door is opened to let him in. Some wealthy families have expensive wine cups especially made for Elijah.

Also worth noting: an empty chair is reserved for Elijah at the Jewish circumcision ceremony.

893. Jonah and the Day of Atonement

The brief book of Jonah is read in its entirety in Jewish synagogues on the annual Day of Atonement. The book, with its story of the reluctant prophet who was swallowed by a whale and went on to preach a message of repentance to the pagan people of Nineveh, is a touching tale of sin and forgiveness, and thus highly appropriate for the Jews' annual festival of divine mercy.

894. contradictory Ecclesiastes

The book of Ecclesiastes had some difficulty in being accepted as inspired Scripture by Israel's rabbis. Why? Though the book is fascinating, it also seems to contradict itself in places. For example, it states that pleasure is useless (2:2) but then tells us to enjoy pleasure (8:15). It states that people already dead are better off than the living (4:2) but later says that a living dog is better off than a dead lion (9:4). It speaks of the greatness of wisdom (2:13) but then asks what advantage a wise man has over a fool (6:8). Had not the book been attributed to the great and wise King Solomon, the rabbis might never have accepted it as divinely inspired.

895. Song of Songs, Holy of Holies

The Song of Solomon, also called the Song of Songs, is one of the least-read books of the Bible. It does not mention God at all, has no moral teaching, and does not even tell an interesting story. It seems, on the surface, to be a pretty blatant celebration of physical attraction—not a bad thing, but hardly "spiritual." But many interpreters seize on the book as an allegory—that is, the book is not about the love between man and woman, but between God and His people, and each verse of the book holds deep spiritual meanings. The noted Rabbi Akiva, around the year A.D. 90, stated that "all the Writings are holy, but the Song of Songs is the Holy of Holies."

896. Philo of Alexandria

Ever wonder how the very secular Song of Solomon got into the Bible? It appears to be a set of poems celebrating physical attraction, but for centuries Jews have interpreted it allegorically, saying that it represents God's love for Israel. Christians have followed suit by saying it represents Christ's love for His church. For the allegorical method of interpreting the Bible we can thank Philo, who lived at the same time as Jesus. Philo was an extremely educated, sophisticated Jew who wanted to make his religion acceptable to Greek and Roman intellectuals. He knew they were put off by the sometimes crude and violent Old Testament stories, so he "cleaned up" these stories by interpreting them allegorically. (For the record, many Greek philosophers did the same thing with Greek myths, which are far more violent and sexual than anything in the Bible.) Philo's method of interpreting the Bible was used by many early Christian scholars.

897. noninstrumental synagogues

If you read the Psalms, you definitely get the impression that music was a big part of worship in Israel. Likewise the books of Kings and Chronicles witness to the role of music in the Jerusalem temple. Harps, drums, tambourines, and other instruments were in abundance. But something dramatically altered this: the destruction of the temple by the Romans in the year A.D. 70. The leaders of Israel ruled that, as a gesture of national mourning, no instrumental music would be played in the synagogues. The custom held for centuries.

898. the ninth of Ab

God's temple in Jerusalem was destroyed twice, and on exactly the same day—650 years apart. The first temple, built by Solomon, was destroyed by the Babylonians. Centuries later, the Romans destroyed the third temple, largely built by Herod the Great. Both destructions happened on the ninth day of the Jewish month of Ab, which Jews still commemorate with a fast.

899. the Wailing Wall

Visitors to Jerusalem, particularly devout Jews, always visit the Wailing Wall. It is all the Romans left of the temple complex that existed at the time of Jesus. The Wailing

Wall, also known as the Western Wall, was a retaining wall around the temple complex, built by Herod the Great.

900. was Jesus literate?

Definitely, yes. We see this in the Gospels, where Jesus reads from the scroll of Isaiah in His hometown synagogue (Luke 4:17). In fact, most Jews then and now were literate, for they placed great importance on each adult male being able to read the sacred words of the Old Testament. Throughout world history, most "common folk" (such as Jesus and His family) have not been literate, nor needed to be, but this was never the case with Jews, who made literacy a top priority.

901. "five fifths"

Traditionally, Jews hold the first five books of the Bible to be the most important part. Genesis through Deuteronomy, also called the Torah and the Law, are referred to as "five fifths of the Law"—that is, the Law in its completeness.

902. "godless" books of the Bible

Two books of the Old Testament—Esther and the Song of Solomon—do not mention the name of God. The

Jewish rabbis accepted the Song as sacred because, though it is a set of love poems, they believed it symbolized the love of God for Israel. Esther was probably accepted as sacred because it was connected with the popular Jewish Feast of Purim.

903. tithing spices

In the New Testament, the Pharisees were known for their keeping of the Law. As faithful Jews, they tithed—in fact, they took tithing so seriously that they tithed even their spices: mint, dill, and cumin. Jesus told them that this fussiness over little details was less important than pursuing justice, mercy, and faithfulness (Matt. 23:23).

904. the poor man's diet

In Bible times, people ate sparingly for the obvious reason: most people couldn't afford to eat well. Meat was a luxury for most, as was good wine. People who could afford to eat well did—such as King Nebuchadnezzar of Babylon. Daniel 1 tells the story of the saintly Daniel and his three Jewish friends who were "interns" at Nebuchadnezzar's court. The four opted for a diet of vegetables and water, turning down the rich foods and wines the king offered them. At the end of three years, they were healthier than the interns who had eaten the king's fare.

905. "eyes of flirtation"

In Jewish tradition dating from well before Christ, women and men sat in separate sections during worship, a situation that was true in the Jerusalem temple and in synagogues. This did not hold true for Christians at the very beginning, but at various periods in Christian history, men and women have sat separately. The Puritans who settled New England did so, believing that they needed to prevent young men and women from "casting eyes of flirtation upon one another during the reading of the Sacred Scriptures."

906. the magic five

The Jews did and do assign great importance to the first five books of the Bible, known as the five books of Moses (Genesis through Deuteronomy). They liked this fivefold division so much that they long ago applied it to the Psalms as well, dividing them into five sections. (These could be called the "five books of David," since David wrote many of the psalms and is the author most associated with the book.)

907. the council at Jamnia

When the Romans destroyed the Jewish temple in A.D. 70, they pretty much ended Jerusalem's role as the center of Jewish life. The Sanhedrin, the great ruling council of the Jews, ceased to function. Sometime around the year 90, a council of Jewish teachers assembled at Jamnia on the coast of Palestine, with the purpose of deciding what was, and was not, sacred Scripture for the Jews. This was significant not only for themselves but for Christians also, since Christians followed the Jews' lead in matters of what was inspired Scripture.

The Jews had determined much earlier that the Law (the first five books of the Bible) and the Prophets (the historical books, plus the Major and Minor Prophets) were definitely inspired Scripture, but the group known as the Writings were still in doubt. Of the Writings, the Psalms were definitely regarded as inspired, but the chief doubts surrounded Ecclesiastes and the Song of Solomon. Ecclesiastes posed some problems because of its cynicism, but its very religious ending and its connection with Solomon helped it gain acceptance. The Song of Solomon was another matter: Did this group of erotic love songs deserve to be taken as Scripture—even if Solomon was the author? The rabbis had the obvious solution: take the love songs allegorically, that is, as exchanges of love between God and His chosen people.

908. the holy tongue

An old Jewish tradition holds that man's original language—the language Adam would have used to utter his first words—was Hebrew. Rabbis did (and still do) refer to Hebrew as "the holy tongue."

909. "Have you not read . . . ?"

Were the people Jesus moved among a *literate* people? Probably so. We know Jesus Himself could read (since He read from the scroll in His hometown synagogue, Luke 4:16), and on several occasions He clinched an argument with his opponents by saying, "Have you not read . . . ?" (see Matt. 12:3; 19:4; 21:42; Mark 2:25; 12:26). This assumes that the Jews of His time were literate enough to read the Scriptures themselves.

910. the master copy

In the days before photocopiers, copying had to be done the old, hard way: by hand. Naturally human nature means errors may creep in. Yet Bible scholars marvel at how faithful the copyists of the Old Testament were. The Jews took their Scriptures seriously, and the sacred words had to be copied from another scroll, not from dictation. The final authority was the master copy of the Scriptures, kept in the Jerusalem temple until the Romans destroyed it in the year A.D. 70. Each synagogue had its own copy of the Scriptures, kept in a cupboard that faced toward Jerusalem.

911. the book people

Christianity took from Judaism a key idea: books are an essential part of religion. The pagan world, such as the

Roman Empire in which Christianity began, had no such concept of religion, which was mostly a matter of rituals and oral traditions. Like the Jews before them, the Christians liked to be able to say, "Look it up—it's in the Book."

912. mass divorce

According to the prophet Malachi, God clearly hates divorce (Mal. 2:16)—but apparently there are exceptions to this. When the Jews were allowed to return from their forced exile to Babylon, the leader Ezra found that many of the Jewish men had defied the laws of Moses and married outside the faith. Ezra called for a period of repentance, then suggested that the men divorce their pagan wives so as to turn away God's wrath. Hundreds of men followed his advice and divorced their idol-worshiping wives (see Ezra 9:1–10:44).

913. circumcision, where timing is everything

The Old Testament commands, and the Jews still practice, circumcising male infants on the eighth day of life. Why the eighth day? For centuries no one knew there was a sound medical reason for this. Apparently there are two specific factors in human blood that allow it to clot safely and quickly, aiding in healing and preventing infection. The two factors are vitamin K and prothrombin, which are believed to be at their highest levels ever on the eighth day of life. In other words, if you are going to cause a newborn child to bleed, the eighth day is the ideal time to do so. Coincidence, or was God's command rooted in the divine knowledge of the human body?

914. the foreskin collection

Israel's neighbors often snickered at the Israelites for their practice of circumcision, and the Israelites often sneered at their neighbors as the "uncircumcised." In one notable story, foreskins were, oddly, the price for gaining a wife. The rising young military star David wished to marry the daughter of King Saul. The king was growing jealous of David's military exploits, so he set David a high price to marry his daughter: one hundred foreskins from the enemies of Israel, the Philistines. In other words, David had to kill one hundred Philistine men in battle—a major task that would likely result in his own death. But David was up to the challenge: he returned not with 100 foreskins foreskins, but with two hundred. (See 1 Sam. 18:17–30.)

915. Purim

This popular Jewish holiday is based on the book of Esther, which tells of the plot of the wicked Persian official, Haman, to exterminate the Jews in Persia. His plot is discovered by a wise Jew, Mordecai, and Mordecai's cousin Esther (who happens to be married to the Persian emperor). Haman is hanged, the Jews defend themselves, and to this day Jews celebrate "the fourteenth day of the month of Adar with gladness and feasting, as a holiday, and for sending presents to one another" (Est. 9:19). The book of Esther never mentions God, and the holiday has a definite secular tone, with heavy drinking as well as eating the triangular fruit pies called "Haman's hats." While the book of Esther is read aloud, the people use noisemakers to drown out Haman's name whenever it is mentioned.

916. no sacred translations

Most Christians would say that a good, reliable translation of the Bible is as trustworthy and sacred as the Hebrew and Greek originals. This is not true for Jews: for them, the Hebrew Bible (they do not read the New Testament, of course) is the only sacred and authoritative Scripture. All translations are, well, just translations. There have been some popular translations into various modern languages, but none of these have ever been officially authorized or approved by any Jewish ruling body. The Hebrew original is the only "real" Bible.

917. Jews and the KJV

Hebrew is, for Jews, the sacred language, the language of their Bible. But there is a problem: most Jews don't read or speak Hebrew. In the 1800s, a Jewish scholar named

Isaac Leeser noted that most American Jews had no choice but to read the Scriptures in the most popular version, the King James Version. Leeser was appalled by this, since the KJV not only contains the New Testament (which Jews do not accept as inspired), but many KJV Bibles contain (in notes) references to Christ in the Old Testament. In other words, Jews were reading from a Christian book. So, in the 1850s, Lesser produced the first American Bible for Jews.

918. Israel in bloom

According to the prophet Isaiah, "He [God] shall cause them that come of Jacob to take root: Israel shall blossom and bud, and fill the face of the world with fruit" (Isa. 27:6 KJV). Much of the land of Israel is, or was, a desolate wilderness. Through irrigation and technology (not to mention a lot of old-fashioned determination), Israel really is blooming and budding today. And as for "filling the face of the world with fruit," Israel now supplies more than 90 percent of the citrus fruit consumed by Europeans.

919. Cromwell and the Jews

In the mid-1600s, the English ousted and executed their king, Charles I, and installed the military genius Oliver Cromwell as Lord Protector. Historians either love or hate Cromwell, but all agree he was sincerely religious and an effective leader. Cromwell has been admired for opening England again to the Jews, who had been forced to leave the country centuries earlier. Cromwell's act wasn't motivated just by compassion: as a devoted Bible-reader, Cromwell believed that Christ's second coming would follow the conversion of the Jews to Christianity, so by readmitting them to a Christian nation, he was (so he thought) helping advance the time of the Lord's return.

19

Potpourri, All Quite Interesting

920. Schulz and his "Peanuts"

Charles Schulz (1922–2000), creator of the "Peanuts" comic strip, was probably the best-known cartoonist of our time. The man who created such memorable characters as Charlie Brown, Linus, Snoopy, Woodstock, and Lucy stated more than once that he had the right to preach in his comic strip, and the "Peanuts" kids quoted the Bible fairly often, reflecting the strip's pro-Bible creator. When the first "Peanuts" TV special, "A Charlie Brown Christmas," aired in 1965, Schulz pressed the producers to allow the character Linus to quote a long passage from the Bible. Schulz won, and the special, which still airs every Christmas, shows that Schulz believed that Luke 2 was the real meaning of Christmas.

921. how many "Lords"?

The names *Yahweh* (always translated as LORD) and *Lord* appear in the Bible a total of 855 times.

922. Christ the communist

In July 2000, Cuban dictator Fidel Castro announced that Jesus was (or had been) a communist. Castro claimed that "Christ chose the fishermen because He was a communist." His brother, Raul Castro, claimed that Jesus was killed "for being a communist, for doing what Fidel defined as revolution."

While Castro's remark got some media coverage, the same remark had been made many times since the 1960s, when the so-called "liberation theologians" tried (unsuccessfully) to combine Christianity with communism. The gospel and Marxism do not mix.

923. four kings

An old tradition has it that the four kings in a deck of playing cards represent four kings in the Bible. Two of them are David and Solomon, while the other two are said to be (pick any two) Hezekiah, Josiah, Nebuchadnezzar, Belshazzar, Melchizedek, Herod, Cyrus, or Sennacherib.

924. no dissection

Using human cadavers in medical schools is an accepted practice today, but it wasn't always so. For many centuries dissecting human corpses was frowned upon because, after all, the New Testament taught that our bodies will be raised whole at the Last Judgment. Thus using them for experiments or for teaching anatomy was unacceptable.

925. Four Spiritual Laws

Millions of copies of this tract have been distributed by Campus Crusade for Christ over the years. The idea is this: present the essence of the gospel simply and convincingly to non-Christians. The laws, as formulated by Bill Bright, are all based on the Bible: (1) God loves you and has a wonderful plan for your life (John 3:16; 10:10); (2) Man is sinful and separated from God, and thus cannot experience God's plan (Rom. 3:23; 6:23); (3) Jesus Christ is God's only provision for experiencing God's love and plan (Rom. 5:8; 1 Cor. 15:3–6; John 14:6); (4) We must individually receive Christ as Savior and Lord in order to know and experience God's plan for our lives (John 1:12; 3:1–8; Eph. 2:8–9; Rev. 3:20). The laws have been criticized as oversimplifying the gospel, yet there is no doubt that this biblically based aid to evangelism has won many converts.

926. Robert Murray M'Cheyne (1813–1843)

The state-supported Church of Scotland experienced its dramatic "Disruption" in 1843, when evangelicals led almost half the church to form the Free Church of Scotland. M'Cheyne was one of the evangelicals. The saintly M'Cheyne served a large church in Dundee, where he was known for his excellent sermons, deep compassion, and tireless visitation of the sick and troubled. One of his biographers wrote that he began every day by reading the Bible. M'Cheyne developed a system for reading through the entire Bible in one year, and it is still widely used.

927. the seven joys of Mary

According to Catholic tradition, the Virgin Mary had "seven joys" in her life, most of them based on events in the Bible: the Annunciation (that she would bear the child Jesus), the Visitation (of Mary to Elizabeth), the Nativity, the visit of the three Magi, the presentation of Jesus in the temple, finding the boy Jesus in the temple, and her assumption into heaven (a Catholic tradition, but not found in the Bible).

928. abortion

The Bible says not a word about this controversial subject. It does, however, show an immense respect for human life, including the life of the child in the womb. Exodus

21:22–25 rules that if a pregnant woman is injured when two men fight, punishment is due. The Bible makes it clear that God "knows" us even before we leave our mothers' wombs (see Ps. 139:13–16; Jer. 1:5). The Didache, an early Christian work almost as old as the New Testament itself, clearly condemns abortion, which was fairly common in the immoral Roman Empire.

929. burning bush as persecuted church

Some of the early Christians had some curious interpretations of the Old Testament. There was a common feeling that every part of the Scriptures had to have some hidden meaning—even if the obvious literal meaning was clear enough. Take the story of Moses' encounter with the burning bush, from which God speaks. Most readers take this story from Exodus 3 at face value: Moses encountered God speaking from a burning bush in the wilderness. But some Christians in the early days saw a deeper meaning: the bush represented the church, suffering under persecution, but not consumed by it.

930. the Holy Sepulchre

The fact is, we don't know exactly where the tomb of Jesus is, but there is a site near Jerusalem that claims to be the place. It lay outside the city walls of Jerusalem, and in the year 336 Emperor Constantine built a church on the site. The present church there dates from about 1810.

931. "embrace and ever hold fast"

For the second Sunday in Advent, the Book of Common Prayer of the Church of England includes this prayer for reading in worship: "Blessed Lord, who has caused all Holy Scriptures to be written for our learning, grant that we may in such wise hear them, read, mark, learn, and inwardly digest them, that by patience, and comfort of thy holy Word, we may embrace, and ever hold fast the blessed hope of everlasting life."

932. the Lindisfarne Gospels

In the British Library in London are the amazing Lindisfarne Gospels. These are some of the best surviving examples of what are called *illuminated manuscripts*—books written out by hand and decorated (often lavishly) with calligraphy and drawings in various bright or metallic colors. The Lindisfarne Gospels were, we think, written out sometime in the 800s by a Bishop Eadfrith. They were, like all Bibles of the day, in Latin.

933. the Bible and perriwigs

The custom of men wearing wigs was quite common in the late 1600s and early 1700s. Many noted clergymen, such as Jonathan Edwards and Cotton Mather, wore wigs when their portraits were painted. Not all Christians accepted this custom, and some said it violated several of God's laws. Writing in the early 1700s, one New England pastor listed several reasons why men should not wear wigs: "Firstly, Adam, so long as he continued in innocency, did wear his own hair, and not a perriwig. Secondly, when the Son of God appeared in the flesh, he did not, from a dislike of his own hair, cut it off and wear a perriwig. Thirdly, the children of God will not wear perriwigs after the Resurrection."

934. how many fishes?

According to John 21, after Jesus' resurrection He led His apostles to an amazing catch of fish—so large they could barely bring it in. For some reason, men of the Middle Ages decided that there were exactly 153 fish in that catch. For years St. Paul's School, a famous school for boys in London, limited its enrollment to 153 students, citing the story in John 21 as the basis.

935. Uchimura Kanzo

Born into the samurai class in Tokyo, Uchimura Kanzo (1861–1930) was converted to Christianity and studied in the United States. He returned to Japan, determined to help spread Christianity there. For thirty years he published a magazine, *Seisho-no Kenkyu* (Biblical Studies). He was noted as a Bible commentator, and also for his somewhat controversial teaching that "there is no organized church in heaven." His disciples helped spread his "non-church movement," which emphasized Christian individualism and the uselessness of clergy.

936. "private interpretation"

For many years, Protestants had a misconception that Catholics were not allowed to read the Bible. Not so. However, what *was* prohibited was "private interpretation" of the Bible—that is, a Catholic could not (without official approval from the church authorities) publish a commentary on the Bible. Also, Catholics were not allowed to read "unauthorized" Bibles—which included any versions produced by Protestants, even the much-loved King James Version. Protestants were, naturally, suspicious of any group of Christians who would shun the KJV. And there were incidents to make Protestants even more suspicious—for example, the case of a Catholic priest who collected all the King James Bibles that had been given to his congregation and publicly burned them.

937. Judas the redhead

If you look at old paintings of Jesus' disciples (such as the many pictures of the Last Supper), you'll notice something: Judas, the traitor, is almost always shown as a redhead. Why? Partly, we assume, because it made him stand out from the other eleven disciples. And, for centuries, redheads have (rightly or wrongly) had a reputation as temperamental, unstable, etc., so naturally the one disciple who proved to be unreliable was (so the artists believed) a redhead. The Bible says nothing whatsoever about Judas's hair color.

938. John Everett Millais

English artist Millais (1829–1896) made his name with portraits and historical pictures, but his first major painting—and most controversial—was *Christ in the House of His Parents*, painted in 1850. People who see it today consider it a pleasant but rather ordinary picture of Jesus, Mary, and Joseph in their home, obviously the working-class home of a carpenter, which Joseph was. But the painting, on display at the Royal Academy of Art, was savagely attacked as "irreverent" and even "blasphemous." One critic wrote that "the attempt to associate the holy family with the meanest details of a carpenter's shop is disgusting." Later generations take a kinder view: Jesus was human, as were His parents, and yes, He did grow up among the "mean details" of a carpenter shop.

939. Joanna Southcott

She was quite the phenomenon of her day, this Methodist woman who believed she had received revelations of the destruction of Satan and the coming of Christ's kingdom. Miss Southcott (1750–1814), an English farm woman, became convinced she was the "woman clothed with the son" (Rev. 12:1) and the bride of the Lamb (Rev. 19). Though a virgin (so she said), she convinced many followers that she was pregnant through the Holy Spirit, but before she could bear the child who would rule all the nations (Rev. 12:5), she died. Some of her faithful followers kept the flame burning into the twentieth century.

940. the *Firing Line* man

William F. Buckley, political commentator, novelist, and longtime host of TV's *Firing Line*, is unashamedly Christian as well as a lover of words and of culture. Buckley has long lamented the decline of a culture where references to the Bible could be sprinkled in books and speeches and be instantly recognized by the audience. Buckley still leavens his own writings with such biblical phrases as "a fallen sparrow" (see Matt. 10:29).

941. Parker the preacher

One of Victorian London's most famous preachers was Joseph Parker (1830–1902), whose congregation built the famous City Temple. During 1885–92, Parker preached through the entire Bible, with his sermons published as a twenty-five-volume set, *The People's Bible*.

942. the Apocalypse of Paul

Paul claimed he knew a man (most likely himself, though we aren't certain) who had been caught up to the "third heaven" (2 Cor. 12:2). Some early Christian used this as the basis for the Apocalypse of Paul, which claims to be the visions Paul had of heaven and hell. While it is definitely not the work of Paul, and has never been accepted as inspired Scripture, the Apocalypse was widely read among the early Christians.

943. the Gilgamesh story

Scholars like to point out that the story of Noah and the Flood in Genesis is similar to flood stories from around the world. To which Bible readers reply, "Doesn't that hint that the story, being universal, is probably true?" One very similar story is the Babylonian tale of Gilgamesh. The hero Gilgamesh meets Utnapishtim, who (like Noah) had built a huge ark that saved him, his family, and animals from a great flood. Like Noah, Utnapishtim sent out birds to see if the waters had receded. And like Noah, Utnapishtim offered a sacrifice once he was on dry land. However, the story differs from the Noah story in many respects, the most notable being that in Genesis God (and there is only one, while the Babylonian tale has several) sends the Flood because of man's immorality.

944. evangelism through Bibles

Evangelists have known for centuries that it is not always necessary for a living person to spread the Word—sometimes the Bible itself is enough. In Korea, for example, Christian missionaries were not allowed in until the 1880s. But before that, Bibles in the Korean language had been smuggled in. When missionaries were allowed into Korea, they found that some of the people there had already become Christians—by reading the Bible.

945. oaths on the Bible

The practice of swearing an oath on the Bible goes back to the Middle Ages. The person taking the oath would swear by a cross, a prayer book, a sacred relic, or the Bible. Usually the person swore with his hand on the object or kissed it after taking the oath.

946. Donne on the ark

John Donne (1572–1631) was one of England's great poets, and also a noted preacher in his day. In a sermon he preached at a wedding, Donne spoke highly of marriage, noting that when God chose to save Noah and his family from the Flood, there were no single people on the ark. In the ark, Donne said, "God admitted only such as were fitted to help one another, couples."

947. sawing in half

Sawing a woman in half used to be standard fare in magicians' acts, but according to the Bible it was sometimes used as a method of capital punishment. The "Faith Hall of Fame" in Hebrews 11 speaks of the many righteous people who have been persecuted, including some who were sawn apart (11:37). This is mentioned nowhere else in the Bible, but outside the Bible an old writing known as the Martyrdom of Isaiah relates that the prophet Isaiah was executed by being sawn apart, at the order of the wicked King Manasseh.

BOOKS AND AUTHORS

948. Flannery O'Connor

One of the twentieth century's best short-story writers, O'Connor (1925–1964) was a Southern Catholic whose stories are populated with truly bizarre characters who sometimes struggle to find faith in a confused world. She often gave biblical titles to her stories, such as "The Violent Bear It Away" (from Matt. 11:12). In her story "The Lame Shall Enter First," a very disturbed young man tears a page from the Bible and eats it.

949. "What would Jesus do?"

One of the biggest-selling books of all time was the 1897 novel *In His Steps* by Charles M. Sheldon. The book's main idea was this: a group of ordinary Christians decide to live their lives by constantly asking themselves the question "What would Jesus do?" Naturally the answering of that question required that the person be familiar with the New Testament, so as to know just how Jesus did respond to certain situations.

A bit of publishing trivia: through an error, Sheldon's copyright for his book was not renewed, which meant that the book became "public domain"—that is, anyone could publish it without having to pay royalties to the author. This proved to be a blessing for the world, for Sheldon's book could be (and was) frequently reprinted and sold cheaply.

950. Caxton and the Bible

Most people know that the first book to be produced on a printing press was the Bible, printed (we think) by Johannes Gutenberg of Germany in 1456. The first English printer of note was William Caxton, who set up his press in London in 1476. Was his first printed work the Bible? No indeed. Caxton printed several notable works, including the poetical works of Geoffrey Chaucer and the King Arthur tales of Thomas Malory. But because of the Constitutions of Oxford (see 229), Caxton could not have printed an English Bible even had he wished to.

951. *The Golden Legend*

This book, written in the Middle Ages, was a collection of lives of saints, including many characters from the Bible. It was written in Latin, probably by an Italian named Jacobus de Voragine. In a day when translations of the Bible into the people's languages was prohibited (or severely restricted), *The Golden Legend* managed to sneak sizable Bible passages into its stories of saintly people from the Bible. William Caxton, England's first printer, could not print an English Bible because of church restrictions, but he did print his own translation of *The Golden Legend*, thus giving the English reading public several Bible passages in English, not only from the New Testament but also from much of Genesis and Exodus.

952. before the Gutenberg Bible

A landmark of Christian—and human—history was Johannes Gutenberg's Bible, printed in Mainz, Germany, in 1456. A little footnote to that notable event: prior to that, in 1454, was the first printed book, also produced by Gutenberg: a Latin version of the Psalms.

953. Bengel's apocalypse

German scholar Johann Albrecht Bengel (1687–1752) was a noted commentator on the New Testament, and many of his writings were incorporated into the *Notes on the New Testament* by Methodist founder John Wesley. Bengel, like many Bible readers, tried to determine the date of the end-time events foretold in the book of Revelation. He predicted that the Millennium (Rev. 20) would begin in 1836. He was wrong (as have been all the predictors so far), but his New Testament notes are still widely read.

954. Vergil's prophecy

The Roman poet Vergil is best known for his *Aeneid*, the epic poem about the origins of Rome. Vergil was one of the greatest writers of Latin, and many early Christians read and admired his work even though he was a pagan. Some readers even believed that Vergil, who died in 19 B.C., had foretold the birth of Christ. In his fourth *Eclogue* are these words: "The maiden returns, Saturn is king again, / A new race descends from on high." Some Christians took "the maiden" to be the Virgin Mary, "Saturn" to be Christ, and the "new race" to be the new community of faith, the church.

955. Stiefel the calculator

Michael Stiefel was a German pastor, a follower of Martin Luther, and also a mathematician. In 1532 he published a small book, *Apocalypse on the Apocalypse: A Little Book of Arithmetic about the Antichrist*. From his reading of the book of Revelation, Stiefel had calculated that the Day of Judgment would occur on the morning of October 9, 1533. On that day many peasants laid their work aside and trudged to the village where Stiefel was pastor. When nothing happened, they bound and dragged him to a nearby village, where some sued him for damages. A few years later, Stiefel published a pamphlet, *A Very Wonderful Recalculation*, in which he admitted he had made a mistake earlier.

956. *The Weight of Glory*

C. S. Lewis, author and lay theologian, published this book in 1949. It takes its title from 2 Corinthians 4:17: "For our light affliction, which is but for a moment, is working for us a far more exceeding and eternal weight of glory."

THE PURITANS

957. the Westminster view of the Bible

In England, Scotland, and America, churches that are part of the Presbyterian tradition look back fondly to the Westminster Assembly of 1647. That body, meeting at Westminster near London, prepared the Westminster Confession of Faith and the Westminster Catechism, both excellent summaries of what is sometimes called the Reformed branch of Protestantism. Regarding the Bible, the Catechism has this to say: "The Word of God, which is contained in the Scriptures of the Old and New Testaments, is the only rule to direct us how we may glorify and enjoy him [God]. The Scriptures principally teach what man is to believe concerning God, and what duty God requires of man." Christians do not have to belong to the Reformed or Presbyterian Church to agree with that powerful statement.

958. twelve pence for swearing

Swearing is so much taken for granted in TV, movies, and pop songs today that we forget it was taken more seriously in the past. Taking God's name in vain (prohibited by the third commandment, Ex. 20:7) was considered an especially vile form of swearing. In certain times and places it has been subject to punishment—for example, in Puritan-dominated New England in the 1600s, and, across the Atlantic, in Puritan-dominated England, where swearing could bring a man a fine of twelve pence, and more for repeat offenders.

959. "Venus's Palace, Satan's Synagogue"

English drama reached amazing heights in Shakespeare's day, but some of the plays impressed people as profane and obscene. Many Christians, particularly the Puritans, objected to the theater in any form. One of the Puritan authors referred to theaters as "Venus's Palace, and Satan's Synagogue." (The phrase "Satan's Synagogue" is from Revelation 2:9 and 3:9.) Christians complained that the theaters were packed while churches sat bare and empty.

960. Puritans and names

The Bible has long been a rich source for parents choosing a name for their child. In England, particularly in the 1600s when Puritanism was at its peak, the Old Testament became popular as a name bank. Thus were put into use many names now familiar (Samuel, Daniel, Joel, Deborah, Hannah) and many that have fallen from use (Abimelech, Melchizedek, Shadrach, Meshach, Abednego, Zerubbabel, etc). It was often assumed that if a person bore an Old Testament name, his parents were probably strict Puritans.

KINGS AND QUEENS AND SUCH

961. the coronation Bible

At the coronation of Queen Elizabeth II in 1953, the young queen was presented with a copy of the King James Bible. The minister doing the presentation stated that it was "to keep your Majesty ever mindful of the Law and the Gospel of God as the rule for the whole life and government of Christian princes, we present you with this

Book, the most valuable thing that this world affords. Here is Wisdom; this is the royal Law; these are the lively Oracles of God."

962. England's king, and the Magi

It has been a custom for several centuries for England's king or queen to enter the Chapel Royal (there are several, in the various palaces where the ruler may live) and offer on the altar gifts of gold, frankincense, and myrrh on January 6, the day known as Epiphany. Traditionally the coming of the three Magi, or wise men, is celebrated not on Christmas but twelve days later, January 6. The three gifts are, of course, the ones brought by the Magi to the child Jesus.

963. prince

We generally use "prince" to refer to the son of a king, but in the Bible, "princes" is a kind of generic term meaning "those in authority" or "rulers" or "big shots." Since God is the ultimate Authority, it is more important to honor and depend upon Him than upon any human power: "It is better to trust in the LORD than to put confidence in princes" (Ps. 118:9). "Do not put your trust in princes, nor in a son of man, in whom there is no help" (Ps. 146:3).

964. *The Book of Sports*

Should Sunday be a day of rest, worship, and spiritual reflection, or should it be a day of worship *and leisure*? In the 1600s, the Puritans in the Church of England pressed for the first option, Sunday as "the Lord's Day," as taught in the Bible. King James I objected to this strict view of the Sabbath, and in 1617 issued a declaration known as *The Book of Sports*. In it he encouraged (but did not demand) that worship be followed by such pursuits as archery, games, even dancing. James issued the declaration for two reasons: he despised the Puritans, and he also believed that a "quiet" Sabbath was not good preparation for men to fight in wars.

965. Victoria and Abraham

In 1901, Queen Victoria of England lay dying. One of her visitors asked the queen if she would be pleased to be in "Abraham's bosom" (a biblical phrase referring to being at the side of the patriarch Abraham—that is, in heaven). The queen solemnly declared, "We will *not* meet Abraham." Victoria, like many Bible readers through the centuries, was disturbed at some of the morally questionable behavior of Old Testament characters, including Abraham, who lied and told the Egyptian pharaoh that his wife, Sarah, was actually his sister.

966. Richard I and the Antichrist

England's great Crusader king, Richard I, is known to history as Richard the Lionhearted. Passing through Italy in the 1190s on his way to the Third Crusade in the Holy Land, Richard paid a visit to the famous Joachim of Fiore, reputed to be a prophet of the end times. Joachim had, supposedly, studied the Bible and calculated when and where the events predicted in Revelation would occur. Richard had a nagging question for Joachim: Where and when would the Antichrist be born? In those days kings took the Bible more seriously than do statesmen today.

THE PRE-GUTENBERG BIBLE

967. the economical book

Scholars have wondered why the early Christians preferred the codex (the early form of book) rather than the traditional scroll. Part of it may have been economy: most early Christians were poor folk, and the codex (which used both sides of the material, while scrolls used only one) were more economical. The codex also traveled better, was easier to carry for missionaries, and also could be "paged" while scrolls could not. To both Jews and pagans, the codex seemed a shocking innovation, something "newfangled" and trendy. But the Christians were on the cutting edge: the codex in time replaced the scroll (as proved by what you are now holding in your hand).

968. "not on papyrus"

Before there was a New Testament there were the eye-witnesses of Jesus, who told what they had seen to others, who passed it on to others, and so forth. The bishop Irenaeus (who lived around A.D. 180) got his knowledge of the Lord thirdhand: he heard the words of the bishop Polycarp, who had heard the words of the apostle John. Polycarp told Irenaeus that the words of the apostle were "not on papyrus but in my heart."

But the original witnesses died off (many of them martyred for their faith), and Christians saw the need to commit the sacred memories to writing. Thus came the New Testament.

969. woman stenographers

In the distant past, there were no women secretaries. What we would call "clerical work" was always handled by men, who served as copyists, scribes, and so forth. The first recorded instance of women doing such work was in Caesarea, Palestine, around the year 220. The noted Bible scholar Origen had set up a *scriptorium*, a hall where people faithfully made copies of the Scriptures. Origen used both men and women—a sign that the early church saw both sexes as capable of dealing with the Word of God.

970. "running hand"

Everyone knows that it is much faster to write in cursive, or "running hand," than to print each letter individually. When the Bible was originally written, ordinary documents were written in "running hand," while more important documents were written in *uncials*, that is, printed in capital letters individually, which took much more time. In the days long before the printing press, copying any document in uncials was pretty time-consuming. Sometime around the year 800 copyists began to use *minuscules* (that is, lowercase) letters, which could be run together, making it much easier and faster to copy the Bible.

971. Rylands Papyrus 457

The John Rylands Library in Manchester, England, contains a small scrap of paper that is a real treasure: the Rylands Papyrus 457, a tiny scrap on which are four verses from John 18. The scrap dates from around the year 135—the oldest copy of any portion of the New Testament.

972. first Bible with chapters

The year 1231 saw a first: a Bible divided into chapters. It was in Latin (the only language for Bibles in those days) and, being done before the printing press era, was hand-copied. The chapter divisions had been introduced by scholar Stephen Langton, a teacher at the University of Paris and later the archbishop of Canterbury in England. There had been some earlier attempts at dividing the Bible into chapters, but Langton's became the standard.

SOME NEW WORDS AND PHRASES TO LEARN

973. *inscripturated*

This word means "put into writing." It has been used by some Bible scholars to speak of how the eternal Word (capital *W*) of God is put into the human words of the Bible—the Word is "inscripturated" in the inerrant words of the Bible.

974. "original autographs"

No, not the signatures of famous people, but the very first Bible writings—that is, the book of Jeremiah as written by Jeremiah himself (or, at least, by a scribe writing down his dictation). Where are they? Nowhere. Even if the archaeologists could dig up some very old manuscripts, there is no way of proving that they were from the actual hand of Moses, David, Paul, Luke, etc.

However, the phrase "original autographs" crops up often in discussions of the Bible's inerrancy. Many people affirm that the Bible *in the original autographs* was totally free from error. The flip side of this belief: minor errors may have crept in over the years due to the carelessness of copyists. It is, in a sense, a way of having your cake and eating it too. You can say that the Bible is totally error-free, and when someone tries to point out an error, you can say, "Yes, but the original autographs had no errors." End of discussion.

975. *curiositas*

It is the Latin word for "curiosity," and early commentators used it to refer to the wrong reason for studying the Bible. As they used the word, it denotes pleasure in acquiring knowledge for its own sake. This, they agreed, is no valid reason to study the sacred Word of God. The great theologian Augustine stated that unless we read the Bible with a view toward growing in faith, hope, and love, we are reading for the wrong reason. (We hope he would not have disapproved of books with titles like *1,001 More Things You Always Wanted to Know About the Bible*.)

976. *Antilegomena*

Several writings almost made it into the New Testament—almost, but not quite. Writing around A.D. 300, the historian Eusebius noted that certain writings (such as the four

Gospels, Paul's Letters, etc.) were accepted by all Christians, everywhere, as genuine and inspired. He called these writings the *Homologoumena*. The *Antilegomena* were writings that were widely read and quoted, but not accepted by everyone as inspired. These included the Acts of Paul, the Shepherd of Hermas, the Apocalypse of Peter, the Epistle of Barnabas, and the Didache. But the Antilegomena also included James, Jude, 2 Peter, and 2 and 3 John, which eventually were accepted as divine Scripture. None of the Antilegomena, even the ones that were never accepted as Scripture, were heretical in the way that various other writings (like the many false Gospels) were.

977. the Seleucids

They aren't mentioned in the Bible, but they certainly influenced it. The Greek-speaking conqueror Alexander the Great died young, leaving an empire to be divided among several successors. One of these was Seleucus, who managed to hold on to Babylonia and Syria, an area that included Israel. Seleucus founded the city of Antioch, mentioned many times in the New Testament. More important, he and his descendants, the Seleucids, maintained Greek language and culture through the region, which is why our New Testament is in Greek. When the Seleucid Empire gave way to the Romans, Greek was still the common language of the region.

978. apologetics

Christianity and the Bible have never lacked for critics. *Apologetics* refers to defending the faith against those critics (and, in the process, perhaps converting them). The earliest apologists for the faith were authors such as Justin Martyr, converted pagans who tried to explain and defend the Bible against pagan critics who sneered at how "barbarous" the Bible was. Some of the greatest theologians and Bible scholars have turned their energies toward apologetics. In the past century, some notable apologists have been C. S. Lewis, the English literary professor who was skilled at explaining the faith to an increasingly secular world. Josh McDowell (in such books as *Evidence That Demands a Verdict*) and Francis Schaeffer (in *How Shall We Then Live*) were also noted apologists.

979. *sensus plenior*

Bible scholars sometimes use this Latin phrase, which means "the fuller sense," referring to the deep meaning of the Bible. The basic idea: the *sensus plenior* is the deeper meaning, intended by God but not necessarily intended by the human authors of the Bible. Put another way, the Bible in some sections has a deeper meaning than its original authors may have known themselves. For example: the prophet Isaiah may not have known that the "Servant Songs" in his book were fulfilled, centuries later, in the life of Jesus of Nazareth. But the *sensus plenior* of the Servant Songs is known to us today.

SOME COMMON MISUNDERSTANDINGS

980. wickedness in high places

In Ephesians 6:12, Paul speaks of Christians doing battle against "wickedness in high places"—or so it reads in some translations. It is clear in the context that Paul is talking about the realm of the supernatural—specifically, war against the devil and his forces. Yet some people have quoted the section on "wickedness in high places" and used it to criticize big government, big business, etc. The New King James Version, which has "wickedness in the heavenly places," is less misleading. (Of course, no one need rule out the possibility that big business and big government might indeed be influenced by demonic forces . . .)

981. unequally yoked

In 2 Corinthians 6:14, Paul warned Christians, "Do not be unequally yoked together with unbelievers." Christians have, correctly, applied this to marriage, believing that Christians should not marry unbelievers. But, over the centuries, some readers have extracted another meaning: people of different races, even if they are Christians, should not marry. This is most assuredly not the meaning that Paul intended.

982. tongues will cease

In his famous "Love Chapter" (1 Corinthians 13), Paul notes that "tongues, they will cease" (v. 8). Some Christians who oppose speaking in tongues (glossolalia) cite this verse as Paul's indication that the practice will die out in time—that is, they were a phenomenon among the first Christians, but no longer needed. This is a wrong interpretation, for in the same verse Paul also notes that knowledge and prophecies will cease—but no one is willing to state that knowledge and prophecies no longer serve a purpose among Christians today.

983. falling into sex

As our culture grows less and less familiar with the Bible, odd ideas are circulated. One of these, which has actually been around for quite a while, is that the original sin of Adam and Eve was sex. As Genesis 3 makes clear, their sin was disobedience of God, defying His command not to eat the forbidden fruit. It is true, however, that there is no mention of Adam and Eve having sexual relations before this occurred (though we need not assume they didn't). We only know they were "naked and unashamed" before their disobedience, not so afterward.

984. Delilah's scissors

In so many paintings, the wily Delilah is shown with a pair of shears or scissors, cutting off the long locks of the Hebrew strongman Samson. An interesting picture—but wrong. So far as we know, shears or scissors were not used in Israel in those days. A knife or razor would have been used. And, as the book of Judges relates, Delilah only served to worm the secret of Samson's hair from him: it was one of the Philistine men who did the shearing, not Delilah (Judg. 16:19).

985. rain on the just and the unjust

In His famous Sermon on the Mount, Jesus observed that God "sends rain on the just and on the unjust" (Matt. 5:45). So many people miss the meaning: they take it to mean that all people, good and bad, receive their share of woes in life. In fact, in the dry land of Israel, always on the verge of a drought, rain was a good thing, the water of life, necessary for crops and for human existence. In the modern world we think of rain as what causes us to cancel picnics and sporting events, but Jesus' words on rain would have had a purely positive meaning for His first hearers.

986. Peter's cursing

In the sad story of Peter denying that he knew Jesus, Mark's gospel notes that Peter "began to curse and swear" (Mark 14:71). Many readers assume that the over-wrought, guilt-stricken Peter was using profanity. In fact, the "swearing" was literal swearing—he was swearing (though it was a lie) that he had no connection with Jesus.

987. an ark, not a ship

Genesis gives us the dimensions of Noah's ark—translated into modern measurements, the ark would have been around 437 feet long, 73 feet wide, and 44 feet deep. While artists have had fun putting the ark into pictures, they usually get it wrong. The ark was, based on the dimensions just given, a long, low barge, one that would have barely risen above the water line. It was, as the name indicates an *ark*—that is, a chest, not a ship in the usual sense. Unlike any normal ship or boat, it had no sail or rudder—and why would it, for with the whole world being flooded, there was nowhere to steer toward.

988. the mercy seat

This was not something to sit on but, rather, the solid gold lid of Israel's ark of the covenant, the gold-covered chest that symbolized God's presence. Over the slab of gold were the two gold cherubim, whose outstretched wings met. God was (spiritually speaking) present between the cherubim, so it was God who was "seated" there. (See Ex. 25:17–22 for a description of the mercy seat.)

989. hate your enemies

"Ye have heard that it hath been said, Thou shalt love thy neighbor, and hate thine enemy" (Matt. 5:43 KJV). So said Jesus. Well, the command to love one's neighbor is in the Old Testament (Lev. 19:18), but what about hating one's enemies? Nowhere in the Bible is this mentioned. In fact, Jesus was doing the obvious thing: referring to human nature, which, left to itself, hates its enemies. God has to tell us to love our neighbors (since we are inclined not to), but hating our enemies comes naturally. Jesus, of course, follows up this famous verse with His command to love our enemies.

990. Sabaoth

No, not Sabbath. The Hebrew word *Sabaoth* occurs in several old Christian hymns (for example, Martin Luther's great "A Mighty Fortress Is Our God" has the line "Lord Sabaoth His name"). Sabaoth was one of the names applied to God. Calling God "Lord Sabaoth" was something equivalent to "Lord of the armies of heaven." The word is used twice in the New Testament (Rom. 9:29; James 5:4).

991. the caduceus

Most people are familiar with the *caduceus,* the medical emblem showing two snakes twined around a pole. It is seen in doctors' offices, on ambulances, and elsewhere, and some people believe the symbol is based on the Old Testament story of Moses lifting up a bronze snake on a pole (see Num. 21). In fact, the caduceus has a Greek origin, not a Hebrew one. The staff with the serpents around it was the symbol of Asclepius, the Greek god of healing, so naturally it became associated with the medical profession.

992. burying my father

Matthew 8:21–22 mentions a would-be follower of Jesus who said to Him, "Lord, let me first go and bury my father." Jesus replied, "Follow Me, and let the dead bury their own dead." This strikes some readers as rather unkind—after all, a dutiful son was making a simple request to bury his father, which Jesus should have respected, right? But scholars familiar with Middle Eastern culture interpret it differently: most likely the man wasn't saying his father had just died—rather, he was saying to Jesus, "I can't follow You until after my father is dead and buried." Obviously Jesus' message was more urgent than that. His reply to the man might have been His way of saying, "Cut the excuses, you're just trying to delay your commitment." The scholars say that even today Middle Easterners use "Let me bury my father first" as a polite way of refusing a request.

993. angels with harps

Revelation 15:2 speaks of the saints in heaven having harps to play, and harps are mentioned many times in the Bible—but not in connection with angels. Despite harps being in heaven, and despite angels portrayed as praising God, the Bible never actually mentions angels with harps. Perhaps the common image comes from John Milton, whose great epic poem *Paradise Lost* describes angel harpists.

994. no room in the inn

Jesus was born in a stable because, as Luke's gospel tells us, there was no room for His family in the inn in Bethlehem (Luke 2:7). We must not imagine that the "inn" was anything like a hotel or motel today. The "inn" in Bethlehem was most likely a large walled enclosure, with roofs to shelter people from the elements.

995. Elijah's double portion

The prophet Elisha was the best friend and protégé of the fiery prophet Elijah. In 2 Kings 2 we read the dramatic story of Elijah departing this earth in a fiery chariot. At their farewell, Elisha requested, "Please let a double portion of your spirit be upon me." Some readers interpret this in a greedy way: Elisha wanting to be twice as great as

Elijah had been. But "double portion" had a definite meaning in ancient Israel: a man's firstborn son received a double portion of the inheritance. Elisha, the spiritual son of the great Elijah, was asking Elijah to treat him as (spiritually speaking) his firstborn and favorite son. Elisha got his request, symbolized by Elijah's mantle falling upon him.

PEOPLE IN GROUPS

996. the Nazis and Paul

In the 1930s and 1940s, the Nazis of Germany referred to the apostle Paul as "the political Jew." In the Nazi view of things, Paul (a Jew) had helped convert Europe to Christianity. This made Europe (so they believed) too Jewish, too Semitic. They believed that, had it not been for Paul and other Jewish Christian missionaries, Europe might have evolved as the Aryan master race.

997. the Christadelphians

The word we usually translate as "church" is *ekklesia* in the Greek New Testament. One Christian denomination that calls its groups "ekklesias" instead of "churches" is the Christadelphians, founded about the time of America's Civil War. As in the New Testament, the group has no paid ministers, and they usually meet in homes or in rented halls.

998. low apostles

For many years the dozen lowest-ranking undergraduates at England's prestigious Cambridge University were known as the "twelve apostles." Did anyone ever recall the words of Jesus, "the last shall be first, and the first last" (Matt. 20:16 KJV)?

999. Moral Rearmament

Largely forgotten today, Moral Rearmament was quite a movement in its heyday, the 1930s and 1940s. At the head of it was a Lutheran pastor, Frank Buchman, who wanted evangelism not only to produce individual conversions but to raise the moral level of the whole world. Buchman and his followers were originally called the Oxford Group but later called Moral Rearmament. One form of their outreach was "house parties," involving dinner, followed by discussions of moral issues of the day. Buchman thought that the Bible and Christianity taught the "Five Cs"—confidence, conviction, confession, conversion, continuance—and the "Four Absolutes"—honesty, purity, unselfishness, and love.

1,000. the Bereans of Britain

One group of Christians who were especially commended in the New Testament were the people of Berea, who "received the word with all readiness, and searched the Scriptures" to see if the apostles were on the right track (Acts 17:10–12). One group of Scottish (and later English) Christians took the name Bereans. The group was founded by John Barclay (1734–1798), who taught that the Bible's meaning had to be interpreted by the witness of the Holy Spirit.

1,001. the Samaritans today

There is still a small community of Samaritans in Israel. They live near Mount Gerizim, which, they say, is the holy mountain of God, and they honor Moses and the first five books of the Bible, the Torah. They preserve a scroll of the Torah that they claim dates from the time of Joshua himself.

Index

Numbers refer to entry numbers, not to page numbers. The main entry for each topic is set in boldface. References to certain broad topics (such as Jesus, Moses, the New Testament, etc.) are so numerous that to list them all would be of little help to the reader.

Kipling, Rudyard 126
Kircher, Athanasius 700
kneading troughs 538
Knoch, Adolph Ernst 278
Knox, John 624, 640
Koresh, David 332
lambs 473
"land o' Goshen" 399
Landmarkism 309
Landor, Walter Savage 106
Langton, Stephen 972
Lanier, Sidney 114
Laodicea, epistle to 852
Last Temptation of Christ, The 75
latitudinarians 202
Latter-day Saints 310-317
Lattimore, Richmond 256
Laubach, Frank 250
Law, Book of the 767
Lawrence, D. H. 141
lawyers 680
lazaretto 406
leeches 458
Lemuel 780
Lent, sacrificing for 170
lentils 509
leopards 468
leviathan 484
levirate marriage 550
Lewis, C. S. 258, 956, 978

life span 699
light, creation of 687, 688
lilies 510
Lincoln, Abraham 113, 382-386, 392
Lindbergh, Anne Morrow 294
Lindisfarne Gospels 932
Lindsey, Hal 338
linen 528
lions 470
"little bird told me" 437
Living Bible, The 329
Livingstone, David 89
lizards 453
locusts 491
lost rivers of Eden 691
Lowell, James Russell 104
Lucifers (matches) 432
Luther, Martin 238, 607-616, 620, 990
lying 717
Lynd, Robert and Helen 46
Macaulay, Thomas Babington 138, 139
Machpelah, cave of 705
Magi 11
Makeda, queen of Sheba 14
makeup 534
man in the moon 10
Man Nobody Knows, The 341

About the Author

J. Stephen Lang is the author of twenty books, including *1,001 Things You Always Wanted to Know About the Bible*, *1,001 Things You Always Wanted to Know About the Holy Spirit*, *The Complete Book of Bible Trivia*, and *The Complete Book of Bible Promises*.

Lang has an M.A. in communications from Wheaton College and is a regular contributor to *Moody*, *Christian History*, *The Christian Reader*, *Discipleship Journal*, and other periodicals.

Also by J. Stephen Lang

1,001 Things You Always Wanted to Know About the Bible But Never Thought to Ask

In this book you'll discover how the Bible has impacted language, U.S. history, worship, music, art, literature, movies, and theater; how the Bible was passed down to us; plus every key person, place, event, and idea in the Bible. Best-selling author J. Stephen Lang's intriguing tidbits will leave you yearning to know more about the world's most fascinating book.

1,001 Things You Always Wanted to Know About the Holy Spirit

What are the fruits and gifts of the Spirit? Why are the flame and the dove symbols of the Spirit? J. Stephen Lang answers these and hundreds of other questions about the Holy Spirit, a subject that has fascinated people throughout the centuries. Lang looks at key Bible passages dealing with the Spirit, great revivals and evangelists throughout history, the charismatic and Pentecostal movements, and the ways in which the Spirit moves in the life of the church around the world.

1,001 Things You Always Wanted to Know About Angels, Demons, and the Afterlife

Lang takes the reader on a fascinating tour through the Bible, Christian belief, folk wisdom, and pop culture, looking at angels, Satan, demons, heaven, hell, and the end times. The book not only looks at controversial issues such as exorcism and reincarnation, but at images found in art, music, movies, literature, and legend. The "unseen world" gets an up-close look that is awe-inspiring, often amusing, and occasionally frightening.